The NEW Greengrocer Cookbook

JOE CARCIONE

Edited by Pete Carcione
(son of Joe Carcione)

Bush Street Press
San Francisco, CA

Made in the United States of America

Library of Congress Cataloging in Publication Data

Library of Congress Control Number: 2010929725

Carcione, Pete The New Greengrocer Cookbook

Bush Street Press
237 Kearny Street, #174
San Francisco, CA 94108
www.bushstreetpress.com
press@bushstreetpress.com

Legal Disclaimer

The information provided in this book is designed to provide helpful information on the subjects discussed. This book is not meant to be used, nor should it be used, to diagnose or treat any medical condition. For diagnosis or treatment of any medical problem, consult your own physician. The publisher and author are not responsible for any specific health or allergy needs that may require medical supervision and are not liable for any damages or negative consequences from any treatment, action, application or preparation, to any person reading or following the information in this book. References are provided for informational purposes only and do not constitute endorsement of any websites or other sources. Readers should be aware that the web sites listed in this book may change.

DEDICATION

I dedicate this book to the spirit of the man known as the Greengrocer, my father, Joe Carcione. His spirit, or should I say passion, was to teach us that produce goodness is dependent on its freshness and taste. Produce is all about freshness, taste, and buying at the right time and season. His five days a week TV and radio spots gave us the knowledge of when a certain fruit or vegetable was at its peak of perfection.

These simple recipes, separated by season, along with bright, healthy, fresh produce, are all we need.

Note: Because of wonderful refrigeration and cooling techniques, we now can have each season twice a year.

CONTENTS

I am very proud of my grandfather and his introduction.
There is not one word that I would change. I think it's perfect!
~ Pete Carcione, grandson

INTRODUCTION
Introduction by Peter Carcione (Grandfather)

When I first introduced my son, Joe, to the produce business more than 40 years ago, I never expected it would lead to writing an introduction to a cookbook. But his mother and I have introduced him to a number of things, and it's only fair to say that in the process of raising Joe, and his brother and sister, they've introduced us to a few things, too. Most of those things have been good, we are happy to say, and among them we count six grandchildren, three of whom also work in produce.

In order to explain the background and experience which cause Joe to become an expert on fresh fruits and vegetables, I'll have to go back into family history. That will also help to explain the reason you will find many of his recipes strongly laced with garlic. Joe loves garlic!

Just before the turn of the century, Joe's mother, Katherine, with her family and I with my family, made the long journey from our separate villages in Sicily to new homes in San Francisco. Here our families became casually acquainted through mutual friends. A few years later, the San Francisco earthquake demolished those homes and our acquaintance became much less casual. Both of our families found refuge on boats owned by my uncles which were tied up at what is now Fisherman's Wharf. Katherine and I were both early adolescents at the time, but the circumstances of the disaster averted any awkward lapses in conversation. To make a long story short, later we were married, and in 1920, I became involved in the produce business.

1

It was very different in those days because, at that time, produce consisted not only of fresh fruits and vegetables, but practically anything that was saleable, including the darndest array of squawking chickens, squealing pigs, and flapping ducks and geese you can imagine. The rabbits confused the inventory, and we even dealt in some wild animals, including raccoons and bobcats. Thanksgiving became a nightmare when dressed turkeys were received in great volume and had to be delivered all over the city.

Fruits and vegetables were difficult to keep fresh without the modern transportation and refrigeration facilities in use today. But even without modern facilities, at least in the Bay Area, fruits and vegetables arrived at the market within twenty-four hours of the time they were harvested. The farmers and growers in the areas north and south of San Francisco would harvest their crops and bring them in by horse and wagon, driving late at night. If they were near a river such as in the Sacramento Valley, the growers would transfer their products to large cargo bots and haul them to market in that manner.

Things improved somewhat by the time Joe joined the business. He had just graduated from high school, and although he wasn't large in stature, he was strong. His first job was trucking stacks of five wooden orange crates that weighed from 80 to 90 pounds each off a truck and hauling them on a hand truck into the stall. For this type of labor, he was to be paid $10.00 a week. Typical of Joe, one week of that was enough. He quickly moved on to bigger and better things.

Joe has always been one of those people who has to know everything there is to know about a particular subject. He wasn't satisfied to just sell strawberries or tomatoes. He had to know where they came from, what was so good about them, what vitamins and minerals they contained and what you were supposed to do with them once you got them in the kitchen. This persistent inquisitiveness, day in and day out, for over 40 years has caused

Joe to accumulate a heck of a lot of information about fresh fruits and vegetables.

I'm sure Joe never imagined at the time that all of the information he was collecting would lead him to writing a daily newspaper column or doing his own daily radio and television spots; that just came naturally. Of course, consumers are interested in the food they buy and the prices they have to pay for them, and he has been well received by his audiences.

In 1967, he began with "Man on the Produce Market" radio spots on KCBS radio with Dave McElhatton and later on KABC, Los Angeles with Michael Jackson and KCRA, Sacramento with Dave Darin He appears three times a day on KRON-TV, San Francisco, and his newspaper column, "The Greengrocer" runs daily in the San Francisco Chronicle. With the publication of his first book, a guide to the selection of fresh fruits and vegetables, The Greengrocer, Chronicle Books, 1972, Joe has become known throughout the United States. Now his TV show is syndicated and is viewed daily in eleven major western cities.

But in the produce business, some things haven't changed at all. The market starts to come alive about 3:00 a.m. every morning Monday through Friday. If you happen to be in South San Francisco near the Produce Mart about that time, you'll be sure to see Joe because that's still when and where his day starts.

Every once in a while, I go down for old time's sake and say 'hello' to my friends. Among all the hustle and bustle of trucks and tractors and crates and cartons, you can smell the wonderful aroma of fresh fruits and vegetables and hear the men greeting the new day and their friends in a dozen different languages. Right in the middle of it all will be Joe, wheeling and dealing and moving those fresh fruits and vegetables that are so dear to his big Sicilian heart.

ABOUT THE GREENGROCER COOKBOOK

The Joe Carcione Cookbook is a great cookbook. I know this, because so many people have used it and told me how much they enjoyed the recipes they found. This book has been out of print for some time, but in the last couple years, many people have asked me where they can get a copy. Most of these people already have the book and like it so much that they would like to get it for family members and friends. After giving it some thought, I realized that when it comes to fruit and vegetables, the authority to many people is still Joe Carcione. Many young cooks know that they must eat fresh fruits and vegetables to be healthy and are looking for simple and easy to prepare recipes from someone they can trust. Now, these young cooks can't be too young because if they were, they wouldn't know Joe. If that was the case, their mom would have to buy the book for them.

I talked about reprinting Dad's book with my brother and sister, and they agreed that it would a worthwhile venture. I believed that nothing should be left out, but because the book was written in 1975, some new knowledge should be added. We now know about anti-oxidants, especially the key antioxidants vitamins A, C, and E. These key antioxidants protect us from sickness, disease, and cancer. The word 'antioxidant' means just what it sounds like—to keep or block oxygen from hooking up with the free radicals or mutations which occur in our bodies constantly. Vitamins A and C are in all fruits and vegetables, and the darkness of their color, red, yellow, orange, green, or blue shows the strength of the antioxidant. We know that genetic improvements have made produce better, more disease resistant, and more prolific without any proven ill effects. We also are growing more organic produce, that is, produce grown without pesticide or chemical fertilizers. None of us wish to eat food which contains pesticides, so buying organic produce is a very good option. It should be known that all produce defends itself by giving off its own pesticide, and under

4

severe circumstances (for example, very warm temperatures), the plant can produce a toxic amount of its own pesticide. It is important to wash everything in water. I think the salad spinner does a great job of cleaning produce. Even though it cannot be proven that organic produce is more nutritious than conventionally grown produce, it definitely can be more flavorful due to the fact that it is grown by smaller growers who can leave it on the vine or tree longer, thereby allowing it to develop more flavor. Also, smaller growers who sell at farmer's markets do not hydro-cool or vacuum-cool and, therefore, don't stop the ripening process. The taste will be better.

I have been in the wholesale produce business for 40 years, and I must say that produce has never been better. We have so many choices available to us.

EAT FRESH AND STAY HEALTHY!

Pete Carcione

SWEETENERS

In reviewing these wonderful recipes, which were all written before 1975, it was noted that a few used corn syrup and raw sugar for sweetening. At first, we thought we should substitute with another sweetener such as agave syrup, maple syrup, or honey.

But, it was decided that this cookbook is so well received and used by many people with success, that we should just suggest the substitutes and leave the decision to sweeten up to you.

Agave Nectar: Derived from the agave plant, a perennial, agave nectar, or agave syrup as it is sometimes called, is often used as a substitute for honey. It is said to be slightly sweeter than sugar. Agave consists primarily of fructose and glucose. Its liquid form makes it a favorite in beverages because of its ability to dissolve completely and quickly. It can also be used in baking and cooking.

Maple Syrup: Produced from the sap of maple trees, it is a natural sweetener which contains more sucrose than fructose. A good source of manganese and zinc, maple syrup is most often used as a topping or syrup. However, it can also be used as a sugar substitute in beverages and works well in other recipes which require baking or cooking.

Honey: A food manufactured by the honeybee, honey is a thick, syrupy sweetener which has about the same sweetness as table sugar. It consists of fructose and glucose, and is considered to be a pure sugar. Used mostly in cooking and baking, it also is spread on breads and pastries and used to sweeten beverages. It should be noted that honey can cause health-threatening bacteria to grow in the immature digestion system of infants, so caution should be used when feeding infants food which contain this sweetener.

FOREWORD

You can ask almost anyone, anywhere in the world, what is most important to them, and right at the top of the list will be good health. Without good health, other things suddenly seem unimportant. But wishing doesn't make it so, unless you believe in fairy tales. Good health is the result of many things, and good eating habits are one of the most important contributing factors.

There is nothing better for your health than fresh fruits and vegetables. First, and most importantly, they taste good, and that by itself contributes to our general well being. They are exceptionally high in vitamins and minerals and provide roughage, bulk, and fibers which are now recognized to be so very important in the daily diet and necessary to good digestion. They are generally low in calories, and as you know, weight control is one of the major medical problems today and obesity is a contributing factor to many other diseases. Good food and good health go hand in hand.

Doctors tell us vitamin C is very important in the prevention of colds. If you believe in vitamins, you don't have to go to a health food or a drug store for them. Go right to the fresh fruit and vegetable counters of your favorite market. Of all the vitamin C available in foods, 95% comes from fruits and vegetables in fresh or processed form and, of course, the fresher, the better. Fifty-two (52%) percent of vitamin A comes from fruits and vegetables. Go directly to the source.

There's no question about the fact that we choose fresh vegetables in our house. We have a couple every day because they have so much more nutrition and flavor when they are fresh.

NATURAL MEANS NUTRITIOUS

There has been a tremendous move toward fresh, natural foods in the past few years, and we have to give the credit to the young folks who are concerned with ecology and nutrition. They want to buy the natural product, and because of this, sales on many fresh fruits and vegetables have increased by 30% or more. Today, people are interested in good food and in vitamins and minerals. They haven't been in the business for 40 years like I have, but they know as much about celery and broccoli as I do. They know celery is low in calories and has vitamin A and vitamin C. They know it's full of bulk and why that is important. It's a good sign that young people are asking questions and want to know what it is all about.

In the last generation, we've witnessed a lot of kids who don't know that peas come from pods or that potatoes are born in the ground. Many of them thought orange juice came from cans and milk from cartons. It's sad, but true. Let them in the kitchen and let them know where their food comes from. Shelling fresh, young peas is a wonderful experience, and they can make these fantastic discoveries for themselves. If there are any peas left when they get done, you can have some of them for dinner!

IT'S UP TO YOU

We have to develop minds of our own about food. For the sake of your family's health, you have to give them the best food available. The average grocer doesn't care, unless he specifically wants to sell fresh fruits and vegetables. He doesn't care if he sells the customer a package of frozen peas, a can of peas, a package of dried peas, or a pound of fresh peas. He doesn't care which one you buy because his only interest at the end of the week is whether he had good business and made a profit. He doesn't care what you bought, and he isn't going to take the time and the trouble to divert his traffic. Why should he break his neck to sell fresh produce?

The consumer can read what the FDA says; they can read that they are buying inferior quality.

ECONOMICS

And I'll tell you something else, compared to the cost of processed foods, you are going to find that fresh produce is not only beneficial from a nutritional standpoint, but, economically, it's far less expensive. It's great to save money and gain a bonus of the flavor and nutrition, too.

If you go in blind and buy only convenience and prepared foods, it is going to cost you a lot more. It's a result of our culture—when people are making more money, the standard of living rises and they want convenience. You have to supply them with food in a convenient form. Just go look at the amount of merchandise that is sold from the frozen food counter, the prepared dinners, the prepared vegetables, desserts, everything. If people would stop to analyze the difference between the price of anything that is processed, compared to the in-season fresh, they would get a big shock. If they bought fresh fruits and vegetables and if they ate more of them instead of junk moods, they would certainly save a lot of money. There is no question about that, and if the price they pay were only in money, it wouldn't be so bad. But they are also paying a high price in loss of nutrition.

Another reason for buying fresh fruits and vegetables is that they are frequently available at bargain prices. They make a great sale item to bring people into the store. You've heard of what is called a loss leader. It's an item they can put on sale at or below cost and not take too much of a beating. For example, if a store puts coffee, sugar, or canned vegetables on sale at a ridiculously low price, people would buy it by the case and store it. Many stores prefer to sell produce at very low price on special because, after all, how many pounds of fresh cherries or peaches or tomatoes can you buy? If you don't eat them within a week, you're going to throw them out. So, that's what's happening now. It's a tremendous value to the average person.

We have gone through a phase of living on canned and frozen produce and need to be re-educated to learn how to buy fresh fruits and vegetables. We don't know what to look for or what to look out for.

THEY TALK TO YOU

You know, people tease me because on my radio and television shows, and in my newspaper column, I say that fresh fruits and vegetables talk to you. You've probably heard that if you talk to your house plants, say 'good morning' to your philodendron and 'good evening' to your Boston fern, they will thrive and grow. Well, I don't know about that, but I do know fresh fruits and vegetables talk to you. They talk to you with their colors and aromas. When a banana, for example, has dark spots on its skin, or sugar spots as they are called in the produce business, it means that the banana has completely converted from starch to sugar. They are fragrant, bursting with flavor and that is when they are easy to digest and assimilate. Let's look at a pineapple. There is a fallacy that if you pull on the leaves and they come out easily, it is ripe, but that isn't so—it may have been bruised. Ninety-nine times out of a hundred, the only way to determine if a pineapple is ripe is by its bright golden color, and when it is ripe you can smell it from a block away. Now, that's talking! The important thing to remember in buying any fresh fruit or vegetable is that is should look fresh. There are different things to look for as far as color and texture are concerned, and we'll discuss those things as we come to each fresh fruit and vegetable in season.

SEASONS

This book is arranged by season and reflects the availability of each particular fresh fruit and vegetable throughout the majority of the country. Naturally, there are differences in the growing seasons from one state to another and from one area to another. As a matter of fact, there are items listed here for summer or fall which are actually available all year long in many parts of the United States. Winter growing areas, such as Florida and the west coast of Mexico, have changed the whole concept of availability of fresh fruits and vegetables. Refrigerated truck and jet air transportation, as well as improved varieties of the fresh fruits and vegetables themselves, provide a great diversity of available produce over long periods of time.

In addition to using the general guide this book produces, take a few moments to look over what is available in the produce department when you are doing your shopping. You will quickly learn from the abundance and from the prices what is in-season and available locally in fresh fruits and vegetables. Then take advantage of that knowledge by serving your family those foods at their finest, when they are ripe and full of nutrition and at their least expensive, in-season price.

SALADS

For your health's sake, start your meal with a salad. It's low in calories and will cut your appetite for large amounts of bread and meat. In Europe, mainly France and Italy, many believe in eating the salad last because it is thought to help with digestion. But, no matter when, what is most important is that you eat your salad.

Salads are easy to prepare because, for the most part, they are eaten raw. The definition for salad is "a dish of greens," but you don't have to stick to iceberg lettuce and tomatoes. You can use almost any combination of fresh vegetables and make an excellent salad. And, of course, fresh raw vegetables contain far more vitamins, minerals, and enzymes than cooked vegetables because every time you cook vegetables, you lose some of the nutrition.

11

Salads put your teeth to work because they require some serious chewing, and that is the best possible exercise your teeth and gums can get. So to take care of your health, start eating more salads – they're loaded with good things for your body and they are low in calories.

SOUPS AND STEWS

I've talked about the fact that raw vegetables contain more nutrition than cooked vegetables. You know, so many people cook their vegetables and throw away the water—then what happens? They throw away the vitamin- and mineral-enriched water and then end up eating vitamin-poor food. My grandmother always said, "For goodness sake, don't throw the pot lickers away," and she was right. You can add a little bouillon and serve it as a clear soup before a meal.

One other way to make sure you get the value of the vitamins and minerals is by using fresh vegetables in soups and stews. This is so important that we have devoted a full chapter to it. Not only do they retain the important body-building nutrients, but you can't find a more satisfying, nourishing, and economical meal than a good soup or stew.

DESSERTS

While we are talking about good health and nutrition, I have to say something about desserts. As far as I'm concerned, the plainer, the better and the better for you. What could be tastier than a fresh, ripe pear or peach or a slice of in-season melon? Or, try a crisp, fresh Gravenstein apple and a slice of good cheese. It is so satisfying and so good for you...so nutritional. Fresh fruit at the end of the meal – it fills you up, not out. These are things that are important.

ENDANGERED FRESH FRUITS
AND VEGETABLES

We've also devoted a chapter to what I call endangered species of fresh fruits and vegetables. There are several reasons—one of the most common being that the growers are using hybrids to produce larger or more attractive produce. For example, you seldom see white corn anymore. When yellow corn was introduced, it looked so great that everyone started buying it. That golden color is attractive, but the white corn is just as nutritious and just as flavorful. And where is the white asparagus and white grapefruit? When the pink or red grapefruit was introduced, people stopped eating white grapefruit. Gooseberries, currants, crabapples, rhubarb, and blood peaches are all also endangered species. In some cases, the growers find they can make more money by growing fruits or vegetables which bring a higher price on the market. The result is that things which used to be familiar items on our table have simply disappeared from the produce scene.

EXOTIC FRESH FRUITS AND VEGETABLES

You know one thing that really keeps life interesting is that there are new and different things to try all the time. When you are too old to try something new, you are really over the hill. But because of newer, speedier transportations, jet air cargo, controlled temperature storage and other innovations, we are finding strange, new things in our fresh produce departments.

Not so long ago, only the coastal states received supplies of fresh tropical fruits like mangoes and papayas. Now they are available throughout the country, but we still think of them as strange, exotic, and exciting. Belgian endive used to be a specialty item only for the wealthy gourmet; it is now available at prices everyone can afford.

There is also Jicama, sometimes referred to as the Mexican potato and pronounced 'Hicama'. And just a short time ago, I saw the strangest fruit I have ever seen in my life; it's called 'carambola', or 'star fruit', and you can have some fun with this one. Every time you slice it, it makes a perfect star. It's fantastic for fancy dishes, and it takes good, too. Because of all these new and unusual foods, we have also included a chapter on exotic fresh fruits and vegetables and hope it will encourage you to try some new things.

As you know, I like things simple and natural. Within the pages of this book, you'll find easy, natural ways to prepare fresh fruits and vegetables. Those are especially my favorites. You'll find them marked with a special sprout symbol, and that means it is a Joe Carcione favorite. But I also know that the ladies, especially, like to fix fancy dishes for special occasions. Many of our readers, listeners, and viewers have sent me their favorites, and we have included many of them. In addition, the real experts of each fresh fruit and vegetable industry have been kind enough to share recipes for their particular product, which have been tested by taste and nutrition experts. Of course, we have included these. It all adds up to good taste, good nutrition, and good sense.

SPRING

SPRING

I think everyone looks forward to spring more than any other season. It is the most distinctive time of change and birth. The long, dormant winter months are behind, and soon the trees will start to bud.

Shortly thereafter, particularly in areas where spring comes earlier than in other parts of the country, young, first lettuce will be coming in and then radish. Particularly in the southeastern states, fresh and tender greens will be arriving. Artichokes and asparagus will also become plentiful once again.

Kids will get more active as the days grow warmer, so it's a good idea to keep a bowl of fresh fruit around to provide nutrition for extra energy. Strawberries will arrive in plenty of time for Mother's Day, and by the time Memorial Day comes, the produce department should be well stocked with beautiful fresh fruits and the tender, young vegetables that always taste best in springtime.

ARTICHOKES

Artichokes are an edible bud of a thistle plant.
They are very low in calories (except for the mayonnaise)
because most of the carbohydrates are in the form
of inulin, a starch that the body handles differently
from other sugars. They are known to be beneficial
for diabetics because the inulin is known to improve
blood sugar control.

Artichokes are becoming more and more popular, and they should because the artichoke is high in nutrition and low in calories. In addition, they are different and fun to eat. You know, you never have much trouble getting kids to eat corn on the cob, and the reason for that is the fact that it's on the cob. If you could put peas on a cob, they would probably love them, too. The artichoke has its own special personality. It, too, is a finger food. When cooked whole, simply pull off the outer leaves one at a time and dip the tender, fleshy end at the base of each leaf in a sauce or dressing. Draw the end of the leaf through the teeth, scraping off the edible part of each leaf and discard the rest.

Continue leaf after leaf until you reach the cone. The tips of these can also be eaten. After removing the core or choke, which is the fuzzy center, you will then have the fleshy bottom or heart to eat with a fork. This is the taste treat of the artichoke.

To cook artichokes, simply stand them upright, and trimming, in a deep saucepan that is large enough to hold them snug. Cook covered, in two or three inches of gently boiling salted water for 35 to 45 minutes until base can be pierced easily with a fork. A few drops of oil and a dash of lemon juice in the water will make the leaves glisten to prevent darkening. Lift out the cooked artichokes and turn them upside down to drain. If the artichokes are to be stuffed, gently spread leaves and remove the choke or thistle-portion from the center with a metal spoon.

17

ARTICHOKES WITH HOT GARLIC BUTTER

4 medium artichokes,
  prepared as directed

1 cup butter
1 large clove garlic, slivered

While artichokes are cooking, melt butter over low heat. Add garlic and continue heating for 30 minutes over very low heat. For clarified butter, strain through several thicknesses of cheese cloth, pouring only the clear yellow liquid through the cheese cloth, or remove garlic and serve.

ARTICHOKES WITH MORNAY SAUCE

4 artichokes, cooked as directed
2 Tbsp. butter or margarine
3 Tbsp. flour
1/2 tsp. salt
dash cayenne

1/2 tsp. dry mustard
1 cup milk
2 Tbsp. grated Gruyere
  cheese (about 1 oz.)
2 Tbsp. light cream

While artichokes are cooking, melt butter. Blend in flour, 1/2 teaspoon salt, cayenne, and mustard. Gradually add milk and cook over low heat, stirring constantly, until thickened. Add cheese and cook over low heat, stirring constantly, until cheese is melted. Stir in cream. Serve hot artichokes with sauce. *Serves 4.*

ITALIAN ARTICHOKE SAUTÉ

6 medium artichokes
boiling salted water
1 Tbsp. lemon juice
2 cloves garlic, finely chopped

freshly ground pepper
1 tsp. oregano leaves
1 tsp. salt
1/4 cup olive oil

Wash artichokes and remove 2 to 3 layers of outer leaves. Trim off 2/3 from top of artichoke and cut in half. Cover and cook artichokes in 2 to 3 inches boiling salted water with lemon juice until tender; 20 to 30 minutes. Drain and remove chokes from center of artichoke halves. In a large skillet, sauté artichokes in heated oil with remaining ingredients until lightly browned.

ARTICHOKES WITH PARSLEY-CHIVE SAUCE

4 artichokes, cooked as
  directed and chilled
1 pkg. (3 ozs.) cream cheese,
  softened
1/2 tsp. salt

1 Tbsp. chopped chives
1/3 cup finely chopped
  parsley
1 Tbsp. milk
1/4 tsp. Tabasco

While artichokes are cooking, combine remaining ingredients; blend well and chill. Serve with parsley-chive sauce. *Serves 4.*

ARTICHOKES WITH BACON-CHEESE DIP

4 artichokes, prepared as
  directed
1 jar (5 ozs.) processed bacon-
  cheese spread
2 Tbsp. lemon juice

1 pkg (3 ozs.) cream cheese,
  softened
3 Tbsp. milk
1/4 cup chopped celery

Combine cheese spread, cream cheese, and milk; beat until well blended. Add celery and lemon juice; mix well. Serve dip with artichokes.

ARTICHOKES DELIGHT

4 artichokes, prepared as
  directed for stuffing
2 Tbsp. butter or margarine
1 Tbsp. lemon juice
1/2 lb. mushrooms, sliced
1 Tbsp. flour

3/4 tsp. salt
1/8 tsp. pepper
1 Tbsp. chopped parsley
1/2 cup milk
1 cup heavy cream
grated Parmesan cheese

While artichokes are cooking, melt butter; add lemon juice and mushrooms. Cook until mushrooms are tender, stirring frequently; reserve a few slices for garnish. Stir in flour, salt, pepper, and parsley. Gradually stir in milk and cream, blending until smooth. Cook, stirring constantly, until sauce thickens. Pour sauce into hot, cooked artichokes. Sprinkle with parmesan cheese. Add mushroom slices and a little parsley, if desired. *Serves 4.*

BEEF STROGANOFF
STUFFED ARTICHOKES

1/4 cup chopped onion
1/4 cup chopped onion
butter or margarine
1 1/2 lbs. beef round steak, cut
   into 2 x 1/2 inch strips
1 & 1/2 cup beef stock
1 Tbsp. chili sauce

2 Tbsp. flour
water
1 tsp. salt
dash pepper
1 cup dairy sour cream
6 medium artichokes,
   prepared as directed

Cook onion and mushroom in 4 tablespoons butter until onion is tender; remove from skillet. Brown beef strips in 2 tablespoons butter in skillet. Add onion, mushrooms, beef stock, and chili sauce. Cover and simmer for 1 hour or until meat is tender. Blend flour with 2 tablespoons cold water to make a smooth paste; add to skillet and cook until thickened, stirring constantly. Stir in salt and pepper. Blend a small amount of gravy with sour cream and return to skillet; blend well. Spoon meat and mushrooms into artichokes; serve gravy as dip for leaves. *Serves 6.*

CHICKEN STUFFED ARTICHOKES

4 artichokes, cooked as directed
1/4 cup grated Parmesan cheese
12 ozs. boned chicken
1/4 cup chopped chives
1 egg, beaten
1/4 cup milk

1/4 cup fine dry bread
   crumbs
1/4 tsp. tarragon
1/4 tsp. oregano
1/2 tsp. salt
1 tsp. paprika

While artichokes are cooking, combine remaining ingredients; mix well. Fill hot artichokes with chicken mixture and arrange in a deep 2 and 1/2-quart casserole dish. Bake covered in a moderate oven (350°F) for 15 minutes. Uncover and bake for 15 minutes longer. *Serves 4.*

GREENS

Watch your produce department for the arrival of fresh, young and tender, locally-grown greens since seasons vary widely throughout the country. Greens are low in calories and contribute vitamin A and bulk to the diet. The use of greens in salads has increased tremendously. They add interesting new flavors, textures, and of course, nutrition.

We have two favorite recipes for cooking greens at our house. We cook them just until tender and add a little garlic, olive oil, salt and pepper, and sprinkle with freshly grated Parmesan or Romano cheese. Another favorite is to cook them in Neapolitan Tomato Sauce, the recipe for which you will find in the section on Tomatoes.

Another family recipe which we refer to frequently is Pesto Sauce made from basil.

PESTO SAUCE

Pick approximately a pint of fresh basil leaves and chop together with 3 to 4 cloves of garlic. When finely chopped, add enough olive oil to moisten. Add salt and pepper to taste. This may be made ahead and stored in a covered dish in the refrigerator for use as needed.

Add Pesto sparingly to salads for added zest. Many Italians add this mixture to spaghetti. After the spaghetti has been cooked and drained, add some butter and the Pesto Sauce together with grated Parmesan or Romano cheese. It is delicious. In the section on Soups and Stews, you will find a recipe for Minestrone which suggests stirring a couple of tablespoons of Pesto sauce into the Minestrone for added flavor.

POWERFUL LEAFY GREENS

*Leafy greens, such as collard, kale spinach, chard,
turnip greens, and mustards, possess just about everything
we need in the form of vitamins and minerals, key
anti-oxidants and fiber. Choose favorite recipes and eat often!*

Leafy greens should not be underestimated! We should learn easy-to-fix recipes and eat them often. Spinach, beets, (beet leaves), and Chard are in the same family and possess large amount of calcium, iron, vitamin A, and Vitamin C. (Spinach, especially, has twice the concentration of iron than most other vegetables.) Kale and other members of the cabbage or cruciferous family, such as mustard greens, turnip greens, and collards, provide excellent levels of vitamin C, potassium, calcium, and iron. It should be noted that the cabbage family possesses sulfur compounds, making them powerful disease and cancer fighters.

SIMPLE RAW KALE & AVOCADO SALAD
Contributed by Kristin Hoppe

*1 large bunch Kale, cut
  chiffonade (sliced in thin strips)
1 small avocado, diced
1 Tbsp. sesame seeds,
  optional*

*1 Tbsp. olive oil
1 Tbsp. Tamari (Wheat Free
  Soy Sauce) or 1 tsp sea salt*

In a large bowl, place kale. Add olive oil and tamari or salt. Massage kale with hands until it becomes soft. Add diced avocado and sesame seeds and toss to combine. Serve immediately!

COLLARD GREEN AND LENTIL STEW
Contributed by Beatrice Johnson

1 bunch of fresh collard greens
1 large onion, diced
1 tablespoon cumin
1/4 cup olive oil
6 cups water
A dash of cayenne pepper

1 cup dry red lentils
4 cloves garlic, minced
2 teaspoons cinnamon
3 teaspoons salt
1 lemon, juiced

Remove the stems from the collard greens (discard). Rinse and thinly slice. Rinse lentils and sort through them for any discolored lentils or pebbles. Heat the olive in large skillet on low flame. Add in onion and cook until brown at edges. Stir in the lentils, water and salt, increase flame and bring to a boil. Lower flame to medium and cover until lentils are tender, about 30 minutes. Stir every several minutes. Add remaining seasonings except for lemon juice and cayenne pepper and simmer for 10 minutes. Remove from heat and stir in lemon juice and cayenne pepper.

YOU WOULDN'T KNOW IT'S VEGAN STEW
Contributed by Zuzy Martin Lynch

1 bunch of kale (chopped)
2 large carrots (chopped)
2 parsnips (chopped)
2 vegetarian sausages cut into
* pieces (eggplant, fennel,*
* fresh garlic, red pepper)*
1/2 teaspoon of garlic powder
1/4 teaspoon of cumin
1 avocado, (for dressing at end)

1 bag of dry beans of choice
* (garbanzo - high fiber)*
1 sweet potato (chopped)
1 lemon (juice)
32-62 ounces water or
* vegetable stock*
1/2 teaspoon of kosher salt
1/4 teaspoon of red pepper

(Continued on next page)

Soak beans overnight or at least 4 hours. Bring beans to a gentle boil in 32 ounces of water or stock. Mix spices together and add about half of spices (spice to your taste along the way). Boil for 1 hour, stir occasionally, and add water or stock as necessary. Add all ingredients and continue gently boiling for 1 hour or until desired level of consistency. Place in a large bowl, top with 2 slices of avocado and an extra squeeze of lemon. *Yields 6 to 8 servings.*

SIMPLY SAUTÉED KALE
Contributed by Zuzy Martin Lynch

1/2 bunch of kale
2 cloves of garlic (sliced)
Sea salt

2 Tablespoons Extra Virgin
  Olive Oil
Pepper

Remove stems at end of bunch of kale and chop. Heat olive oil in saucepan. Add garlic slices and sizzle for a few seconds to release flavors. Add a pinch of sea salt and pepper to olive oil. Add chopped kale and continuously toss with tongs for 4 to 5 minutes (until medium tender). Serve as delicious side dish or healthy snack! *Yields 2 servings.*

RAW KALE SALAD
Contributed by
Simla Somturk Wickless

For the salad:

1 bunch kale, stems removed,
leaves rolled up and sliced into
very thin strips
3 to 4 Tbsp. toasted pumpkin seeds
1/4 cup pomegranate seeds

3 to 4 Tbsp. goat/sheep feta
or goat cheese, crumbled
(optional if sensitive to
dairy)

(Dressing recipe on next page)

For the dressing, per bunch of kale:

Juice from 1 whole lemon
1 Tbsp. olive oil

2 Tbsp. Dijon mustard
Sea salt, to taste

Place all the salad ingredients in a large salad bowl. Combine and whip (with a fork) the dressing ingredients. Toss salad with dressing, and enjoy! *Serves 2 generously.*

Optional:
*other (ideally seasonal) fruit such as apples, pears, oranges, tangerines, or persimmon
*other seeds or nuts

OPA GREENS!
Contributed by Alexandra I. Lopez

2 (1 pound) bunches of assorted
  greens like kale or rainbow
  chard
1/4 cup apple cider vinegar
1/4 cup fresh mint, finely chopped
1/4 cup toasted walnuts, roughly
  chopped

2 shallots, minced
1 teaspoon red pepper flakes
2 tablespoons olive oil
1/4 cup fresh dill, finely
  chopped
1/2 cup crumbled feta cheese
Salt and pepper to taste

Remove leaves of greens from stems and cut into thin strips, stems cut into 1/2 inch pieces. In a large stock pot, heat olive oil over medium heat. Cook shallots until fragrant and slightly tender, about 3 to 4 minutes. Add in the chopped stems and pepper flakes and cook for 5 minutes. Add in the cut leaves and vinegar, cover pot and cook for another 5 to 7 minutes or until greens are tender and most of the liquid has evaporated. Remove greens from heat, add in the fresh herbs and walnuts, and season with salt and pepper to taste. Top cooked greens with crumbled feta cheese. Great served over polenta. *Serves 4.*

25

SWISS CHARD
Contributed by Bruce Reizenman

2 bunches Swiss Chard
1 Tablespoon butter
8 each garlic cloves, peeled
  and sliced thin

1 Tablespoon olive oil
1/2 yellow onion, peeled,
  diced
Salt & pepper to taste

Remove ribs from Swiss chard and slice. Rinse chard and place in a colander to drain. Chop roughly.

In a large skillet, heat olive oil. Add onion and garlic. Cover and cook over medium low heat. Add to chard ribs a small amount of salt. Replace the cover and cook for 5 more minutes. Add chard leaves and cook for an additional 8 to 10 minutes until chard is wilted and cooked. Add extra salt and pepper to taste. *Serves 6.*

SAUTÉED SWISS CHARD
Contributed by Deborah Dal Fovo

2 & 1/4 pounds/1 kilo Swiss chard
8 tablespoons/113g butter
Kosher salt

1/4 cup extra virgin olive oil
1 shallot, finely minced
freshly ground black pepper
  to taste

Tear or cut the dark green leaves from the Swiss chard stalks, reserving the stalks for another use (see recipe for Gratinéed Swiss Chard Stalks with Parmigiano, page 27). Soak the leaves in a large bowl of cold water for 5 minutes then rinse thoroughly under cold running water to remove any soil.

Transfer the chard leaves to a large sauté pan and sprinkle with 1 teaspoon salt. Add 1 cup of water, cover and place over medium heat. Cook the chard leaves for 6 to 7 minutes until tender, stirring occasionally as they reduce. Remove the cooked leaves from the pan and drain in colander if needed. When the chard has cooled slightly, transfer to a cutting board and chop into large pieces or wide ribbons.

Heat the olive oil, butter and minced shallots in a large skillet over medium heat. Cook the shallots, stirring, for about 2 minutes until soft and translucent. Add the chopped chard leaves and toss to coat with the cooking oils. Season to taste with salt and pepper, then sauté for 3 to 4 minutes, stirring occasionally. Serve hot or warm as an accompaniment to meats and poultry. *Serves 6.*

 ## GRATINÉED SWISS CHARD STALKS WITH PARMIGIANO
Contributed by Deborah Dal Fovo

2&1/4 pounds/1 kilo Swiss chard
Freshly grated Parmigiano
   Reggiano cheese

4 tablespoons/65g butter
Kosher salt and freshly
   ground black pepper to
   taste

Preheat the oven to 400°F/200°C. Bring a large pot of water to a boil over high heat. When the water boils, add a handful of salt and return to a full boil.

Tear or cut the leaves off the Swiss chard stalks and reserve leaves for another use (see recipe for Sautéed Swiss Chard, page 26). Wash the stalks thoroughly under cold running water. Trim ends off stalks and discard. Cut the stalks into uniform pieces of approximately 1 inch by 4 inches. Drop the chard stalks into the boiling water and reduce the heat to medium. Boil the chard for 20 minutes until tender, then drain well.

Generously butter the bottom and sides of a shallow baking dish. Arrange one layer of chard stalks in the baking dish. Dot the chard with butter and sprinkle with grated cheese. Place another layer of chard stalks over the cheese, building another layer in the same manner as the first. Repeat with all the chard and finishing with a final layer of grated cheese.

Place in the upper half of the hot oven and bake for 10-15 minutes until a golden crust forms on surface. Remove from oven and cool for 15 minutes before serving warm as a side dish. *Serves 6.*

SAUTÉED SWISS CHARD WITH LEMON & GARLIC
Contributed by Cindi Avila

1 bunch of green Swiss chard
2 tablespoons olive oil
Salt
Fresh ground pepper

1 tablespoon lemon juice
2 tablespoons of minced garlic

Boil medium pot of water. Cut off bottom of stems (below the leaves). Once water comes to a boil, add all of the Swiss Chard. This is just to blanch them (cook quickly to retain color). Leave in pot for just 1 minute. Strain in colander and immediately shock with cold water to stop the cooking.

Heat olive oil in large sauté pan over medium heat. Cut leaves off white stalks. Dice stalks into small pieces (about 1/4 wide). Add stalk pieces to hot pan. Add garlic to pan.

Chop leaves into 2-inch pieces. Add to pan. Stir to make sure olive oil and garlic are evenly distributed. Add lemon juice, salt and pepper to taste. Cook for just about a minute. Serve immediately.

NUTRIENT RICH
RAINBOW SALAD
Contributed by Connie Umbenhower

The following salad is delicious and filled with amazing health benefits and a rainbow of colors.

In addition to wholesome carrots, apples, and nuts, one serving of this salad contains nutrient-rich kale and Swiss chard loaded with minerals and vitamins A, C, and K; Red, yellow and green bell peppers high in antioxidants, phytochemicals, and lycopene, known to fight heart disease, stroke, and cancer; and cilantro, which is a powerful cleansing agent, good for the digestion, and full of antibacterial qualities.

2 cups red Swiss chard, chopped
1 cup celery, chopped
1 cup red apple, chopped
1 cup yellow pepper, chopped
1/2 cup finely chopped cilantro

2 cups kale, chopped
2 cups Romaine lettuce, chopped
1 cup red pepper, chopped
1/2 cup shredded carrots
1/4 cup slivered almonds

Wash vegetables and apples thoroughly, prepare and drain using a salad spinner so salad is nice and dry. Mix thoroughly in a large bowl. Sprinkle slivered almonds over the top of the salad and serve with your favourite dressing.

GRILLED ROMAINE WITH
AGED BALSAMIC AND OIL
Contributed by Diem Doonan

Salad:
2 Romaine hearts, washed, dried, cut lengthwise
(Continued on next page)

2 to 3 Tbsp. shaved Parmigiano Reggiano

Dressing:

1/4 cup aged balsamic vinegar
Sea salt and fresh ground pepper
to taste

1/3 cup extra virgin olive oil
(save 1 Tbsp. for grilling)

Brush cut side of romaine heart with olive oil and lay face-down on grill over medium high heat. Once romaine is slightly charred or the middle is slightly limp (about 2 to 3 minutes), remove from grill onto plate. Drizzle with balsamic, olive oil, and season with salt & pepper. Garnish with shaved slices of Parmigianno Reggiano. *Servings: 2 entrée salads or 4 sides.*

SWEET RAINBOW CHARD
Contributed by
Simla Somturk Wickless

1 bunch rainbow chard
1 small sweet potato or jewel
yam, scrubbed and largely
diced into bite-size pieces
3 to 4 Tbsp. mirin (sweet rice
vinegar)
1/4 to 1/2 cup broth or
filtered water

1 medium yellow onion,
peeled and chopped into
half moons
2 Tbsp. extra virgin olive oil
2 to 4 swigs of Umeboshi
plum vinegar, to taste (salty
and sour, yum!)

Prepare rainbow chard, washed, with stem ends cut off but rest of stems included, chopped, or torn into bite-size pieces – stems and leaves separate, if possible. If not, don't worry about it. Use a large sauté pan with high edges, as the rainbow chard takes up a lot of room before it deflates in size. A heavy-bottomed stainless steel pot works well.

Heat the olive oil in the sauté pan over low-medium heat for 1 to 2 minutes. Add onions, stir for 1 to 2 minutes. Add sweet potato, stir for 1 minute, then let cook for about 10 to 15 minutes, stirring every 3 to 4 minutes to prevent burning. Add the chard stems and stir in, letting it cook for another 5 minutes. Lastly, add the chopped chard leaves plus 1/4 to 1/2 cup of broth or filtered water. Add both vinegars, to taste, and let simmer until sweet potatoes are cooked through, about another 10 minutes or so.

Serve over any type of grain. Fantastic served with pan-roasted, simply seasoned chicken breast and a brown and wild rice medley. *Serves 6 to 8.*

SPINACH

Popeye is right! Spinach has the ability to restore energy.
It has twice as much iron than most other greens, and its strength
of carotenes and chlorophyll make it a great cancer fighter.

About this time of year (depending on your area's spring season), you will find nice young and tender spinach available, and usually at a very reasonable price. Many people are trying raw spinach salad, and they are enjoying it. There is a real difference in the flavor and taste of raw spinach in comparison with cooked spinach.

"JEANNE'S GREENIE"

6 slices bacon   *One bunch of fresh spinach*
2 hard boiled eggs

Rinse spinach in salt water, then fresh water, to remove all sand. Shake well and pat dry with paper towels. Tear into bite-size pieces in salad bowl. Fry bacon until crisp, drain and crumble into small pieces over the spinach. Dice hard boiled eggs over spinach. Keep chilled until ready to serve. Just before serving, add vinegar, olive oil, salt and pepper to taste. Try different kinds of vinegar (red wine, garlic, tarragon, etc.) for variety.

FIELD SALAD

2 avocados, sliced   *1/2 cup pepitos, peanuts,*
10 ozs. fresh spinach   *pistachio or pine nuts*
1 lb. bacon, cooked crisp and   *Italian salad dressing*
  crumbled

Rinse, drain, and tear spinach. Chill in bowl or plastic bag. Arrange avocado slices with bacon and nuts on spinach in salad bowl. *Serves 6 to 8.* Note: Watercress may be substituted for half the spinach.

SPINACH WITH GARLIC

Prepare and chop spinach. Instead of white sauce, simmer in a brown sauce, made as follows:

1 Tbsp. butter
1 Tbsp. flour
1/2 cup strong bouillon

1 clove garlic, mashed
salt and pepper to taste

Brown the butter. Mix in the flour smoothly. Add bouillon and stir over low heat until thickened. Then add garlic and seasoning. Combine chopped spinach with the brown sauce and simmer, tightly covered, for 15 to 20 minutes. *Serves 6.*

SPINACH WITH SWEET CREAM

3 lbs. spinach, cleaned and
*   parboiled in salted water*
*   for 5 minutes*
1 Tbsp. butter
dash of sugar

1 Tbsp. flour
1/2 cup sweet cream (milk, if
*   preferred)*
salt and pepper to taste

Drain parboiled spinach and rinse under cold water to restore color. Chop fine and press through a sieve. Melt butter, blend in flour, add cream, and stir until smooth. Season, add spinach, and simmer tightly covered for 15 to 20 minutes. Note: Serve garnished with slices of hard cooked egg, if desired. *Serves 6.*

SWEET-SOUR SPINACH

1 lb. spinach
1 large onion
2 Tbsp. shortening
2 Tbsp. flour

2 Tbsp. brown sugar
1 tsp. salt
1 cup tomatoes
1/2 cup cider vinegar

Wash and drain spinach. Shred or chop leaves and stems. Brown diced onion in shortening. Stir in flour and blend till light brown. Add vinegar in which sugar has been dissolved. Add salt. Stir till smooth. Add tomatoes and chopped spinach and cook for 3 minutes. *Serves 4.*

SPINACH AU GRATIN

3 lbs. spinach
7 Tbsp. butter
1/4 to 1/2 lb. kefalotiri cheese,
  grated
toasted bread crumbs
3 eggs, either hard cooked or
  1 egg, beaten raw (optional)

Bechamel Sauce
1 can evaporated milk
1 can water
1/4 cup butter
1/2 cup flour
salt and pepper to taste

Clean and wash the spinach; cut each leaf until 3 to 4 pieces, and drop into rapidly boiling water. Let the spinach boil for 3 to 4 minutes, then strain it; press out all excess fluid and return it to the pot. Melt 5 tablespoons of the butter, pour it over the spinach.

To prepare the sauce, pour the evaporated milk and water (measured in the milk can) into a pot; scald and keep hot. Melt the 1/4 cup butter in another pot. Blend in the flour. Add the hot milk, stirring constantly until the mixture is smooth and thick. Season with salt and pepper. Cool slightly, then stir in the beaten egg, blending it in well.

Spread a thin layer of the Bechamel in a buttered pan; sprinkle with a little cheese. Spread the rest of the Bechamel over all; sprinkle with the remaining cheese and then with the bread crumbs. Melt the remaining 2 tablespoons butter and drizzle over the casserole. Bake in a preheated 400°F oven for about 20 minutes.

Note: You may add the hard-cooked eggs to this, if you like. Slice them and place them on the spinach before adding the final layer of sauce. Or beat the uncooked eggs and mix them with the spinach before you layer that into the casserole.

SPINACH MEAT BALLS ITALIANO

1 lb. spinach
1 lb. ground beef
1/2 ground pork
1/4 cup chopped parsley
1/4 cup bread crumbs
2 eggs
1/2 chopped onion

1 clove chopped garlic
2 Tbsp. chopped sweet basil
1/2 cup Parmesan cheese
salt and pepper to taste
6 Tbsp. olive oil
6 ozs. tomato sauce
6 ozs. water

Cook spinach and drain real dry. Squeeze out all of the water and chop. Add all other ingredients except tomato sauce and oil. Mix well and make into meatballs and brown in oil.

When browned on both sides, add tomato sauce and water and simmer covered for 45 minutes. Serve with steamed rice.

SPINACH PUDDING

2 lbs. spinach, cleaned
4 eggs, separated
2 rolls
1 & 1/3 cups milk

salt to taste
dash of mace
1/4 cup butter
2 Tbsp. bread crumbs

Soak rolls in milk. Steam spinach for 3 to 5 minutes. Drain and grind. Beat egg yolk until creamy, add rolls, salt, mace, and spinach. Fold in stiffly-beaten egg whites.

Grease a covered pudding well, sprinkle with bread crumbs. Pour in mixture, cover, and cook in a pan of boiling water for about 45 minutes. Serve with melted butter and fried bread crumbs. *Serves 4 to 6.*

SPINACH ARTICHOKE DIP
Contributed by Cindi Avila

1 bag fresh spinach
1 cup lowfat mayonnaise

1 can artichokes
1/2 cup parmesan cheese

Preheat oven to 350 degrees. Blanch spinach by putting in a pot of boiling water for 1 minute. Immediately remove and place in colander. Run cold water over spinach (you can also use frozen spinach that has been defrosted and drained). Chop artichokes into small pieces. Combine all ingredients in a small casserole pan and thoroughly mix. Bake for 25 minutes. Serve hot with crackers.

SPRINGTIME SPINACH SALAD
Contributed by Dole Nutrition Institute

1/2 lb. fresh Dole asparagus or 1 pkg. (10 oz.) frozen asparagus tips
1 pint fresh Dole strawberries, sliced
2/3 cup crumbled feta or blue cheese

1/4 cup water
1 pkg. (6 oz.) Dole baby spinach
1 cup julienne-sliced Dole red onion
1/2 cup bottled raspberry vinaigrette or red wine vinaigrette

Break off woody ends of fresh asparagus (the bottom 1" to 1-1/2") and discard. Cut asparagus into 1" lengths. Place in microwavable dish with water. Microwave on high 3 minutes. Immediately rinse asparagus under cold water 1 minute; drain well. Place asparagus, spinach, strawberries, onion and cheese in large bowl. Toss ingredients with salad dressing; serve immediately. *Serves 6.*

ROASTED FENNEL SPINACH SALAD WITH CHICKEN
Contributed by
Dole Nutrition Institute

3/4 lb. fennel, cut in half
1 & 1/2 lb. grilled chicken
  breast, cut into chunks
1 jar (6 oz.) marinated artichoke
  hearts, drained
2/3 cup shredded Dole carrots
1/3 cup slivered almonds,
  toasted

1 pkg. (6 oz.) Dole baby
  spinach
1 can (14 oz.) artichoke
  hearts, quartered and
  drained
1 & 1/2 cups fat-free Mango
  Vinaigrette

Preheat oven to 375°F. Place fennel on baking sheet coated with cooking spray. Bake for 45 to 60 minutes or until tender. Cool slightly; cut into cubes.

Combine fennel, spinach, chicken, artichoke hearts, and carrots in large bowl. Pour Mango Vinaigrette (see below) over salad. Toss to coat. Sprinkle with almonds. *Serves 6.*

Mango Vinaigrette:

3/4 cup Dole frozen mango
  chunks, thawed
3/4 cup orange juice
1 & 1/2 Tbsp. honey

1/3 cup Dole frozen
  raspberries, thawed
2 & 1/2 Tbsp. rice vinegar

Place above ingredients in blender or food processor. Cover; blend until smooth. *Makes 1 and 3/4 cups.*

PARSLEY

Parsley is extremely rich in chlorophyll and carotenes.
This combination and its high vitamin C content makes
parsley very healthy and a great cancer fighter.

Let me tell you about this little powerhouse of nutrition! It's amazing, but 3 and 1/2 ounces of parsley is one of the finest sources of protein. Three and a half ounces contain 6 grams of protein and is very high in iron. That same 3 and 1/2 ounces gives over 700 units of potassium, 8,500 units of vitamin A, and 172 milligrams of vitamin C. It's really fantastic!

But how can we get people to eat parsley? We see a sprig of it beside our entrées, but most people just throw it away. I don't think parsley should be thought of as a decoration or ornamentation or only as a garnish. It can be included along with your other greens. There's another way—the way my children and I enjoy it.

Mince a bunch of parsley and a clove or two of garlic, depending on how you feel about garlic. At our house, we use two or three cloves, and mince it very, very fine, add a little bit of olive oil, salt and pepper to taste, and then grate a little fresh Romano or fresh Parmesan cheese and mix it all together. We call it Parsley Sauce, and it's absolutely fantastic on steak, fish, or fowl. It's also good on salads as a dressing.

FENNEL

Fennel, also known as Anise, has a mild licorice flavor, and its fern is used as a traditional fish herb. It also works well on lamb and in omelets and salads. Its bulb is crunchy and slightly sweet, adding a refreshing contribution to any cuisine.

PAN-SEARED SCALLOPS WITH FENNEL, WATERCRESS AND ORANGE SALAD
Contributed by Zuzy Martin Lynch

12 U10 dry sea scallops
2 oranges
1 lemon, juiced
2 Tablespoons olive oil

1 head of fennel
1 small bunch of watercress, washed and trimmed
Kosher salt and pepper

Split and core fennel. Thinly slice fennel (about 1/16 inch wide) with mandoline, if available. With a knife, remove skin and pith of the oranges. Cut the oranges into segments (otherwise known as supremes). Reserve any juice, strained to remove seeds.

In a large skillet, over medium-high heat, heat a thin layer of vegetable oil. Season scallops with salt and pepper. Place scallops in pan, careful not to crowd scallops. Cook for about two minutes, then turn scallops over and cook an additional two minutes.

While scallops are cooking, toss fennel, orange segments and watercress with the lemon juice, reserved orange juice and olive oil. Season with salt and pepper. When scallops have finished cooking, remove from heat, place three scallops on each plate. Divide salad evenly among the four plates. *Makes 4 servings.*

FENNEL, ORANGE AND POMEGRANATE SALAD
Contributed by Alexandra I. Lopez

*2 small fennel bulbs, quartered,
cored and thinly shaved
lengthwise
1/2 cup pomegranate seeds
2 tablespoons cilantro,
finely chopped
1 teaspoon agave nectar
Juice of one lime*

*1 cup jicama, peeled and
cut into thin matchsticks
2 oranges (Navel, Cara Cara,
Blood) peeled and cut into
segments
2 tablespoons extra virgin
olive oil
Salt and freshly ground black
pepper to taste*

In a small bowl, whisk together lime juice, agave, and olive oil with salt and pepper.

Toss fennel and jicama in the vinaigrette. Gently mix in the orange segments, pomegranate seeds and cilantro. Keep salad chilled until ready to serve. *Serves 4.*

LETTUCE

Lettuce is a good source of chlorophyll
(the darker the green, the better), and vitamin K,
which is known for its bone-strengthening ability.

Handle a head of lettuce gently. If it gives a little bit or has some spring to it, you know you have a nice, young head of sweet lettuce that's very, very good to eat. If it is white or hard, it has become old on the plant, and it's bitter. Also, be sure to check out the leaf lettuce. You will find that the Butter and Red and the Romaine lettuce are really excellent, too, as far as quality is concerned. And the change once in a while will help you appreciate the different flavors and textures of the various lettuces.

You'll find that some varieties are softer and far more tender than others, and you may be surprised to know the leaf lettuces contain more vitamin C and vitamin A than the crisp head variety, such as iceberg. To get the utmost from iceberg, select only those with outside leaves that are beautiful, bright and green.

GREAT PLAINS SALAD

2 heads fresh iceberg
   lettuce
1 & 1/2 cups sliced zucchini
2 cups julienne cooked beef
   (about 3/4 lb.)

1/3 cup corn oil
3 Tbsp. vinegar
1 tsp. onion salt
1/2 tsp. coarsely ground
   black pepper

PENNSYLVANIA DUTCH-STYLE LETTUCE

1 medium head fresh lettuce
1 beef bouillon cube
1/2 cup water
1/8 tsp. pepper

3/4 tsp. sugar
5 slices bacon
3/4 cup sliced green onions
1/3 cup vinegar

(Continued on next page)

Reserve outer lettuce leaves to line salad bowl; tear remaining lettuce into bite-size pieces. Cook bacon until crisp; crumble and drain on absorbent paper, reserving drippings in pan. Add green onions, vinegar, sugar, bouillon cube, water, and pepper. Bring to a boil and toss with lettuce and bacon. *Makes 4 servings.*

NEW ENGLAND CREAMY CLAM ICEBERG

1 head fresh iceberg lettuce
1 can (4 ozs.) minced clams,
* drained*
3/4 cup real mayonnaise
1/4 cup finely chopped parsley

1 Tbsp. lemon juice
2 tsp. white dinner wine
* (optional)*
3/4 tsp. salt
generous dash pepper

Core, rinse, and drain lettuce thoroughly; chill. Mix all remaining ingredients. Cut lettuce into wedges; chill any remaining lettuce for use another time. Spoon dressing over wedges. Store any remaining dressing in refrigerator for use later in the week. *Makes 5 to 6 servings.*

U.S. CHICKEN SALAD ICEBERG

1 head fresh iceberg lettuce
2 cups cubed cooked chicken
1 Tbsp. chopped green pepper
2 Tbsp. capers

2 Tbsp. chopped pimiento
1/3 cup real mayonnaise
salt
pepper

Core, rinse, and drain lettuce thoroughly; chill in disposable plastic bag or crisper. Remove outer leaves for serving cups. Cut remaining lettuce lengthwise into halves; place cut-sides down on board and cut into bite-size pieces. Lightly mix chicken, green pepper, capers, pimiento, and mayonnaise. Add cut lettuce; toss lightly. Season to taste with salt and pepper. Heap into lettuce cups. *Serves 4.*

STUFFED LETTUCE

6 large green lettuce leaves
6 slices dry bread
1 cup milk
1/2 lb. mushrooms, chopped
4 Tbsp. melted butter

2 egg yolks
1 Tbsp. chopped parsley
1/2 tsp. salt
1/2 cup sour cream
1/2 cup chicken stock

Scald lettuce leaves briefly to wilt. Soften bread slices in milk, squeeze out excess milk and press through sieve. Cook mushrooms with half the butter, parsley, and salt. Combine with the bread and cold egg yolks and cream. Spread the mixture on each lettuce leaf and roll up. Arrange closely together in a buttered baking dish, add chicken stock and bake in a hot oven (400°F) for 20 minutes. Remove to serving dish; pour remaining butter over lettuce rolls and serve.

CARROT STUFFED LETTUCE

1/4 cup grated, peeled carrot
3 Tbsp. sour cream
1/4 tsp. Worcestershire sauce
1 tsp. lemon juice
1/2 tsp. salt
3 Tbsp. minced peeled tomato

3 oz. pkg. cream cheese
1 Tbsp. minced green pepper
1 Tbsp. minced green onion
1 Tbsp. minced celery
2 tsp. minced parsley
1 large head iceberg lettuce

Blend cream cheese, sour cream, Worcestershire sauce, lemon juice, and sauce. Add minced vegetables. Hollow out the core and center of the lettuce. Stuff with carrot vegetable cream cheese filling. Wrap lettuce in aluminum foil. Chill for 5 or 6 hours. Slice crosswise and serve. *Serves 6.*

SALAD OF BUTTER LETTUCE WITH PERSIMMONS, ROASTED GOLDEN BEETS, ORANGES, POMEGRANATE SEEDS AND CITRUS-HONEY DRESSING

Contributed by Bruce Riezenman

With the many starches we serve at our Thanksgiving dinner, a refreshing salad filled with wonderful seasonal ingredients is always welcomed.

I like to toss the butter lettuce very gently with my favorite olive oil first. It flavors and protects the delicate greens from the acid in the dressing, keeping them crisp longer. Top with the rest of the ingredients (or pick what looks best at your local farmer's or neighborhood produce market). I love beets, but not the way red beets stain everything they touch, which is why I suggest golden beets for this salad.

1 head butter lettuce, washed, core removed
1/3 bunch chives, cut into 1/2 inch pieces
2 each Hachiya Persimmons, core removed, top core removed, quartered, then cut into thick slices
1 Tbsp. extra virgin olive oil
1/2 cup Citrus-Honey Dressing (see recipe following)

1 pound golden beets, cut into wedges, pan-roasted and peeled (1 large beet)
1 each pomegranate, whole
2 each oranges, peeled, then quartered, then cut into thick slices (option: peel, then separate the orange meat from the membranes that separate them: these are called supremes.)

Prepare the beets: I have a simple way to cook beets. With the skin still on, wash the outside, trim the ends, and cut into wedges (8 or 12, depending on the size of the beet). Place in a small sauté pan with 1/4 cup of water, a pinch of salt, and a pinch of sugar. Cover and simmer gently for 8 to 10 minutes. Check and toss occasionally. If the water evaporates or is absorbed, add a small amount of water, cover and cook until they are easily pierced with a knife, but not mushy. Let them cool for 10 minutes on the counter. While they are still warm, rub the skins off with a paper towel. They will come off quickly and easily. Allow to cool or chill for later use.

Pull apart the leaves of butter lettuce from each other, wash and dry completely. Toss the leaves with olive oil, and arrange nicely on 4 chilled plates by stacking the leaves loosely on top of each other. Arrange and/or sprinkle the persimmons, beets, and orange segments on the salad. Drizzle with the Citrus-Honey Dressing.

Break open the pomegranate, being careful not to get the juice (it stains!) on your clothing. Separate the red seeds from the white membrane and sprinkle on the salad. Finish with the chopped chives, and if you like, some toasted slices or chopped almonds. Serve and enjoy! *Serves 4.*

CITRUS VINAIGRETTE
Contributed by Bruce Riezenman

Grated zest and juice of one large orange (to yield at least 1/2 cup juice)
1/2 cup olive oil
1 clove garlic, minced
1/4 teaspoon coarse sea salt

Grated zest and juice of one lemon
2 Tablespoons honey
1 scallion, minced
1 teaspoon minced fresh ginger

In a small jar, mix all ingredients together and shake well. Allow to sit at least 20 minutes for flavors to bloom. Shake again and serve with your favorite salad. *Eat well!*

RADISHES

*Radish is a member of the cabbage family,
and along with those benefits, the radish is an
excellent source of vitamin C and potassium.*

Here is a bright and colorful little goodie from the ground that makes a very tasty vegetable dipper or will brighten any salad. It is extremely decorative, and, with a little bit of practice, you can learn to quickly carve a radish into a flower that not only looks good, but is good enough to eat.

SPRING PICNIC SALAD

1 head lettuce	*1/2 tsp. seasoned salt*
2 medium size tomatoes	*1/2 tsp. dry mustard*
1 green pepper	*1/2 tsp. paprika*
8 to 10 radishes	*1/2 tsp. chili powder*
2 or 3 green onions	*2 Tbsp. lemon juice*
1 tsp. sugar	*2 Tbsp. vinegar*
	1/2 cup corn oil

Core, rinse, and drain lettuce thoroughly. Wash remaining vegetables; trim radishes and onions. Place lettuce along with other vegetables in a plastic bowl with cover or in a plastic bag. Chill. Combine sugar, seasoned salt, mustard, paprika, and chili powder in a small plastic bowl or jar with cover. Stir in lemon juice and vinegar. Add oil; cover and shake to blend. Carry plastic containers to picnic. Just before serving, tear lettuce into bite-size pieces, cut tomatoes into wedges and green pepper into strips, and slice radishes and onion; combine in plastic bowl. Shake dressing to blend; pour over vegetables. Toss lightly. *Serves 6.*

ASPARAGUS

Asparagus is rich in minerals and low in calories,
and it is very rich in protein.

Asparagus is a member of the lily family, of which there are 150 different species. Some are ornamental, and some are edible and include such plants as onions, garlic, leeks, lilies, tulips, hyacinths and gladiolas. So you can see, asparagus comes from a pretty good family.

There is very little work to fixing asparagus. Just rinse it in a little water and boil or steam it for a few minutes, and it's ready to eat. Try it with garlic and butter or cooked in Neapolitan Sauce. It ranges in all different sizes, from jumbo down to the very, very thin size that is called spaghettini, which is the favorite of the Italians. It is especially good in omelets. But large or small, always look for bright green, fresh asparagus as soon as possible because, like fresh sweet peas, it loses sugar very quickly. However, if you put it in a plastic bag in the refrigerator, it will keep for at least four or five days.

CREAMED ASPARAGUS

2 lbs. fresh asparagus
1 can cream of asparagus
  soup
1/2 cup Half and Half cream

1 tsp. lemon juice
1 beaten egg
1/2 cup slivered, blanched
  almonds, toasted

Slice fresh asparagus with long, slanting cuts about 1/2 inch thick. Cook in small amount of boiling, salted water until just barely tender. Drain. Combine next 4 ingredients in sauce pan and heat thoroughly. Add the asparagus and almonds. Serve in 6 patty shells or over toast points.

DEEP-FRIED ASPARAGUS

2 lbs. asparagus
salt
2 eggs, beaten

1 to 2 cups flour
fat

Cook asparagus in slightly salted water until half done. Chop off top half of stalks and tie together in bundles of 5 or 6. Dip in beaten egg and then roll in flour. Fry in deep fat. The stubs and cooking water can be used for soup. *Serves 4.*

ASPARAGUS CASSEROLE

2 lbs. fresh asparagus
4 Tbsp. butter
2 Tbsp. flour
2 cups milk

1/4 tsp. fresh ground pepper
salt
4 hard-cooked eggs
1/2 cup cracker crumbs

To prepare fresh asparagus: Slice with long, slanting cuts about 1/4 to 1/2 inch thick. Cook in small amount of boiling, salted water until just barely tender. Drain. Melt two tablespoons butter, blend in flour. Add milk and cook, stirring constantly until mixture comes to a boil and thickens. Add salt to taste and pepper. Arrange half of the cooked asparagus and the 4 eggs, sliced, in the bottom of an 8 x 8 x 2 inch baking dish. Cover with half of the white sauce. Top with the remaining asparagus, then the rest of the white sauce. Sprinkle cracker crumbs on top and dot with 2 tablespoons butter. Bake in 350°F oven for 30 to 35 minutes or until hot and bubbly. *Serves 6.*

HUNGARIAN STYLE ASPARAGUS

2 lbs. asparagus
salted water
1 tsp. sugar

3 Tbsp. butter
1 pt. sour cream
1/2 cup bread crumbs

(Continued on next page)

Peel asparagus and boil until tender in salted water to which a little sugar has been added. Drain. Butter an ovenproof dish. In it, place half of the sour cream and bread crumbs, then asparagus, then cream and bread crumbs again. Bake in 325°F oven for about 30 minutes. *Serves 4 to 6.*

ASPARAGUS TIPS WITH BUTTER

Cut the asparagus into 2-inch lengths and tie them together in bundles. Cut remainder into bits the size of peas. Plunge them into boiling salted water and cook them quickly, to preserve color. Thoroughly drain them; mix with butter and serve the asparagus bunches on top.

They may be served in small patty crusts, or in small tarts crusts, with a few tips on each.

ASPARAGUS WITH HOLLANDAISE

2 bunches asparagus,	*water as required*
trimmed	*1 tsp. salt*

Sauce:

1/2 cup butter	*1/2 cup hot asparagus liquid*
1/4 tsp. salt	*1 Tbsp. lemon juice*
3 egg yolks	*cayenne pepper, if desired*

Cook the trimmed asparagus, standing up, in quickly boiling water with the salt. The tips should not be in the water, but should be steamed for about 15 minutes by putting a smaller pot over the top of the one with the water. Drain well, reserving the liquid.

For the sauce, work the butter until creamy, adding the egg yolks one at a time, then the lemon juice and salt. Just before serving, add the asparagus liquid and stir quickly. Cook in top of a double boiler until thick, stirring constantly. Add a dash of cayenne pepper, if you wish. Serve over the drained asparagus. *Serves 4 to 6.*

EAT-YOUR-VEGETABLES SALAD

1 head lettuce
12 cooked spears fresh
 asparagus
6 radish roses
1/2 pt. plain yogurt

1 Tbsp. minced fresh chives
1 Tbsp. bottled mixed salad
 dressing
1 tsp. sugar
1/2 tsp. salt

Core, rinse and thoroughly drain lettuce; chill in plastic bag. For dressing, blend yogurt, chives, salad seasonings, sugar, and salt; chill. At serving time, cut lettuce head crosswise into "rafts"; cut each in half. (Store remaining lettuce for later use.) Place each half-slice on a salad plate and top with asparagus spears and radish rose. Spoon dressing across each salad. *Makes 6 servings.*

ASPARAGUS QUICHE

1 & 1/2 lbs. fresh asparagus
pie shell
slices bacon
1/8 tsp. nutmeg
1/8 tsp. salt
dash of pepper

4 eggs
1 1/2 cups Half & Half cream
1/2 lb. natural grated Swiss
 cheese
mushrooms (optional)

To prepare fresh asparagus: Snap off and discard woody base of stalks. Slice with long, slanting cuts 1/2 inch thick. Cook in small amount of boiling, salted water until just tender. Drain.

Prepare pie shell and bake for 10 minutes at 400°F. Reduce heat to 375°F. Sauté bacon, cut into small pieces. When crisp, remove and drain on paper towel. Sprinkle the bottom of the pie shell with bacon, Swiss cheese, and then the asparagus.

With a rotary beater, beat eggs, cream, nutmeg, salt, and pepper. Beat until just combined and pour over the ingredients in the pie shell. (If you wish, reserve 1/4 cup asparagus to decorate the top after the mixture has been poured in.) Bake for 40 minutes or until a knife inserted 1 inch from the pastry edge comes out clean. Serve immediately.

ASPARAGUS AND WILTED GREENS IN BLOOD ORANGE, WITH HERBED EASY "AIOLI"
Contributed by Aaron French

1 bunch asparagus
2 tablespoons olive oil
1 to 2 blood oranges, juiced
Salt and pepper, to taste

1 small bunch of at least two kinds of hearty greens, such as rainbow chard and mustard greens

Start a large pot of well-salted water to boil. Break off bottoms of asparagus. Blanch asparagus in boiling water for 45 seconds. Shock asparagus in bowl of cold ice water. Set aside.

Rinse greens, remove stems as necessary, and slice in 1/2-inch strips. Heat olive oil in large sauté pan with lid. Add greens and stir for about 30 seconds. Add 1/8 cup blood orange juice (or other citrus juice if unavailable), cover, and remove from heat. Leave covered for several minutes until greens are wilted. Add salt and pepper, if desired, and arrange in thin layers on plate. Top with asparagus spears, and serve with herb aioli (recipe below).

EASY HERB "AOILI"
Using mayonnaise as a base makes this aioli variation foolproof, while the fresh herbs add seasonal flavor.

1/2 cup mayonnaise
1/4 tsp kosher salt
3/4 cup olive oil
1/4 cup fresh herbs (seasonal choice), stems removed

2 tsp minced fresh garlic
1/4 tsp pepper
1 egg yolk

Place all ingredients except the olive oil in a small food processor, and turn on. Slowly pour the olive oil into the running processor slowly to emulsify the oil into the mayonnaise mixture.

POTATOES

Potatoes are an excellent source of many nutrients,
including potassium and vitamin C.

More potatoes are eaten than any other vegetable, and they are the most valuable crop in the world. Yet, the sale of processed potatoes has surpassed the sale of fresh potatoes in the last couple of years, and that's a real shame.

As far as I am concerned, there is nothing as convenient to cook as a potato, and I always tell people to cook them with the skin on. If a recipe calls for peeled potatoes, parboil them first. It doesn't affect the flavor, and you will gain so much more nutrition.

Potatoes are recommended to provide bulk in the diet, for the easily digestible protein they contain, and for their mineral and vitamin content. In fact, they contain vitamin C, and people get from 20% to 30% of their minimum daily requirement of vitamin C from eating potatoes, not that potatoes contain so much vitamin C, but because of the fact that so many people eat so many potatoes.

A lot of people are misled to believe that potatoes are fattening, but that is not true. The only thing that is fattening about a potato is the stuff that many people put on it. But you know, two-thirds of a cup of macaroni contains 100 calories, two-thirds of a cup of rice contains 135 calories, and two-thirds cup of potatoes contains only 75 calories. The calories you get from potatoes are absolutely packed with vitamins and minerals. Insofar as starch content, bread contains 52% starch and potatoes 18%.

Before we get into our delicious potato recipes, I want to tell you about "new potatoes," as they are called, with the thin white or red skin. They should be showing up in your market any day now and they are a taste treat! You cook them, skin and all, and they are excellent cold in salads with tomatoes and beans, a little garlic, a little olive oil and maybe a couple of hard-boiled eggs. Or if you want them hot with your meal, just steam them and add a little garlic and oil, maybe a little fresh parsley and they are really delicious.

PARSLIED POTATOES

potatoes to serve 4
1/4 cup butter or margarine
1/4 tsp. salt

few grains pepper
1/4 cup chopped parsley
2 Tbsp. lemon juice

If "old" potatoes are used, parboil, skin and quarter them. If these are new potatoes, use small ones, leaving the skin on. Cook in boiling, salted water until tender, about 25 minutes. Drain. Add butter, salt, pepper, parsley, and lemon juice. When the butter has melted, spoon some of the mixture over each serving of potatoes.

MA'S SCALLOPED POTATOES

6 medium potatoes
3 medium onions
5 Tbsp. flour
1 & 1/2 tsp. salt

1/4 tsp. pepper
5 Tbsp. butter or margarine
1 & 1/2 to 2 cups milk

Pare potatoes and onions; cut in slices 1/8 thick. Into a greased casserole dish, put a layer of potatoes, then a layer of onion slices. Sprinkle with flour, salt, and pepper. Dot with butter or margarine. Repeat until potatoes and onions are used.

Add milk almost to top of potatoes. Cover and bake in slow oven at 300°F, for 2 hours, or until potatoes are soft throughout. Remove cover during last half hour of cooking. (Slow oven prevents milk curdling or boiling over. If potatoes become too dry, add more milk.) *Serves 6.*

POTATO BISCUITS

1 medium potato, peeled and
cooked
3/4 cup flour
1 Tbsp. baking powder

1 tsp. salt
1 Tbsp. diet margarine
6 Tbsp. skim milk

Put potato through ricer or mash. Set aside.

In large bowl, stir together flour, baking powder, and salt. With pastry cutter or 2 knives used scissor-fashion, cut in margarine. Stir in potato, then milk, blending lightly with fork. Spoon into 12 mounds on a non-stick cookie sheet.

Bake at 400°F for 15 to 20 minutes or until golden brown. *Makes 12 biscuits.*

OVEN-BROWNED POTATOES

Wash and parboil potatoes for 10 minutes. Remove skin and place in pan with roasting beef or lamb. Turn potatoes 2 to 3 times. Bake for about 40 minutes or until tender and serve on platter with meat.

POTATO DUMPLINGS FOR STEW

2 cups mashed potatoes
1 egg
1/4 cup flour

1 Tbsp. minced onion
1 Tbsp. chopped parsley
1/2 tsp. salt

In a small bowl, combine all ingredients, mixing well. Drop by rounded spoonful on top of hot stew. Cover and simmer for 20 minutes. *Makes 12 dumplings.*

PERFECT POTATO SALAD

5 medium potatoes
garlic
1 medium onion, thinly sliced
2 Tbsp chopped parsley
4 Tbsp chopped cucumber

2 Tbsp chopped green pepper
salt and pepper
French dressing
mayonnaise

Boil potatoes in jackets. Peel and slice or dice into garlic-rubbed bowl. Add onion, parsley, cucumber, and green pepper. Season with salt and pepper. Add French dressing and toss salad lightly. Cover and allow to chill for 6 to 8 hours. Just before serving, add desired amount of mayonnaise. Yield: 6 portions. (May be garnished with paprika-sprinkled onion rings, cucumber, tomato, or other vegetables.)

CAESAR POTATO SALAD

1 egg
1/4 cup Italian dressing
1/4 cup grated Romano cheese
1 Tbsp. Worcestershire sauce
2 tsp. prepared mustard

1 tsp. salt
4 medium potatoes, cooked
    and cubed
4 pitted ripe olives, sliced

In a large bowl, with wire whisk, beat together egg, Italian dressing, cheese, Worcestershire sauce, mustard, and salt until well blended. Add potatoes and olives; toss to mix well. Refrigerate to chill. *Makes 8 servings.*

YOGURT POTATO SALAD

1 cup plain yogurt
2 tsp. prepared mustard
2 tsp. horseradish
2 cups cooked cubed potatoes
(Continued on next page)

1/2 cup sliced celery
1 medium cucumber, sliced
1/4 cup sliced onion
1 Tbsp. chopped chives

In large bowl, combine yogurt, mustard, and horseradish. Add remaining ingredients; toss to mix well. Refrigerate to chill. *Makes 8 servings.*

DUTCH POTATO SALAD

1/2 pound bacon	dash of pepper
2 Tbsp. flour	4 large potatoes, cooked,
2 Tbsp. sugar	and sliced
1 tsp. dry mustard	1/2 cup chopped celery
2/3 cup vinegar	1/3 cup chopped green
2/3 cup water	onions and tops
1 tsp. salt	Kielbasa or knackwurst

Heat oven to 350°F. Cut bacon into 1-inch pieces; fry until crisp. Drain off fat; set bacon aside. Combine 1/3 cup bacon fat, flour, sugar, and mustard in medium-size saucepan; stir until smooth. Add vinegar and water. Cook over medium heat, stirring constantly, until thickened; remove from heat. Stir in salt and pepper. Arrange half the hot potatoes in a shallow baking dish. Sprinkle with half the celery, green onions, and bacon. Pour over half the dressing. Repeat with remaining ingredients. Heat for 25 minutes or until heated through. Top with sausage. *Makes 6 servings.*

ITALIAN CHICKEN POTATOTORE

1 broiler-fryer (about 3 lbs.),	1 cup tomato juice
cut up	1 tsp. salt
2 medium potatoes, peeled and	1/2 tsp. oregano
diced	dash pepper
1 small onion, sliced	dash garlic powder

Bake chicken pieces, skin-side up, at 350°F for 30 minutes or until golden brown, basting occasionally with pan juices. Drain off any accumulated fat. Add remaining ingredients, cover and bake for 30 minutes more or until chicken and vegetables are tender, basting frequently during cooking. *Makes 6 servings.*

RAGOUT OF BEEF

2 lbs. lean, well-trimmed
round steak, cubed
3/4 cup chopped onion
2 tsp. salad oil
1 lb. tomatoes
1/2 cup red wine
2 tsp. Worcestershire sauce
2 beef bouillon cubes
celery

2 Tbsp. flour
2 tsp. salt
1 tsp. paprika
dash pepper
dash garlic powder
4 medium potatoes, peeled
and cubed
1 cup coarsely chopped

In a large, heavy non-stick Dutch oven, brown meat and onions in oil. Drain off any accumulated fat. To meat and onions, add 2 cups water and remaining ingredients, except potatoes and celery. Cover and simmer for 1 hour or until meat is almost tender.

Add potatoes and celery. Cook for 30 minutes more or until meat and vegetables are tender. *Makes 8 servings.*

TURKEY AND POTATO BAKE

2 medium potatoes, thinly
sliced
2 cups cooked diced turkey*
*or 2 cups cooked, diced ham
or chicken

1 can condensed cream
of celery soup
1/2 cup milk
1 medium onion, sliced

In a non-stick 8-inch square baking pan, arrange in layers, as follows: potatoes, turkey, onion slices. In a small bowl, blend soup and milk; pour over casserole. Cover and bake at 375°F for 45 minutes. Uncover and bake for 15 minutes longer or until potatoes are tender. *Makes 4 servings.*

DANISH PORK CHOPS

6 center cut pork chops, well
  trimmed
2 medium potatoes,
  quartered
2 chicken bouillon cubes
1 tsp. salt

1 tsp. curry powder
dash pepper
1 cup coarsely chopped apple
1 Tbsp. lemon juice
liquid sugar substitute
  (optional)

In a large, heavy, non-stick skillet, brown pork chops on both sides. Drain off any accumulated fat. Add potatoes, bouillon cubes, salt, curry powder, pepper, and 2 cups water. Cover and simmer for 45 minutes or until pork chops are almost tender.

Add apples and lemon juice; simmer for 15 minutes more. Just before serving, stir in a few drops of sugar, if desired. *Makes 6 servings.*

POTATO-CRUST HAM AND CHEESE

2 cups mashed potatoes
2 Tbsp. prepared mustard
1 lb. cooked ham, cubed

1/2 cup cottage cheese
2 slices cheddar cheese,
  crumbled

Mix mashed potatoes and mustard. Spread evenly in bottom of non-stick 8-inch square baking pan. Add ham cubes in a layer on top of potatoes.

In electric blender, blend cottage cheese and Cheddar cheese until fairly smooth. Spread over ham. Bake at 350°F for 30 minutes or until casserole is heated through. *Makes 5 servings.*

POTATO YEAST ROLLS

4 cups milk (1 qt.)
1 cup mashed potatoes
1 cup sugar
1 cup butter or margarine
1 tsp. salt

2 yeast cakes or 2 pkgs. dry
  granular yeast
1 tsp. soda
2 tsp. baking powder
11 cups sifted, all-purpose
  flour

Mix and heat to boil: milk, potatoes, sugar, butter or margarine, and salt. Cool in large bowl until lukewarm. Add yeast, dissolved in small amount of lukewarm mixture. Mix and sift soda, baking powder and flour; add enough to liquid mixture to make stiff batter. Let rise for 1 hour. Add remaining flour; mix and knead. If you wish to use dough at once, let rise to double bulk, knead, shape, and bake. If you wish to store all or part of dough, place in large bowl, cover and put in refrigerator. When ready to use, knead down. Cut off desired amount and shape into rolls (Parker-house, cloverleaf, etc.). Let rise for 1 to 1 and 1/2 hours, or until double in bulk. Bake in moderately hot oven, 400°F, for 15 to 20 minutes. *Makes about 6 dozen rolls.*

POTATO PUDDING PUFFS

3 medium potatoes, cut up
1 egg
1 small onion, diced

1/2 tsp. salt
1/4 tsp. baking powder
dash pepper

In electric blender on "grate" setting, blend potatoes with 1/2 cup water for a few seconds. Pour into fine strainer, pressing potatoes against sides with back of spoon to drain off all liquid possible. Return potatoes to blender; add remaining ingredients. Blend on low speed for a few seconds. Spoon into 9 small non-stick muffin pan cups, filling each two-thirds full. Bake at 350°F for 45 minutes. Serve immediately. *Makes 9 puffs.*

POTATO CANDY

3/4 cup cold mashed potatoes 1 & 1/2 tsp. vanilla
4 cups confectioners' sugar 1/2 tsp. salt
4 cups shredded coconut, chopped 4 sq. baking chocolate

Mix potatoes (plain mashed, no butter, milk or salt added) and confectioners' sugar. Stir in coconut, vanilla, and salt; blend well. Press into 1 large, or 2 small, pans so that candy will be about 1/2 inch thick. Melt chocolate over hot water. (Do not allow water to boil. If chocolate gets too hot, it may be streaky when hardened.) Pour chocolate on top of candy. Cool and cut in squares. (For variation, make haystacks by forming white mixture into cones 1 inch high. Allow to stand uncovered for 20 minutes. Dip base of each cone in melted chocolate; place on waxed paper until chocolate hardens. *Makes about 100 small haystacks.)*

CURRY
Contributed by Connie Umbenhower

You can make a nice curry in the crock pot by placing all the ingredients into it and letting them slow cook. It only takes about fifteen minutes to get all the ingredients together, and this curry will be hot, delicious, and ready in a few hours.

2 large potatoes, chopped
 into cubes
2 large tomatoes, chopped
2 cups celery, chopped
1 cup vegetable broth
1 teaspoon garam masala
 powder
1 teaspoon fresh ginger, minced

1/2 of a cauliflower, broken
 into small florets
1 can (15 1/2 ounces)
 garbanzo beans
1/2 cup water
1/2 teaspoon ground turmeric
1/2 teaspoon cayenne pepper
1/4 cup red onion, finely
 chopped

(Continued on next page)

Optional: Add lean ground beef, browned. Put all ingredients in crock pot and cook on low for six hours. *Serves six.*

POTATO, PARSNIP AND APPLE PUREE
Contributed by Bruce Riezenman

1 lb. parsnips, peeled and chopped (yield after peeling)

1 lb. baking potatoes, peeled and chopped (yield after peeling)

Cook in boiling, salted water until soft.

3/4 lb. granny smith apples, peeled and chopped (yield after peeling)

1/4 cup water

Combine and cook covered until soft.

1/4 cup milk
salt and pepper to taste

4 Tbsp butter, cold, chopped

Combine parsnips, potatoes, apples (in water), milk, and salt and pepper. Puree VERY smooth in food processor. Add butter at the end and adjust for salt.

Garnish with a GENEROUS amount of fried julienne of parsnips (golden brown and salted!) *Yield: 4 cups*

STRAWBERRIES

Strawberries are very high in vitamin C and A. Its high vitamin C content enables its iron to be fully absorbed by the body. They are very good for those who are iron deficient.

Spring time is strawberry time. As far as I'm concerned, you can give me strawberries and cream. That just happens to be my weakness, and I'd eat it every day of the week if I could.

For the kids, cut a few strawberries and add them to their cereal in the morning, or put four or five strawberries into the blender with a glass of milk in the afternoon. It's really a fantastic drink and will give the kids a little more milk, more fresh fruit, and more nutrition.

On the average, fresh strawberries contain 59 milligrams of vitamin C for every 3 and 1/2 ounces. Actually, the vitamin C content depends on the amount of sunshine they receive when growing. There have been instances where the vitamin C content was as high as 99 milligrams for 3 and 1/2 ounces. You know the amazing thing is fresh strawberries with the caps on will retain their vitamin C content whether they are stored at room temperature or under refrigeration. But once they are capped, not only do they lose vitamin C, but they start to deteriorate in a hurry. Now, when you lose valuable nutrition, you're losing something, so all I can say is, keep on eating fresh strawberries until just before you are ready to prepare them.

STRAWBERRY FRAPPE

2 pts. fresh strawberries	*1/4 cup sugar*
1 pt. vanilla ice cream, softened	*1/4 cup lemon juice*
1 cup cold milk	*1 qt. crushed ice*

Puree strawberries in electric blender. Combine lemon juice and strawberry puree; stir in milk. Add sugar and ice cream; beat, or

63

blend in electric blender. Pour over ice into chilled glasses. Serve with straws. *Makes 8 servings.*

VERY ADULT STRAWBERRY FLIPS

2 pts. fresh strawberries
4 eggs
6 Tbsp. lemon juice
1/2 cup sugar

1 cup vodka
red food coloring, as desired
cracked ice

Puree strawberries in electric blender at high speed. If desired, strain puree through double thickness of cheesecloth or fine sieve to remove seeds. Return to blender; add eggs, lemon juice, sugar, vodka, and good coloring. Blend for about 15 seconds, turning off occasionally and using spatula to redistribute mixture. Pour into tall glasses over cracked ice. *Makes 8 servings.*

SUMMER FRUIT SALAD

salad greens
1 avocado
2 Tbsp. lemon juice
3 cups cantaloupe balls
1 cup fresh pineapple cubes

1 cup washed, hulled straw-
berries
8 ozs. cheddar cheese, cut in
strips
Honey-Nut Dressing

Line a shallow salad bowl with greens. Peel avocado and cut in lengthwise strips; sprinkle with lemon juice. Combine cantaloupe, pineapple, and berries and fill bowl. Garnish with cheese and avocado. Serve with dressing. *Serves 6.*

Honey-Nut Dressing: Mix 1 cup mayonnaise, 2 tablespoons honey, and 2 tablespoons slivered almonds.

HOT STRAWBERRY SAUCE FOR ICE CREAM

2 pts. fresh strawberries　　*2 Tbsp. cornstarch*
1 cup sugar　　　　　　　　*3 Tbsp. Cointreau or orange*
water　　　　　　　　　　　　*juice*

Puree 1 pint strawberries. Cut remaining pint of strawberries in halves. Combine sugar and 1 cup water in saucepan and bring to boil; reduce heat and simmer for 5 minutes. Stir in strawberry halves and pureed berries. In a small dish, blend cornstarch and 2 tablespoons water. Stir in strawberry mixture in saucepan. Heat and stir until sauce boils, 1/2 minute. Cool slightly and stir in Cointreau or orange juice. Serve over ice cream. *Makes 3 cups sauce.*

STRAWBERRY MOLD

1 box (3 ozs.) strawberry-　　*1 cup sliced or halved fresh*
flavor gelatin　　　　　　　　*strawberries*
2 Tbsp. sugar　　　　　　　　*2/3 cup heavy cream,*
　　　　　　　　　　　　　　　whipped

Dissolve gelatin and sugar in 1 and 1/2 cups hot water. Chill until thickened, but not firm. Fold in berries and whipped cream. Chill until firm. *Serves 4 to 6.*

STRAWBERRIES CHANTILLY

1 & 1/2 to 2 pts. strawberries　　*1 Tbsp. confectioners' sugar*
2 cups heavy cream　　　　　　　*2 Tbsp. light rum*
1/2 cup grated sweet cooking
chocolate

Hull berries and arrange in bowl. Whip cream until foamy and barely thickened. Fold in remaining ingredients and chill. Serve as sauce for berries. *Makes 6 servings.*

MAPLE SOUR CREAM AND STRAWBERRIES

1/2 pt. (1 cup) dairy sour cream　　*2 pts. strawberries, sliced*
1/4 cup maple-blended syrup　　　*and sweetened to taste*
chopped nuts, optional

Stir together sour cream and syrup until well blended. Spoon sour cream mixture over strawberries. If desired, sprinkle with chopped nuts. *Makes 4 to 6 servings.*

BAKED CUSTARD WITH STRAWBERRY SAUCE

4 large eggs　　　　　*3 cups milk*
1/3 cup sugar　　　　*1 tsp. vanilla extract*
1/4 tsp. salt　　　　　*sweetened, sliced*
strawberries

Beat eggs slightly and stir in sugar and salt. Scald milk and gradually stir into egg mixture. Add vanilla and pour into six 6-ounce custard cups or a 1 and 1/2-quart glass casserole dish. Set in shallow pan and add 3/4 inch hot water. Bake in preheated 325°F oven for 45 minutes for small custards or 1 and 1/4 hours for casserole, or until small spatula comes out clean when inserted in center of custard. Remove from hot water, cool, then chill. Unmold small custards, and large one, if desired. Serve with berries. *Serves 6.*

ICE CREAM SUPREME

1 pt. strawberries, hulled　　*1 pt. vanilla ice cream,*
1/3 cup sugar　　　　　　　*softened*
1/4 tsp. almond extract　　　*1/2 pt. whipping cream*

Mash and sweeten strawberries. Whip cream, adding sugar and almond extract. Fold in softened ice cream and strawberries. Pour into an 8-inch square pan and freeze until firm. *Serves 10 to 12.*

STRAWBERRY CREAM CAKE

1 cup sifted cake flour
1 tsp. baking powder
1/4 tsp. salt
grated rind of 1 lemon
2 eggs, separated

sugar
1 qt. strawberries
3/4 cup heavy cream,
  whipped and sweetened

Sift together first 3 ingredients. Add 1/2 cup cold water and rind to egg yolks and beat until tripled in volume. Gradually beat in 3/4 cup sugar. Slowly beat in dry ingredients. Beat whites and 2 tablespoons sugar until soft peaks form. Fold in flour mixture. Pour into 2 ungreased 8-inch layer-cake pans. Bake in preheated 350°F oven for 25 minutes. Invert on racks and cool. Remove cakes. Wash and hull berries; reserve 18. Slice and sweeten remainder; put between layers. Top each serving with whipped cream and whole berries.

STRAWBERRY SHORTCAKE

3 cups all-purpose flower
3 & 1/4 tsp. double-acting baking
  powder
sugar
1 & 1/4 tsp. salt

1/2 cup soft shortening
1 egg, well beaten
2/3 cup milk (about)
3 pts. strawberries
heavy cream

Mix flour, baking powder, 3 tablespoons sugar, and the salt in bowl. Cut in shortening. Add egg and enough milk to make a soft dough, mixing with fork. Knead lightly about 20 turns on floured board. Divide in thirds. Pat out each third in greased 9-inch round layer-cake pan. Bake in preheated 450°F oven for about 15 minutes. Wash and hull berries. Cut in halves and sweeten to taste. Put shortcake layers together with berries between and on top. Serve with cream. *Serves 6 to 8.*

FRESH STRAWBERRIES WITH BALSAMIC SYRUP
Contributed by Deborah Dal Fovo

1 pint fresh ripe strawberries
1 tablespoon good quality
  Balsamic vinegar
Sprigs of fresh mint to garnish,
  optional

2 tablespoons sugar
8 small fresh mint leaves,
  wiped clean with a damp
  cloth

Rinse the strawberries under cold running water to remove any soil. Hull strawberries, then cut the fruit into slices lengthwise. Place strawberry slices in a mixing bowl and sprinkle with sugar and balsamic vinegar. Gently toss the strawberries to evenly coat with sugar and vinegar.

Set strawberries aside to macerate for at least 1/2 hour, until a syrup has formed. Tear the mint leaves into pieces and add to the strawberries, tossing gently to combine. Spoon into individual dessert cups and serve immediately, each garnished with a sprig of fresh mint, if desired. *Serves 4.*

SUMMER

SUMMER

Summer's here! This is the time all the good, fresh, and familiar fruits and vegetables that we haven't seen for about eight to nine months, at least not at reasonable prices, start coming back, and they look really good.

I can remember, many, many years ago, whenever the first peach, the first apricot, or the first cherries came into season, my father would bring them home. Then at dinnertime, my grandmother would always offer a toast: "Cose Nove," new things— she would say it in Sicilian. "Saluti per tutti," good health for all. A toast to the new season. You know, in those days, there weren't any jet airplanes bringing in fresh peaches and strawberries each day of the year. It used to be an event when you got something new—an absolute event when all of a sudden, you would have new plums, new tomatoes, and new spring peas.

But maybe we should really toast the new season now, because when in-season, you can buy all the fresh fruits and vegetables at very reasonable prices. Now, that's something to toast. Father's Day is coming, and it might be a good time to do that; when we are honoring dad, I'm sure he would like to toast anything that won't cost as much for the next few months.

This is a good season for salads, and there'll be plenty of the lettuces—iceberg and all the leaf lettuces, romaine, butter, red and bib—and, of course, radishes, fresh green onions, celery, and wonderful red tomatoes. They certainly make a cool and refreshing salad for your barbecue table.

When most people plan a tossed salad, they go right for the lettuce and tomatoes. That's fine, but remember, with iceberg lettuce, after you strip all those leaves off, you don't have too much nutrition. You can pack twice as much nutrition into your salad if you add one shredded carrot, and maybe a half a bell pepper and a couple sprigs of parsley. Not only will you have a more flavorful salad, but you will add more zest and certainly a lot more nutrition.

Another thing to remember on these hot days is there are several vegetables that are very good when they are served cold, like broccoli and green beans. You might plan to cook enough for two meals. Serve them hot for the evening meal and the next day you can serve them cold in a salad.

Summertime is the time for corn on the cob, and the melons will be coming, too; first the cantaloupe and watermelon, and later the varietal melons. The blueberries will be in at this time of year, and we really have some great recipes for blueberries. In the fresh vegetable counters, you'll find ripe, red tomatoes and fresh sweet peas, fresh new potatoes, and toward the end of summer, the green bell peppers will be turning red.

Keep lots of fresh ripe peaches and apricots, nectarines, and plums around. They say it's an ill wind that blows no good, so even though the weather gets hot and maybe a little uncomfortable, it may be a good incentive to eat more fresh fruit and fresh vegetable salads. When you do, you will be subtracting calories from your meals and adding a tremendous amount of nutrition, more vitamins and more minerals, and something that many of us get too little of that is very important—roughage, cellulose and fibers. The body needs it. It's time to change your eating habits; it's summertime.

APRICOTS

Apricots are a delicious source of vitamin A,
potassium, magnesium and iron.

This is the best time to eat apricots on the West Coast because those with the finest flavor should be in the stores in mid-June. For the most part, they'll probably be gone after the 4th of July. But this is not so for the rest of the United States. They will be starting later, mid-July, and you can enjoy them through August and into September.

Apricots go back to about 2200 B.C., when they used to grow wild in China. Today, they still grow wild in some parts of China. They say the famous golden apples referred to in Greek mythology were actually apricots.

Apricots are nature's gift to good health. They are known for their high concentration of vitamin A, which maintains healthy skin and eyes and aids in resistance to disease. They also provide good amounts of vitamin C for growth and maintenance of teeth and bones. The blood builder, iron, is also sufficiently present in apricots.

So, while you have the chance, while the apricots are at their delicious best and reasonably priced, make the most of them. A real tasty, flavorful apricot must be a golden yellow color, and this is one of the very, very few fruits that I recommend soft. If they are too firm, go ahead and buy them and take them home, but give them a couple of days to soften. Apricots and persimmons are the same consistency, and they are the only fruits I recommend soft. They're great to eat out-of-hand, but we also have some interesting and tasty recipes so you can take full advantage of the short time they are with us. Remember, the next season is a long way away.

FRESH APRICOT SAUCE

1 lb. unpeeled, sliced or   *1/2 cup sugar*
chopped, fresh apricots   *1 pinch salt*
1 tsp. fresh lemon juice

Put all ingredients into blender at high speed for 20 seconds. Or thoroughly blend all ingredients with mixer, then force through fine sieve. The sauce keeps for weeks in the refrigerator, months in the freezer. *Makes about 2 cups.*

MINTED FRESH APRICOTS

1/3 cup sugar   *3 cups sliced, fresh apricots*
1/3 cup fresh lime juice   *fresh mint for garnish*
2 Tbsp. chopped, fresh mint

Combine sugar, lime juice, and mint in saucepan. Bring to boil. Strain. Cool. Add apricots. Chill for 2 to 3 hours. Serve in sherbet glasses, garnished with fresh mint. *Makes 6 servings.*

CALIFORNIA WALDORF SALAD

10 fresh, ripe apricots   *1/4 cup mayonnaise*
3 large apples, cut into bite-   *2 cups sliced celery*
     sized pieces   *1/2 cup dark, seedless raisins*
3 Tbsp. lemon juice   *2/3 cup chopped walnuts*
1/4 cup dairy sour cream   *crisp salad greens*

Reserve 3 apricots for garnish; cut the remaining apricots into bite-size pieces. Sprinkle apricots and apple with lemon juice to prevent darkening. To prepare salad dressing, blend together sour cream and mayonnaise. Toss apricots, apples, celery and raisins with dressing. Chill for several hours. At serving time, add walnuts to salad and toss. Spoon into a lettuce-lined salad bowl. Cut reserved apricots in half and arrange around edge of salad. *Serves 8.*

TERIYAKI SLIM 'N' TRIM SALAD

1/4 lb. fresh spinach
1/2 lb. fresh apricots, halved
and pitted
1/3 lb. white chicken meat,
cut in pieces
1/3 lb. lean roast beef, thinly
sliced

1/3 cup sliced scallions, cut
in 1-inch pieces
1/3 cup sliced celery
4 medium mushrooms, sliced
* Paprika Dressing
** Oriental Dressing

Arrange spinach, apricots, chicken, beef, scallions, celery, and mushrooms in groups on large platter. Serve with Paprika Dressing and Oriental Dressing. *Serves 4.*

*Paprika Dressing: Combine 1/4 teaspoon each dry mustard and paprika, 3/4 teaspoon salt, 1 teaspoon sugar, 1 beaten egg, 1/4 cup mild vinegar, and 2 tablespoons olive or salad oil in top of double boiler. Cook, stirring constantly, over simmering water until mixture thickens. Remove from heat and cool.

**Oriental Dressing: Combine 2 tablespoons lemon juice, 2 tablespoons soy sauce, 2 teaspoons sugar, and 1/2 teaspoon finely chopped crystallized ginger.

FLAME APRICOTS

Heat contents of one 10-ounce jar of red currant jelly in chafing dish until smooth and thoroughly melted. Add 9 fresh apricots (about 3/4 pound), halved, and heat until apricots are hot, spooning sauce over apricots while heating. To flame, heat about 1/2 cup brandy in small saucepan, ignite, then pour over apricots and sauce in chafing dish. After flame has burned out, spoon sauce and apricots over vanilla ice cream in individual dessert dishes.

APRICOT COBBLER

Filling:

1 lb. fresh apricots, halved

1 egg

1 cup sugar

1/4 cup shortening

Topping:

1 cup flour

1/2 tsp. salt

2 tsp. baking powder

Sprinkle over apricots, bake at 350°F for 30 minutes. Delicious served with whipped cream.

FRESH APRICOT A LA RUSSE

3 cups sliced, fresh apricots

1 cup sour cream

1 to 2 Tbsp. sugar

1/4 to 1/2 tsp. grated lemon peel

6 fresh apricot slices

Place sliced apricots in each of 6 sherbet glasses. Combine sour cream, sugar, and lemon peel; spoon over apricots. Garnish with additional fresh apricot slices. *Makes 6 servings.*

BAKED APRICOT PUDDING

3 cups fresh apricots (sugar to sweeten)

3 eggs

1 cup sugar

1 Tbsp. of water

1 cup flour mixed with tsp. baking powder

Put sweetened apricots in a buttered baking dish. Beat eggs, add sugar and flour and enough water so the dough won't be too stiff. Pour over apricots. Bake in a moderate oven for 30 to 40 minutes. *Serves 6.*

CHÈVRE-STUFFED APRICOTS
Contributed by Zuzy Martin Lynch

2 ounces "chevre" style goat cheese

1/4 cup roasted, unsalted almonds

1 cup dried Turkish apricots, about 22 total

Cut/chop each almond into 3 to 4 pieces. Scoop 1/2 teaspoon of goat cheese and form a small ball, pushing 3 or 4 almond pieces into it. Open up the apricots, keeping them joined on one side and fill them with the cheese and nut ball. Press the apricot halves together to seal. Serve. *Yields 6 to 8 servings.*

GREEN BEANS

Green beans contain very little calories per serving,
while providing excellent nutrition and dietary fiber.

There was a time when we used to call green beans or snap beans 'string beans', but you don't hear that very often anymore. The growers have developed them so nicely from a commercial standpoint that you will find very, very few beans with any strings at all. Now, they're snap beans and green beans, and they're beautiful.

Of course, my favorite green bean is the Italian bean, no question about it. Now, the Italian bean or the Fagiolini Italiani, as we call it, is a remarkable bean, and I certainly hope you will take the time to go into the supermarket and ask for this fine bean by name. If they don't happen to have it, they certainly can get it. In fact, it's so fantastic that it is just coming into its own as a frozen food item. It is a flat bean, about 5 to 7 inches long, and it is good even when the beans themselves burst through the pod. Now, I know that's not a good sign for other beans, but for this bean, it is.

Until four or five years ago, this bean was known and enjoyed mostly by people from the Mediterranean countries because they were the only ones who knew how good it is. After all, it did grow in their native land. It is soft when it is cooked, and it has a distinctly different flavor and texture from any other bean. You can cook it in tomato sauce, or it lends excellent flavor in a stew. It's fantastic served cold in a bean salad with tomatoes. It's great served with Pesto sauce and freshly grated Romano or Parmesan cheese.

Anyway, regardless of the variety, be sure to look for a nice bright bean, a young bean. If they feel hard, it means they've been too long on the vine. Years ago, when the old-time Chinese buyers would come to the street to buy, they would put their hands into a crate of beans. If the beans felt soft to them, they would talk price with the vendor. But if the beans felt hard, they wouldn't even talk about the price because they wouldn't want them. They knew the hard beans were not as young and wouldn't be as tender or as flavorful as the young beans.

Don't forget, do yourself a favor and buy enough for two or three meals because leftover refrigerated beans make an excellent salad with a few tomato wedges or slices, a little olive oil, vinegar, and of course, a little garlic.

TASTY GREEN BEANS

3 lbs. fresh green beans
1 & 1/2 cups oil
2 medium onions, minced
1 & 1/2 lbs. ripe tomatoes,
    peeled and strained

2 Tbsp. minced parsley
salt and pepper to taste
water as needed

Wash the beans and break them in half or slice them lengthwise. Place in a large pot of cold water. Heat the oil in a large pot and sauté the onions in it until soft and limp; add the tomatoes (or diluted tomato paste), and bring to a boil. Drain the beans and add them to the pot. Add the parsley, salt, pepper, and enough water to barely cover the beans. Cook over medium heat until the liquid is absorbed, but the oil remains (30 to 45 minutes). *Serves 6.*

BULGARIAN GREEN BEANS

2 to 3 onions
1/4 cup oil
paprika to taste
1 lb. green beans, broken in
    pieces
2 carrots, peeled and sliced thin

4 tomatoes, peeled and
    quartered
2 green peppers, membrane
    removed, seeded and
    chopped
chopped herbs to taste

(Continued on next page)

Cut onions into rings, and cut rings in half. Fry in hot oil until golden; sprinkle with paprika, then add beans and carrots. Simmer for about 45 minutes.

Add tomatoes and peppers. Simmer for another 15 minutes. Sprinkle with herbs. *Serves 4 to 6.*

GREEN BEANS PAPRIKA

1 lb. green beans   *1 clove garlic*
2 Tbsp. vinegar or lemon juice   *1 bay leaf*
brown sugar to taste   *dash of allspice*

Cut beans diagonally or lengthwise. Cook in very little water in covered saucepan for 5 minutes. Add the other ingredients, cook for 3 minutes longer. Remove garlic and bay leaf. Serve hot or cold. *Serves 6 to 8.*

GREEN BEAN CASSEROLE

3 Tbsp. butter   *1 lb. fresh green beans,*
2 Tbsp. flour   *cooked and French sliced*
1/4 tsp. sugar   *1/2 lb. graced mild cheddar*
1/2 tsp. grated onion   *cheese*
1 cup dairy sour cream   *1/2 cup cornflake crumbs*

Melt 2 tablespoons butter, add 2 tablespoons flour. Cook gently, remove from heat. Stir in sugar, grated onion, and sour cream, then fold in the beans. Place in a 2-quart casserole, cover with cheese, then with crumbs which have been mixed with the remaining tablespoons of butter. Bake in a 350°F oven until hot and bubbly.

Also, sliced water chestnuts may be added with beans. *Serves 8.*

SWEET-AND-SOUR GREEN BEANS

4 slices bacon
1 Tbsp. flour
1/2 cup chicken broth
2 Tbsp. vinegar

2 Tbsp. sugar
1 Tbsp. minced onion
3/4 lb. green beans,
   cooked and drained

In a medium skillet, cook bacon until lightly browned. Remove bacon, drain, crumble and reserve. Remove all but 2 tablespoons bacon drippings from skillet. Blend flour into drippings in skillet. Stir in chicken broth, vinegar, sugar, and onion. Cook, stirring constantly, until mixture thickens and comes to a boil. Add green beans and reserved bacon. Heat. Serve immediately. *Serves 4.*

FRIED GREEN BEANS

1 lb. tender green beans
1 cup flour

1 cup olive oil
salt

Parboil string beans for 10 minutes and drain well. Roll in flour and fry in hot olive oil until crisp and golden brown. Sprinkle with salt and serve immediately. *Serves 4.*

GREEN BEAN SOUFFLE

1 lb. green beans
2 qts. boiling water
1/2 tsp. salt

1 cup thick cream sauce
2 Tbsp. grated Parmesan
   cheese
4 egg whites

Wash beans and cook in boiling salted water 20 minutes, or until tender. Drain and pass beans through strainer. Mix with cream sauce and cheese. Beat egg whites until stiff and fold gently into bean mixture. Pour into greased casserole and bake in moderate oven (375°F) for 25 minutes. Serve immediately. *Serves 4.*

GREEN BEAN PUDDING

1 lb. green beans
2 Tbsp. butter
1/4 tsp. salt
1 cup cream sauce

2 eggs, lightly beaten with 2
Tbsp. grated Parmesan
cheese
2 Tbsp. fine bread crumbs
2 Tbsp. butter

Wash green beans and cut into very small pieces. Boil in water for 18 minutes and drain. Place beans in saucepan with butter and salt and cook gently for 5 minutes. Remove from fire and add cream sauce, eggs, and Parmesan.

Grease a 1-quart mold and sprinkle with bread crumbs. Pour in bean mixture, top with more bread crumbs and dot with butter. Bake in hot oven (400°F) for 45 minutes, or until mixture is firm. Remove from oven and let stand for 4 minutes before unmolding. *Serves 4.*

CRISP GREEN BEANS
Contributed by Cindi Avila

1 lb. fresh green beans
(wash and trim ends)
1/2 cup slivered almonds

3 tablespoons olive oil
2 tablespoons minced garlic

Put green beans in pot and cover with water. Heat on high and let boil for 5 minutes. In the meantime, heat olive oil and garlic in a pan on medium heat. Add beans when ready and almonds. Mix and serve immediately.

MUSHROOMS

Mushrooms provide a decent amount of protein,
vitamin D, and folic acid.

Everybody is going for mushrooms. Sales are nothing but spectacular! Though they are most frequently served with meats, they deserve a more prominent role. High in protein and phosphorus, they also contain riboflavin, niacin, calcium, and even some copper and iron. Best of all, they contain only 20 calories per cup.

When you look at mushrooms in your produce department, the price per pound may sound high until you start weighing them. Then, you find there are generally over 6 cups of mushrooms to a pound, and that's a lot of mushrooms. For cooking, you can save money by buying the small size mushrooms, because when you cook them, they shrink anyway. As long as they are bright and clean and look fresh and beautiful, the flavor and nutrition are there. Of course, if you are going to stuff the mushrooms, they you need the large, dollar or steak size mushrooms.

Fresh mushrooms will keep in the refrigerator for about 5 days. Keep them in a paper bag or put them on a plate and, to help retain moisture, cover them loosely with a damp paper towel.

MOSTLY MUSHROOM SALAD

1 lb. fresh mushrooms	*2 Tbsp. salad or olive oil*
1 cup diced celery	*1 Tbsp. wine vinegar*
1 cup diced green pepper	*2 tsp. salt*
2 Tbsp. finely chopped onion	*1/8 tsp. ground black pepper*
	2 Tbsp. lemon juice

Rinse, pat dry, and slice mushrooms (makes about 5 cups). In a salad bowl, place mushrooms, celery, green pepper, and onion.

82

Combine remaining ingredients and pour over vegetables; toss gently. Serve immediately. *Serves 6.*

MUSHROOM AND TURKEY CLUB SALAD

1 lb. fresh mushrooms
lettuce leaves
2 cups diced, cooked turkey, chilled
1 and 1/2 cups cooked green beans, chilled
1 cup cherry tomatoes, halved
1 medium cucumber, sliced

2 ribs celery, sliced
2 stuffed green olives, sliced
1/4 cup cocktail vegetable juice
1 Tbsp. lemon juice
1 Tbsp. salad oil
3/4 tsp. salt
1/8 tsp. red pepper sauce

Rinse, pat dry and slice mushrooms.

Line a large salad bowl with lettuce leaves. Arrange mushrooms, turkey, green beans, tomatoes, cucumber, celery, and olives in clusters.

Combine remaining ingredients. Just before serving, pour over salad ingredients; toss gently. *Serves 6.*

SLIM SHRIMP SALAD

1/2 lb. fresh mushrooms
3 cups shredded lettuce
2 cups diced, cooked shrimp, chilled
1/2 cucumber, peeled and sliced

6 cherry tomatoes, halved
1/4 cup sliced scallions
1/4 tsp. Italian seasoning
1/4 cup Italian salad dressing

Rinse, pat dry and slice mushrooms (*makes about 2 and 1/2 cups*). In a salad bowl, combine mushrooms with lettuce, shrimp, cucumber, tomatoes, scallions, and Italian seasoning. Pour salad dressing over all; toss gently. Serve immediately.

BROILED STUFFED MUSHROOM CAPS

*1 lb. (12) large fresh
mushrooms
1 cup soft fine bread crumbs
1/2 cup finely chopped
tomatoes
1/4 cup shredded sharp
American cheese
2 Tbsp. finely chopped parsley*

*1 & 1/2 tsp. salt
1/4 tsp. ground thyme
1/8 tsp. ground black pepper
4 Tbsp. butter or margarine,
melted
1 tsp. lemon juice
1/4 cup buttered bread
crumbs*

Rinse and pat dry mushrooms. Remove stems from mushrooms and chop very fine; set caps aside.

Combine stems with bread crumbs, tomatoes, cheese, parsley, salt, thyme, black pepper, and 2 tablespoons of the butter.

Sauté mushroom caps in remaining 2 tablespoons of the butter and lemon juice. Fill caps with bread crumb mixture. Sprinkle buttered crumbs over tops. Place on baking sheet and broil for 5 to 8 minutes. Serve as an hors d'oeuvre or meat accompaniment.

SAVORY STUFFED MUSHROOMS

*1 lb. medium-size fresh
mushrooms
1/2 cup butter or margarine
1 cup minced onions*

*1/2 cup chopped parsley
2 Tbsp. lemon juice
1 tsp. salt
1/4 tsp. ground black pepper*

Rinse, pat dry, and halve fresh mushrooms and set aside. In a large skillet, melt butter. Add onions and sauté for 2 minutes. Add mushrooms and sauté for 5 minutes. Stir in parsley, lemon juice, salt, and black pepper. Serve hot over toasted, sliced French bread. *Serves 8.*

TRUITES DE RIVIERE A LA
M-G-M GRAND HOTEL

4 boneless trout 10-12 oz.
1 Maine lobster (cooked)
12 oz. cooked shrimp
16 oz. fresh mushrooms
8 oz. crab meat

4 oz. chives
12 oz. chopped fresh shallots
4 medium tomatoes
8 oz. dry white wine

Prepare a diced mixture with lobster, cooked shrimp, crab meat, and mushrooms, sautéed in butter with shallots and chives, and 4 oz. white wine. Season to taste with salt and pepper.

Lay the boneless trout on a buttered platter with chopped shallots. Put about 1 large tablespoon of the preceding mixture on top with a tomato and a mushroom button. Bake in the oven for about 25 minutes. Before serving, pour some "Beurre noisette" (brown butter) over the fish, garnish with Parisienne Potatoes and fresh parsley, and serve with a nice cold white wine.

MUSHROOM ONION CASSEROLE

5 cups sliced fresh mushrooms
3 Tbsp. butter or margarine
1 Tbsp. lemon juice
4 cups sliced onion rings
2 Tbsp. butter or margarine
salt

ground black pepper
3 cups diced tomatoes
2 cups soft bread crumbs
3 Tbsp. butter or margarine,
*   melted*

Using fresh mushrooms (approximately 2 lb.) sauté 3 minutes in 3 tablespoons butter and 1 tablespoon lemon juice. Sauté onion rings in 2 tablespoons butter until transparent. Turn into 10 x 6 x 2 inch baking dish. Layer mushrooms over the onions and sprinkle lightly with salt and pepper. Cook tomatoes with 1 cup soft bread crumbs and season with salt and pepper. Pour over mushrooms. Toss 1 cup bread crumbs with 3 tablespoons melted butter and sprinkle over top. Bake in preheated moderate oven (350°F) for 30 minutes. *Serves 6.*

STEAK AND MUSHROOM DELIGHT

*2 lbs. boneless beef round,
shoulder or chuck steak,
cut into 1-inch cubes
3/4 cup dry sherry
1/2 lb. fresh mushrooms
1/2 cup flour
1 Tbsp. dry mustard
2 tsp. salt*

*5 Tbsp. oil or shortening,
divided
1 lb. tomatoes, broken up
1 cup diced carrots
1 cup small white onion
2 Tbsp. brown sugar
2 Tbsp. Worcestershire sauce
1/8 tsp. ground black pepper*

Place meat in a snug-fitting bowl. Add sherry. Cover and marinate in the refrigerator for 6 hours. Drain thoroughly; set meat aside. Rinse, pat dry, and slice mushrooms (makes about 2 1/2 cups); set aside. Place in a plastic or paper bag flour, mustard, salt and black pepper. Add meat, a few pieces at a time, and coat thoroughly. In a large skillet, heat 2 tablespoons of the oil. Add meat and brown on all sides. Add additional oil as needed. Stir in reserved mushrooms, along with the tomatoes, carrots, onions, brown sugar, and Worcestershire sauce. Cover and simmer for 1 and 1/2 hours, stirring frequently. *Serves 6.*

CHICKEN MADEIRA

*1/2 cup butter
4 cups fresh mushrooms
sliced
3 lbs. chicken, cut up
1 tsp. garlic salt*

*1/4 cup brandy
3/4 cup Madeira
1/2 tsp. fines herbes
1/2 cup Half & Half
1/2 cup chopped green onion*

Melt butter in large frying pan until bubbly. Sauté mushrooms until browned; remove and reserve. Brown chicken in pan. Sprinkle with garlic salt during browning. Carefully pour brandy over chicken and flame. Add Madeira and fines herbes. Cover lightly and cook for 20 minutes until almost all liquid has cooked off. Remove chickens to serving platter. Add Half & Half, green onion, and mushrooms to pan. Cook, stirring constantly until thickened. Serve over chicken. *Makes 4 servings.*

MUSHROOM TURKEY NEWBERG

1/2 lb. fresh mushrooms,
  sliced
3 Tbsp. butter
3 egg yolks, slightly beaten
1 cup light cream
1/2 tsp. salt

1 tsp. ground marjoram
ground black powder
2 cups cooked turkey, cut
  in cubes
1/4 cup chicken stock
toast points or patty shells

Rinse, pat dry, and slice fresh mushrooms, (about 2 and 1/2 cups). Heat butter in a small skillet. Add mushrooms and sauté for 5 minutes or until golden brown; set aside. In top of a double boiler, combine egg yolks, cream, salt, marjoram, and black pepper. Cook over hot water (not boiling) until custard consistency, stirring constantly. Add turkey, chicken stock, and sautéed mushrooms; blend well and cook for about 3 minutes longer. Serve immediately on toast point. Garnish with paprika, if desired. *Serves 6.*

MUSHROOM SHRIMP SUKYAKI

3/4 lb. fresh mushrooms
1/4 cup salad oil
2 cups sliced celery
2 large green peppers, sliced
2 large onions, sliced
1/2 cup beef broth or water

1/2 cup soy sauce
2 Tbsp. sugar
1 Tbsp. dry sherry
1 lb. peeled and deveined
  shrimp
hot cooked rice

Rinse, pat dry, and slice fresh mushrooms (makes 3 & 3/4 cups); set aside. In a large skillet, heat oil. Add celery, green peppers, and onions. Sauté for 5 minutes or until onions are pale gold. Combine broth, soy sauce, sugar, and sherry. Gradually add to sautéed vegetables. Bring to boiling point. Add reserved mushrooms and shrimp. Return to boil; reduce heat and simmer for 8 to 10 minutes longer or until shrimp turn pink. If desired, thicken sauce with 1 tablespoon cornstarch blended with 1 tablespoon water. Blend into mixture and cook until clear and slightly thickened, stirring. Serve with hot cooked rice. *Serves 6.*

MUSHROOM FU YUNG

1/2 lb. fresh mushrooms
3 Tbsp. oil
3/4 cup sliced onions
1/2 cup thinly sliced celery
1 cup bean sprouts, rinsed
* and drained*
1 cup chicken broth

6 eggs
2 & 1/2 Tbsp. cornstarch,
* divided*
2 Tbsp. soy sauce, divided
3/4 tsp. salt
1/16 tsp. ground red pepper

Rinse, pat dry, and slice fresh mushrooms. In a large skillet or wok, heat oil. Add mushrooms, onion and celery; sauté for 5 minutes. Remove to a large bowl. Add bean sprouts; set aside. In a large bowl, beat eggs. Add 1 1/2 tablespoons of the cornstarch. 1 tablespoon of the soy sauce, salt and red pepper; mix well. Add to mushroom mixture; mix thoroughly. Spoon approximately 2 to 3 tablespoons of mushroom egg mixture on a lightly greased griddle or skillet. Cook until brown, turning once. Remove to platter; keep warm. Repeat until all mushroom egg mixture is used. In a small saucepan, combine remaining 1 tablespoon cornstarch and 1 tablespoon soy sauce and the chicken broth. Cook, stirring until thickened. Serve sauce over Mushroom Fu Yung. *Serves 6.*

ONIONS

Onions become sweet when caramelized. They possess beneficial sulfur compounds and are known to lower blood sugar.

Onions are available all year around, but they are milder and sweeter when they are young. Red Italian onions are a member of the Bermuda onion family, which are the flat type onion. They are very, very sweet this time of year.

We have a lot of good recipes for onions, but I think what the man likes best is sliced red onions, marinated in a little olive oil and vinegar and salt and pepper for 3 or 4 hours. Put in enough vinegar to cover the onions. If you do this in a bowl, you're going to waste too much vinegar. At our house, we put them in a plastic bag, which flattens out and, therefore, covers the onions very well. Serve it with steak, chicken, or whatever you're having for dinner, and people are liable to eat more onions than anything else.

CREAMED ONIONS

*4 medium onions, sliced
  lengthwise
6 Tbsp. butter
4 Tbsp. flour*

*1/2 tsp. salt
2 cups milk
1 cup Cheddar cheese*

Boil onions in large amount of salted water till tender. Drain well. Melt butter in a large saucepan, blend in flour and salt. Add milk. Cook, stirring constantly, until mixture is thickened and bubbly. Add cheese, cook until melted. Add the onions to the sauce and heat. Taste for seasoning. Serve in individual sauce dishes. *Serves 6.*

SPANISH NOODLES

3 cups chopped onions (large)　　*2 cups beef bouillon or*
1/4 cup butter or margarine　　　　*consommé*
8 oz. thin uncooked noodles　　　　*salt and pepper*

Sauté onions in butter for 2 or 3 minutes; add noodles and stir. Continue cooking for 5 minutes. Add bouillon; cover and simmer, stirring occasionally until noodles are tender, about 30 minutes. Salt and pepper to taste.

For a special added touch, garnish with chopped chives, parsley, or grated cheese. *Serves 6.*

STUFFED ONIONS

6 medium onions　　　　　　*2 Tbsp. chopped pecans*
4 Tbsp. butter　　　　　　　*1/4 tsp. salt*
4 Tbsp. light cream　　　　　*dry bread crumbs*
4 Tbsp. chopped ripe olives　*paprika*

Peel onions. Cut a thick slice from the top of each, reserve. Cut out the center of each onion and reserve. Cook onion shells in a large amount of boiling, salted water until tender (about 20 to 25 minutes). Remove from water and drain upside down. Brush outside of shells with salad oil and sprinkle with paprika.

Chop reserved onion coarsely. Cook in butter until tender. Stir in cream, olives, pecans, and salt. Spoon into the onion shells. Sprinkle each onion with bread crumbs, drizzle with melted butter. Dash with paprika and bake at 350°F for 20 minutes. *Serves 6.*

GLAZED ONIONS

18 medium-sized onions
8 cups boiling water
2 tsp. salt

4 Tbsp. butter, melted
3 Tbsp. sugar

Peel onions and cook, uncovered, in boiling water to which 1 1/2 teaspoons salt have been added, for 20 minutes. Drain. Put in baking dish.

Mix melted butter, sugar, and remaining 1/2 teaspoon salt together. Pour over onions. Bake, uncovered, in moderate oven (350°F) for 1/2 hour, or until glazed and lightly browned. Baste onions frequently with butter mixture during baking. *Serves 6.*

CHEESE SCALLOPED ONIONS

3 large onions, cut in 1/2-inch
slices
1 cup of 1/2-inch cubes process
American cheese
4 slices buttered toast, cut in
1/2-inch cubes

1/4 cup butter or margarine
1/4 cup enriched flour
2 cups milk
1/2 tsp. salt
1/4 tsp. pepper
2 beaten eggs

Cook onions in boiling, salted water till tender, about 10 to 15 minutes, stirring occasionally to separate into rings. Drain well, place 1/2 the onions in 2-quart casserole. Add 1/2 the cheese and 1/2 the toast. Repeat layers of onion and cheese.

Melt butter, blend in flour. Stir in milk gradually. Cook, stirring constantly, until thick. Add salt and pepper. Add a little of hot mixture to beaten eggs; gradually stir into hot mixture. Pour sauce over layers. Top with remaining toast cubes. Bake in moderate oven (350°F) for 30 minutes. *Serves 6 to 8.*

BEACHCOMBER CASSEROLE

2 lbs. ground beef
1 medium onion, chopped
1 small green pepper, chopped
1 & 1/2 lbs. fresh tomatoes

6-oz. can tomato paste
1 Tbsp. salt
1/4 tsp. pepper
8-oz. pkg. shell macaroni,
cooked

Dice and cook fresh tomatoes. Break meat into 1-inch pieces. Brown over medium heat in a large skillet. Add onion and green pepper and sauté lightly. Add tomatoes and mix. Combine tomato paste, salt, and pepper and add to meat mixture. Mix well. Add macaroni. Spoon into a 2 and 1/2-quart casserole. Bake in a preheated 350°F oven for 45 minutes. Stir occasionally. *Serves 8.*

SAVORY ONION LOAF

6 cups soft bread crumbs
3/4 cup diced celery
1 & 1/4 cups chopped onion
3/4 lb. bulked pork sausage

1 slightly beaten egg
3/4 cup milk
2 Tbsp. chopped parsley

Mix bread crumbs, celery, onion, parsley, sausage, beaten egg, and milk together until well blended. Shape into loaf with the hands. Put in greased baking dish. Bake uncovered in moderate oven (350°F) for 1 hour, or until brown. *Serves 6.* This also makes a savory onion stuffing for roast turkey, duck, breast of lamb or veal.

ONION STUFFED FISH

1 cup finely chopped onion
1/4 cup finely chopped celery
1/3 cup butter or margarine,
melted
2 cups stale bread crumbs
1 tsp. salt
1/2 tsp. poultry seasoning

1/8 tsp. black pepper
2 fish steaks, 1 lb. each
salt to taste
pepper to taste
2 tsp. lemon juice
melted butter or margarine

Sauté onion and celery in butter or margarine until vegetables are limp and transparent. Add bread crumbs and cook until lightly browned. Blend in seasonings. Wipe fish with a damp cloth and sprinkle with salt, pepper, and lemon juice. Place half the fish in bottom of a buttered baking dish. Spread stuffing over the top. Top with remaining fish steak. Break with melted butter or margarine. Bake in preheated moderate oven (350°F) for 30 to 40 minutes or until fish is flaky. *Serves 4.*

SWISS STEAK

2 & 1/4 lbs. round steak
(1 inch thick)
3 Tbsp. flour
1 & 1/2 tsp. salt
2 Tbsp. fat

1 & 1/2 cups thinly sliced
onions
3 cups tomatoes, sliced
1/4 tsp. pepper

Cut steak into suitable pieces for serving. Pound in mixture of flour, salt, and pepper. In a heavy skillet or Dutch oven, brown on both sides in hot fat. Remove meat; put onions in skillet. Cook until lightly browned. Return steak and add tomatoes. Cover and cook slowly for 1 and 1/2 hours, or until tender. *Serves 6.*

A steak—even a very special one—takes on a new glory when it's rubbed with the cut side of a raw onion before it's broiled.

ONION CUCUMBER SALAD

2 mild onions
2 large cucumbers
1/2 cup Tarragon vinegar

1/4 cup cold water
1 tsp. sugar
salt and pepper

Peel and cut onions and cucumbers into thin slices. Cover with salted ice water and let stand in refrigerator for several hours. Drain and add remaining ingredients. *Serves 8.*

PEAS

Green peas are a good source of vitamin C
and carotenes (Vitamin A).

There's no question about the fact that fresh peas are selling better now than they have for many years. However, the sales today are absolutely nothing when compared with the sale of fresh peas in the 1930s and 1940s. The freezing of peas is what actually ruined the sale of fresh peas because it is so convenient for people, just as it practically eliminated the sale of fresh oranges for juice and fresh lima beans. But thank goodness, right now both the fresh peas and the fresh orange juice are making a comeback.

If you really want to find out just how good peas actually are, buy some fresh green peas, shell and cook them for about 15 minutes and serve them with a little butter. Believe me, you'll wonder why you haven't tried fresh peas before. But, just like fresh corn or fresh asparagus, peas begin to lose their natural sugar once they are picked, so it is important to use them as soon as you possibly can. Once shelled, they should be used immediately, if possible.

There are two good reasons to go back to fresh peas: for flavor and nutrition. Peas are very high in iron, so women should take heed, because women require a lot of iron. Parsley is also a good source of iron. Here is a wonderful dressing for anything: chop a bunch of parsley with a little garlic and some cheese. Use it as a dressing on fresh peas and you have a wonderful tasty dish, which will be exceptionally high in iron.

I have told you other fresh fruits and vegetables talk to you...well, you're not going to believe this till you try it yourself, but peas sing. When the professional buyers used to come down into the market, they would hit the sack of peas with their hands and rub it to see if the peas would squeak. When peas are fresh, they're stiff and crisp, and when you rub them together, they squeak, or as we say, sing.

You know, one of the fondest memories of my childhood is of my mother sitting there, shelling peas. There's nothing so sweet as sweet peas. They're as sweet as candy. I can remember my grandmother shelling peas—she dropped the pods into her apron and the peas into a bowl. All the kids would be eating the peas and she would be chasing us away.

You know, at night when they're watching TV or listening to the radio, get children started shelling peas. Then put the peas in a plastic bag, and seal them and use them the next day. They'll be excellent.

My mother has an old Sicilian recipe called Pasta e Pisedi. She used to make this dish of peas cooked in a little tomato sauce and then with spaghetti, and it's absolutely delicious. I know this will be a new way of eating fresh peas for a lot of people because they are used to them boiled or steamed, but try this, Pasta e Pisedi, with a roast or fowl. It's a wonderful dish. It's Sicilian and I know you are going to like this combination.

PASTE E PISEDI

3 cloves garlic
1/4 cup olive oil
1/2 onion, sliced
2 lbs. fresh peas

6 or 7 tomatoes, blended
1/2 lb. spaghetti
grated cheese-Parmesan or
Romano

Put oil in frying pan and fry onions first, for 5 minutes, then add sliced cloves of garlic and let fry until garlic is lightly tanned. Place peas in the pan with garlic and onion and sauté together for about 5 minutes, stirring 2 or 3 times. Add blended tomatoes and bring to boil. Cover and simmer for about 1/2 hour. Strain spaghetti, which has been cooking in another pot, and add the peas and tomato sauce to the hot strained spaghetti. Mix together and serve with freshly grated Parmesan or Romano cheese.

GREEN MEDLEY

2 cups shelled fresh peas
2 Tbsp. butter or margarine
1 Tbsp. salad oil
4 cups diagonally sliced celery

1/2 cup sliced stuffed green
  olives
1/2 tsp. salt
1/4 tsp. ground black pepper

In a large skillet, heat butter and oil. Add celery; cook and stir for 5 minutes. Add peas; cook and stir for 5 minutes longer. Blend in olives, salt, and black pepper. Cook and stir for 1 minute longer. *Serves 8.*

SAUTEED GREEN PEAS

1 lb. (2 cups shelled) fresh
  peas
1/2 cup salted, boiling water
1/4 cup butter

1 Tbsp. flour
1/2 cup milk
1 Tbsp. minced parsley

Simmer peas in water for 5 minutes. Drain. Sauté in butter until tender (5 to 15 minutes). Dust with flour, stir in milk. Bring to a boil, add parsley. Peas may also be sautéed with other vegetables: carrots, kohlrabi, cauliflower, lettuce hearts, etc. *Serves 2 to 3.*

CREAMED PEAS IN ONION CUPS

12 medium-sized onions
6 cups boiling water
2 tsp. salt
3 Tbsp. butter

2 Tbsp. flour
few grain pepper
1 cup milk
1 & 1/2 cups shelled, cooked
  peas

Peel onions and cook, uncovered, in boiling water to which 1 and 1/2 teaspoons salt have been added, 30 minutes, or until almost tender. Drain. Scoop out centers with sharp paring knife to form cups. Put in baking dish with 2 tablespoons butter, melted. Bake in hot oven (400°F) for 30 minutes, or until lightly browned, basting frequently with melted butter. Meanwhile, melt remaining tablespoon butter in saucepan. Blend in flour, remaining 1/2 teaspoon salt, and butter. Slowly stir in milk. Boil for 2 minutes, stirring constantly. Add peas and heat thoroughly. To serve, fill onion cups with creamed peas. *Serves 6.*

MINTED GREEN PEAS

2 cups shelled fresh peas
1/4 tsp. salt
few grains sugar
1/2 cup cold water

2 Tbsp. chopped fresh mint
leaves
1 Tbsp. butter

Place fresh peas in saucepan and add cold water, salt, and sugar and cook tightly covered, 5 to 7 minutes over moderate heat (or two minutes in pressure cooker). Just before serving add butter and chopped mint; shake the pan to distribute evenly. Remember when marketing, that it takes about 3 pounds unshelled peas to serve 4.

PEAS LATHEROS

4 & 1/2 to 5 lbs. peas
1 & 1/2 lbs. ripe tomatoes,
  peeled and strained
4 scallions

1 1/4 cups oil or 1 cup butter
3 Tbsp. chopped dill
salt and pepper to taste
water as needed

Shell, wash, and drain the peas. Chop the white part of the scallions into small pieces and the green part into large pieces. Heat the oil in a large pot. Add the scallions and cook until soft, but not browned. Add the peas and brown very lightly. Add the tomatoes, dill, salt, and pepper. Add enough water to half cover the peas. Cover the pot. Cook over medium heat until only the oil remains and the liquid has been absorbed (about 45 minutes). *Serves 6 to 9.*

EASY GRAIN SALAD
Contributed by
Simla Somturk Wickless

This recipe was born when I was staring at a bunch of leftovers in my fridge one day, wondering what the heck I was going to eat for a quick but satisfying lunch on a busy day... Sounds like a lot of ingredients, but it's really just a bit of this and a bit of that. Aim for organic ingredients.

1 cup cooked quinoa or any other favorite grain, freshly cooked or leftovers
2 Tbsp frozen shelled edamame, straight from the bag
1-2 leaves of any leafy green, torn into bite-size pieces, raw, lightly steamed or sautéed in 2 Tbsp water for 5 min.
1 Tbsp parsley, washed and de-stemmed, or finely chopped with stems on
Drizzle of olive oil (about 2 tsp)
Salt & Pepper, to taste

1/4 cup frozen shelled peas or frozen snap peas
1 Tbsp frozen sweet corn, straight from the bag
2-3 heaping Tbsp of drained, canned garbanzo beans (chickpeas) or any other canned beans on hand
1 Tbsp slivered almonds or raw pumpkin seeds or pine nuts
1 Tbsp lemon juice or more, to taste

Prepare quinoa/other grain. If using leftovers, sprinkle with 3 to 4 tablespoons of water and place in small pot over low heat to warm up the grain. Stir to evenly distribute the added water. In a small skillet, break leafy greens into bite-size pieces, and sauté in 2 tablespoons water for 5 minutes (if cooking; otherwise, leave raw). Add sautéed greens and all other ingredients to pot of grains. Stir and keep on low to low-medium heat until heated through. Serve warm in the winter or cool in the summer – Enjoy! *Single serving as a main dish, or 2 servings as a side dish. Double the recipe for bigger servings or more people as this dish goes fast!*

Variations:

- Add shredded chicken, turkey, tofu, tempeh, whole egg (like the egg in fried rice) or other healthy, lean protein of choice for added protein content.

- Use flax seed oil instead of olive oil or sprinkle with 1 tablespoon ground flax seeds or add 1/4 to 1/2 of an avocado for added healthy Omega 3 fats.

TOMATOES

Tomatoes supply a good amount of vitamin C and potassium. They also possess lycopine, a strong anti-oxidant. Tomatoes are more valuable when cooked, unlike most vegetables that are more valuable raw. (Tomatoes are members of the nightshade family and could aggravate those with arthritis).

You hear a lot of people who say tomatoes don't taste as good anymore, and I suspect they used to grow their own tomatoes. There is no question that when you walk into a garden and rustle the leaves of a tomato plant, it emits a beautiful aroma that makes you want to eat tomatoes. The fact is you can't beat tomatoes right off the plant when they are ripe. And you can buy them that way from about June to September. The complaints come during the winter months. But tomatoes are available all year around now because of the winter growing areas in Florida and the west coasts of the United States and Mexico. You can eat tomatoes 12 months a year, but now is the time to enjoy good, ripe locally-grown tomatoes.

My wife slices a fresh tomato with a little olive oil, sprinkles it with a little parsley, a bit of garlic and oregano. Sometimes, she puts a sardine with a caper on it. We have been enjoying fresh tomatoes like that all our lives, but one day I came home when she was just putting them on the table and they smelled so good. I said, "Gee, Babe, that's good. We should make a recipe out of that." Believe me, it really brings out that flavor of the fresh ripe tomato.

Before we go on, I want to give you the recipe for my Neapolitan Tomato Sauce. You will find it referred to many times in this book. This delicious all-purpose sauce is one of the foundations of all good Italian cooking—for vegetable dishes, spaghetti, or casseroles. You can make it in 15 minutes and use it right away, or it can be stored in the refrigerator or frozen for use as needed.

NEAPOLITAN TOMATO SAUCE

12 fresh tomatoes
4 cloves garlic
1 medium white or yellow
  onion

1 bay leaf
3 Tbsp. olive oil or salad oil
salt and pepper

Blend 12 fresh tomatoes in electric blender. Remove to saucepan, bring to boil, and then reduce heat to simmer. Meanwhile, heat 3 tablespoons olive oil or salad oil in frying pan. Slice 4 cloves of garlic and sauté slowly in oil until golden brown. Pour hot tomato mixture into the garlic mixture and add 1 sliced onion, 1 bay leaf, salt and pepper to taste.

For vegetable dishes, simmer for about 15 minutes and add your favorite fresh vegetable-zucchini, carrots, peas, beans, eggplant, or even hearts of artichokes and continue cooking until tender.

For spaghetti sauce, simmer slowly for 1 hour. That's your basic Neapolitan Tomato Sauce.

STUFFED FRESH TOMATOES

For a real tasty, cool luncheon, here are some ideas that taste and look great. Select fresh and firm, well-shaped tomatoes. Wash and dry each tomato and slice downward from the top to approximately 1/2 inch from base. Spread the 6 or 8 sections outward and place on a bed of lettuce in individual salad bowls. Place approximately 1/2 cup of any of the following fillings in the center of the fresh tomato.

FRESH TOMATO-TUNA SALAD

6 ozs. flaked, white tuna
2 Tbsp mayonnaise
1 tsp. chopped green onion

1 tsp. chopped pickle
salt and pepper to taste

FRESH TOMATO-SEAFOOD SALAD

2 cups crab meat, shrimp, or
lobster
1/2 tsp. salt
dash of black pepper
juice of 1 lemon

3 hard cooked eggs,
optional
1 cup chopped celery
1/2 cup diced cucumber
mayonnaise to moisten

Sprinkle lemon juice, salt and pepper over seafood. Combine seafood, celery, and cucumber, with small amount of mayonnaise. Place large scoop in center of tomato. Arrange hard-cooked egg slices around edge as garnish.

FRESH TOMATO-CHICKEN SALAD

3 cups cooked, cubed chicken
1/2 cups dice celery
1 tsp. salt
mayonnaise to moisten

3 hard cooked eggs
(optional) (quartered)
3 sweet pickles (chopped)

Combine all ingredients in small amount of mayonnaise. Spoon into tomato center.

You know, I like tomatoes best fresh with other fresh vegetables, but they are good baked, fried, and broiled, too. Here are recipes, some come from the Carcione kitchen and some which our radio and television audiences have shared. We've tried them all at our home, and these are our favorites.

CRUNCHY FRIED TOMATOES

4 firm, ripe tomatoes
1 egg, beaten
1 cup dry bread crumbs

1/2 cup butter or margarine
salt and pepper to taste

Slice tomatoes into 3/4 inch slices and dip into beaten egg and then into crumbs. Fry tomatoes in large skillet in hot butter until golden brown on each side. Season to taste.

STUFFED BAKED TOMATOES

These make a great side dish with your entrée. Some people like fresh tomatoes baked, leaving the skin on, others want the skin removed. If you want to remove the skin, dip the tomato into boiling water for just a minute, then run cold water over it, and the skin is easy to remove. Cut off the top and scoop out small amount from center, then stuff firmly with your favorite filling.

STUFFED TOMATOES

6 fresh, firm tomatoes   1 tsp. salt
1 & 1/2 cups soft bread crumbs   1/2 tsp. pepper
2 Tbsp. fat

Make stuffing using the centers you have scooped from the tomatoes, bread crumbs, melted fat and seasonings. Mix well. Sprinkle each tomato with salt and pepper and fill with stuffing, packing firmly. Arrange tomatoes in shallow baking dish, top each with dab of butter and bake in moderate oven over 350°F to 375°F, for about 20 minutes until tender.

STUFFED BAKED TOMATOES
WITH FRESH VEGETABLES

6 fresh, firm tomatoes   1/2 cup grated American
2 cups freshly cooked spinach,   cheese
   broccoli or other vegetable   2 beaten eggs
2 Tbsp. chopped onion   1/2 cup milk
1/2 cup buttered bread crumbs

Mix all ingredients except bread crumbs and stuff tomatoes firmly. Place tomatoes in shallow baking dish, dot each with butter and sprinkle with bread crumbs. Bake in moderate oven, 350°F, for about 20 minutes until tender.

SCALLOPED TOMATOES

4 medium fresh tomatoes
3 or 4 slices toast (cubed)
1 tsp. grated onion
1/4 tsp. pepper

1/4 cup melted butter or
margarine
1 tsp. salt

Scald tomatoes and remove skin, quarter and simmer in saucepan until tender, about 5 minutes. In greased 1-quart casserole dish, alternate tomatoes and toast cubes, finishing with layer of toast. Sprinkle with grated onion, seasonings and pour melted butter over top. Bake in moderate oven (375°F) till heated through, or about 20 minutes.

BROILED TOMATOES NAPOLI

4 large firm, ripe tomatoes
1 cup fresh bread crumbs
1/4 cup melted butter

2 Tbsp. Parmesan cheese
1/2 tsp. Italian Herbs

Wash tomatoes, remove stems, cut into halves and place on large broiler pan cut-side up. Toss crumbs lightly with butter, Parmesan cheese and Italian Herbs. Spoon crumb mixture into tomatoes. Place under the broiler 10 inches from the source of heat, for 4 to 5 minutes, until tomatoes are heated through and crumbs well-browned. Serve at once. *Makes 4 servings.*

DEVIL'S TOMATOES

6 fresh tomatoes
1 Tbsp. flour
1 cooked egg yolk
5 Tbsp. butter
1 whole egg

2 tsp. powdered sugar
1 tsp. mustard
2 Tbsp. vinegar
salt and pepper

Sprinkle peeled, slice tomatoes with flour, salt, and pepper and fry in butter. Keep hot while making sauce, as follows: Mash egg yolk and cream with butter and whole egg. Mix in other ingredients.

Cook in double boiler and stir continuously till sauce thickens. Pour over tomatoes and serve.

FRESH TOMATO-EGG SALAD

3 hard cooked eggs, chopped   *3 ozs. cream cheese*
2 Tbsp. chopped green onion   *1/4 cup mayonnaise*
1/4 cup chopped green pepper   *salt and pepper*
1/2 med. fresh chopped cucumber   *paprika*

Blend cream cheese and mayonnaise, salt and pepper, adding small amount of cream, if necessary. Mix well with eggs, fresh onion, green pepper, and cucumber. Spoon into tomatoes. Top with sprinkle of paprika.

TOMATOES WITH GROUND BEEF STUFFING

6 large fresh, firm tomatoes   *1/4 cup chopped celery*
1/2 lb. lean ground beef   *1/4 cup green pepper*
1/2 cup cracker crumbs   *1/3 cup water*
1/4 cup grated American cheese   *salt and pepper to taste*

Scoop out center of 6 firm, fresh tomatoes. Using centers, combine with all other ingredients. Stuff tomatoes and place in shallow greased baking dish. Bake in moderate oven, 350°F for 30 minutes.

Here are other ways to fix tomatoes for a great side dish:

TOMATO OMELET

3 small fresh, ripe tomatoes   *6 eggs*
4 Tbsp. butter   *salt and pepper*

Brown tomatoes cut in small pieces in frying pan with salt and pepper to taste, cooking until tomato is reduced to pulp. Remove from pan. Beat eggs with small amount of salt and pepper and pour into center of frying pan. Lower heat and allow to cook until set to your taste. Spread tomatoes on top of the omelet, fold in half. Flip omelet to firm tomato filling. Serve immediately with hash browned potatoes.

HEIRLOOM TOMATO AND SUMMER VEGETABLE GRIDDLE-STICKERS
Contributed by Aaron French

1/2 cup carrots – grated
1 cups heirloom tomatoes, diced
1 cups heirloom tomatoes
2 tsp. pepper
1/2 tsp. brown sugar
1/2 tsp. ginger powder
1 package wonton wrappers

1 cup summer squash,
  diced fine
2 Tbsp. fresh ginger, grated
2 tsp. salt
1/2 tsp. dry mustard
2 Tbsp. sesame oil
Canola oil for cooking

Bring heavy skillet to medium heat and add all ingredients. Stir as needed, and reduce heat to low after 5 minutes. Cook on low for another 10 minutes and then drain through colander to remove all liquid.

Wrap 2 Tbsp. portions of vegetables in wonton wrappers, pinching the edges into triangles. Cook on high heat in lightly greased pan, flipping once, until golden and crispy on both sides (about 5 minutes total). Serve with Griddle-Sticker Sauce (recipe below).

GRIDDLE-STICKERS SAUCE
1/2 cup organic ketchup
1 tsp. sesame oil
2 dashes Tabasco, or to taste
1/4 cup sour cream

1/4 cup green onion, diced
  fine
1 Tbsp. soy sauce

Whisk all ingredients together and serve with Heirloom Tomato and Summer Vegetable Griddle-Stickers.

CABBAGE

*Cabbage contains many vitamins and minerals
and possess the strong sulfur compounds that make
cabbage a great cancer fighter.*

Here is a vegetable that is really underrated. It's a shame because cabbage is a good source of vitamin C, iron, and potassium, and it provides roughage the body needs. It is also surprisingly low in calories, so it is ideal for the weight watcher. Per capita, consumption of cabbage has declined 50% in the last 30 years. I really don't know what the reason is unless cabbage carries the stigma of being the poor man's vegetable. But its low price should be to its credit because you can use it in stews and salads, make coleslaw, and it is delicious just boiled with a little butter or cream sauce. Although it is most abundant in late summer, cabbage is usually available all year round, and it is one of the least expensive vegetables you can serve at any time.

CABBAGE A LA CARCIONE

3/4 head of fresh cabbage   *4 tbsp grated Romano cheese*
1 cup Neapolitan Tomato sauce   *salt and pepper*

Combine shredded cabbage and Neapolitan Tomato Sauce and simmer for 8 to 10 minutes until cabbage is tender. Do not overcook. Season to taste. Sprinkle each serving with grated Romano cheese. *Serves 4.*

FRIED CABBAGE

3 small heads cabbage   *2 eggs, beaten*
pepper to taste   *1 & 1/2 cups bread crumbs*
1 cup flour   *2 cups fat*

Halve cabbages. Cut out cores. Cook for 20 minutes in salted water. Squeeze dry and flatten like cutlets. Season with pepper.

Dip in flour, beaten egg, and bread crumbs. Fry in deep fat until golden brown. *Serves 6.* Note: Celery or eggplant slices may be prepared the same way.

CABBAGE IN SOUR CREAM

1 medium head cabbage
(3 to 3 & 1/2 lbs.)
1/2 cup cold water
2 cups sour cream
2 Tbsp. butter

1/2 cup mild vinegar
1/2 cup flour
1/2 cup sugar
salt to taste

Shred cabbage and add water. Cook in frying pan for 5 minutes. Drain off excess liquid. Add sour cream and butter. Blend flour, vinegar, and sugar and stir in. Cook for 3 minutes longer. Add salt. *Serves 6.*

STUFFED CABBAGE ROLLS

1 head cabbage
1 lb. lean ground beef
3 Tbsp. onion, chopped
1/2 tsp. garlic salt
2 cans tomato sauce

1/2 tsp. pepper
1/2 tsp. oregano
1 cup bread crumbs
2 eggs
3 Tbsp. grated Parmesan
cheese

Boil 12 large cabbage leaves in salted water until soft. Sauté ground beef with onion. Add garlic salt, pepper, oregano, bread crumbs, eggs, and cheese. Cook for 1 or 2 minutes. Divide filling equally on cabbage leaves. Fold sides over and roll up. Place rolls in buttered baking dish. Cover with tomato sauce and sprinkle each roll with a little salt and pepper. Cover and bake for 1/2 hour at 300°F.

GERMAN COLESLAW

1 head cabbage
3 carrots
3 green onions
6 Tbsp. mayonnaise

1 tomato
1 green pepper
1 bunch radishes

Grate cabbage, carrots, cut up tomato, onions, green pepper, and radishes. Combine and add dressing. Salt and pepper to taste.

CABBAGE DUMPLINGS

1 medium cabbage
2 Tbsp. oil
4 hot rolls
1/2 cup milk
3/4 lb. (3 sticks) butter

2 egg yolks
2 eggs, beaten
1/4 cup flour
2 qts. salted water
grated cheese (optional)

Remove core and hard ribs from cabbage and chop leaves very fine. Fry in oil for 10 minutes. Cube 2 rolls and dry in 4 tablespoons butter until golden. Soak the other 2 rolls in milk and put through strainer. Beat 14 tablespoons butter with egg yolks until soft. Slowly add whole eggs, flour, and cabbage. Season and add fried roll cubes and strain roll mixture. Knead well. Shape small dumplings; cook in boiling salted water until they rise to the surface (about 10 minutes). Cook for 3 to 4 minutes more. Remove and strain. Pour remaining melted butter over, or sprinkle with grated cheese, or use both. *Serves 4 to 6.*

SKINNY CORNED BEEF AND CABBAGE

4 lbs. corned beef round*
2 to 3 cloves garlic, minced
3 bay leaves

4 medium potatoes, peeled
and quartered
1 large head cabbage, cut in
wedges

In large kettle or Dutch oven, place corned beef, garlic, and bay leaves; add water to cover. Heat water to boiling; skim surface. Cover and simmer over low heat for about 4 hours or until meat is

109

almost tender. Remove cover and skim off all surface fat. Add potatoes, cover and cook for 15 to 20 minutes. Add cabbage and simmer until meat and vegetables are tender, about 10 minutes more. *Makes 8 servings.*

*Ask your butcher for corned beef round instead of brisket; it's far less fattening!

GERMAN RED CABBAGE

1 medium-size red cabbage,
  finely sliced
1 large onion, chopped
3 Tbsp. butter
1 bay leaf
4 whole cloves
2 Tbsp. vinegar

1/2 cup water
4 tart apples, peeled and cut
  in slices
1 tsp. salt
1 Tbsp. sugar
3 Tbsp. dry red wine

Brown the onion in butter, add the cabbage and stir until it is also slightly browned. Add bay leaf, cloves, vinegar, water, apples, and salt. Cover and simmer for about 45 minutes, or until the cabbage is tender. Add sugar and wine, then cook for 5 minutes longer. *Serves 8 to 10.*

CORN

*Corn is a grain which provides essential fatty acids,
vitamin E and some protein.*

What's better than corn on the cob? Use your hands! You know, the fresher the corn, the sweeter it is, because corn loses its sugar almost immediately. So it is important that you buy, cook, and serve it as soon as possible. If you do have to hold it a day or two, put it in a plastic bag to keep the moisture in. That will keep it as fresh as possible.

To select corn, just like everything else, you have to use your eyes. Look for a fresh green color on the outside leaves and husk. Check the stem ends to see that they are not dried out. The kernels should be a bright, light yellow color, and they should be well filled and plump, never dented.

BOILED CORN-ON-THE-COB

1 to 2 cobs for each portion   *2 tsp. salt to each qt. (5 cups)*
water   *of water*

Remove the husks and silky threads and rinse the cobs. Put the cobs into boiling salted water and cook until the corn feels tender, about 10 to 20 minutes. Lift out the cobs and drain them. Serve with creamed butter.

SOUFFLE OF CREAMED CORN

Cook the cut corn in water or steam; rub it quickly through a sieve; put it into a saucepan with a small piece of butter, and quickly dry it. This done, add sufficient fresh cream to this puree to make a somewhat soft paste. Thicken this paste with the yolks of 3 eggs per pound of puree, and combine it with the whites of 4 eggs beaten to a stiff froth. Pour into a soufflé form and cook as you would an ordinary soufflé.

SOUFFLE OF CORN WITH PAPRIKA

Before crushing the corn through a sieve, add to it 2 tablespoons of chopped onion fried in butter, and a large pinch of paprika per pound of corn.

CORN FRITTERS

2 cups cooked corn kernels　　1/2 cup flour
2 eggs　　　　　　　　　　　1/2 cup milk or water
1/2 tsp. salt　　　　　　　　　shortening for frying

Beat eggs, add salt, flour, and liquid to make a smooth batter. Add corn kernels and drop by the spoonful in deep, hot, melted shortening. Fry till nicely browned on both sides. Drain well. *Serves 4.*

CORN O'BRIEN

3 cups corn, cooked　　　1 Tbsp. flour
1 onion　　　　　　　　1/2 cup milk
1 large green pepper　　　1/4 tsp. salt
2 Tbsp. butter　　　　　　dash of white pepper

Cut corn from cob. Dice onion and green pepper. Sauté in butter till lightly browned. Blend in flour, stirring lightly for 1 to 2 minutes, add milk slowly to blend smooth. Add cooked corn and season to taste. Cook for 3 minutes. If uncooked corn kernels are used, sauté with browned onion and pepper before adding milk in which flour has been blended smooth. Cook over low heat for 5 to 10 minutes till corn is tender. *Serves 4.*

CUCUMBERS

Cucumbers contain important minerals.
They are a good source of silicon, which is known to
improve the complexion and health of the skin.

You know the old saying "cool as a cucumber" is not just a lot of words. It is a fact that cucumbers on the vine are 20% cooler than the outside air.

We are seeing more and more of the hothouse or hydroponically grown cucumbers on the market, and they are selling at very reasonable prices. They come wrapped in plastic, and there's no question about the fact that it is a large cucumber and too much for the average family salad, but with the plastic wrap they will keep for a long period, at least a week. Leave the plastic on the part you didn't use and cover the exposed end with plastic wrap because once cut and exposed to the air, it will deteriorate rapidly. These hothouse cucumbers are called the non-repeaters. They're seedless, burpless, non-bitter, and you can eat skin and all and enjoy it.

Cucumbers are great in warm weather, so cooling in a salad, and when it comes to calories, cucumbers are very, very low; I'd say about 15 calories to every 3 and 1/2 ounces.

DILLED CUCUMBERS AND AVOCADO

1/3 cup each: vinegar and
salad oil
1 & 1/2 tsp. salt
1/2 tsp. dill weed
1/4 tsp. onion salt
dash each: pepper, garlic powder

2 medium cucumbers, pared
and thinly sliced
3 or 4 unpeeled avocados,
halved
salad greens

Combine vinegar, oil and seasonings; pour over cucumbers in shallow dish. Chill for several hours or overnight, turning

113

occasionally. Arrange avocado half-shells on salad greens and fill with cucumbers. *Serves 6 to 8.*

SAUTÉED CUCUMBERS

Peel 3 average-sized cucumbers and cut into 1/4-inch slices. Soak in ice water for 2 hours. Dry on paper towel.

Melt 3 tablespoons butter and 3 tablespoons oil in heavy skillet. Coat the cucumbers in flour and sauté at medium heat until they are brown on both sides. Sprinkle with salt and pepper. Serve with lemon butter.

To make lemon butter: Melt 1/4 cup butter, add 1 & 1/2 tablespoons lemon juice. (Optional: add 2 tablespoons finely chopped parsley.)

CREAMED CUCUMBERS

Peel and slice the cucumber. Parboil and drain the pieces. Partially cook them in butter; moisten with boiling cream, and finish the cooking in the cream.

STUFFED CUCUMBER AU GRATIN

1 green or white cucumber	*2 Tbsp. butter or margarine*
(1 & 1/2 to 2 lbs.)	*salt*
water	*white pepper*
2 tsp. salt to each qt. of water	

Stuffing
1/2 lb. fresh mushrooms,
  chopped

Gratin Top
1 Tbsp. butter or margarine
2 Tbsp. grated cheese

Wash and peel the cucumber. Cut it into two halves lengthwise and remove the seeds carefully using a teaspoon. Blanch the cucumber halves by parboiling them for a few minutes in salted water. Drain. Fry the mushrooms in butter or margarine. Season to taste. Put the cucumber halves onto a greased, fireproof dish and fill them with

114

mushrooms. Dot with pats of butter and sprinkle grated cheese on top. Bake in oven (425°F) until lightly browned, about 10 minutes. Serve with boiled rice or boiled potatoes. *Serves 4.*

CUCUMBERS IN CREAM IN TOMATO CUPS

4 medium-sized cucumbers　　*1 cup heavy cream*
1 tsp. salt　　*salt*
6 medium-sized tomatoes　　*pepper*
salt　　*2 Tbsp. chopped parsley*
1/4 cup butter or margarine

Pare cucumbers; cut in half lengthwise; scoop out seeds. Cut into 1/2-inch cubes; place in bowl; sprinkle with 1 teaspoon salt. Toss a few times. Let stand for 1 hour. Drain. Dry.

Heat oven to 325°F. Slice tops off tomatoes. Use a spoon to scoop out pulp, seeds, and juices. Sprinkle insides of tomatoes lightly with salt. Set aside.

Melt butter or margarine in large skillet over medium heat. Add cucumbers. Cook for 2 to 3 minutes, tossing or stirring frequently. Add cream. Bring to boiling; reduce heat. Simmer for 10 minutes or until cream is reduced by half and cucumbers are tender. Correct seasoning to taste. Remove extra juices from tomatoes. Spoon cucumber mixture into tomato shells. Set in shallow baking dish. Bake for 20 minutes or until tomatoes are tender. Sprinkle with parsley. *Makes 6 servings.*

CUCUMBER TOMATO DISH

2 medium cucumbers　　*dill (chopped)*
4 tomatoes　　*3 Tbsp. butter*
salt and pepper　　*lemon juice or vinegar*

Pare cucumbers, cutting toward stem end. Chop up cucumbers and tomatoes. Season well and sauté in butter. Before serving, add a dash of lemon juice or vinegar. *Serves 4.*

STUFFED CUCUMBERS

3 large cucumbers   salad dressing
3 tomatoes   lettuce leaves

Without paring cucumbers, cut off each end squarely. Cut in half. Scoop out insides and dice. Chop up tomatoes. Add salad dressing to cucumber and tomato mixture and blend well. Fill each half. Set upright and serve on lettuce leaves. *Serves 6.*

CRISP MARINATED SALAD
Contributed by Elaine Murphy

1 English cucumber, cut into   2 tomatoes
   medallions and then quartered   1/4 cup celery, crosscut
1/4 cup red onion, thinly sliced   1/2 cup coarsely chopped
                                         parsley

Dress with:
1/4 - 1/2 cup fresh lemon or   1/4-1/2 cup extra virgin olive
   lime juice   oil
1 or 2 tsp. salt   1/2 tsp. fresh ground pepper
1/2 tsp. thyme   2 cloves fresh garlic, finely
1/2 tsp. oregano   grated

Additions for Variations:
- *1/8 cup capers or 1/4 cup pitted Calamata olives, cut in half lengthwise (this and Feta make it very much like a Greek salad)*
- *1/2 cup shredded carrots*
- *1/2 cup crumbled Feta cheese or other goat cheese*
- *1 or 2 cubed avocados*
- *1 or 2 cups cooked peeled shrimp*

Put all ingredients in a container with a tightly fitting lid, and refrigerate for at least 30 minutes before serving (an hour is better). This salad will last for three days or so in the refrigerator (not if you add the shrimp or avocados, though) and can have greens added to it and tossed before serving, if desired.

JICAMA – CUCUMBER SALAD WITH CITRUS DRESSING
Contributed by
Simla Somturk Wickless

1 medium jicama, peeled and cut into matchsticks
1/2 small red onion, peeled, quartered, and sliced into very thin moons
leaves from 1/3 bunch of fresh mint, washed, finely chopped
1/2 tsp sea salt; more later, to taste
2-3 cranks freshly ground pepper

2 medium cucumbers, peeled halved horizontally, and cut into thin half moons
leaves from 1/2 bunch of cilantro, washed, finely chopped
the juice of 1 lime
1 large or 2 small oranges, peeled, cut into wedges without the membranes
1 tsp. canola oil

Gently 'massage' the red onions with the sea salt, to mellow out their acidity and flavor (both my grandmothers' trick). Add the remaining ingredients. Toss! Add more sea salt, to taste.

Variations

- Great with shredded chicken
- Add 1/2 bunch of watercress for a peppery kick
- Spice it up with some chili powder
- Add some sweet color with some red paprika powder (caution: nightshade)
- Add pumpkin seeds for crunch and protein

PICKLED CUCUMBERS AND GRAPES
Contributed by Aaron French

*1 cucumber, peeled and
 sliced thin**
1 jalapeno, seeded and sliced thin
1/4 cup turbinado sugar

1 cup seedless grapes
6 cloves whole garlic
1 cup rice vinegar
1 Tbsp. salt

* Many homegrown cucumbers might not need to be peeled.

Combine all ingredients and let marinate in refrigerator overnight.
Serve as an appetizer, perhaps with some hard cheese and crackers.
Will keep in refrigerator for up to 4 days. *Makes enough as a side
for 6, or 2 to 3 meal-size salads.*

EGGPLANT

Eggplant is known to lower blood cholesterol and improve digestion. (Eggplant is a member of the nightshade family and may aggravate those with arthritis).

Eggplant is not as popular as some of the other fresh vegetables, probably because many people don't know how to prepare it. You can't just boil an eggplant like you would green beans or zucchini. However, once people learn to prepare eggplant, they really do enjoy it and, incidentally, sales are up and the number of fields have increased quite a lot in the past few years.

Select a firm eggplant that has a bright, shiny, purple-black skin and a green calyx. The calyx is the stem cap where it connects and overlaps part of the plant at the top. Avoid soft, shriveled, or dull looking eggplant. A dull, dark eggplant is trying to tell you it has been around too long.

Although it is used as a vegetable, eggplant is actually a fruit. It fits the definition of a berry since it consists of a pulpy fruit with one or more seeds. You see, we come up with these oddities once in a while. Here is a fruit used like a vegetable that is really a berry. How do you like those apples?

There are simple ways to enjoy eggplant. I like it raw. Just mix a little bit of olive oil, salt and pepper together and dice slices of raw eggplant in it and eat as finger food. It is very tender and tasty.

FRIED EGGPLANT

*1 medium eggplant, peeled
and cut into 1 and 1/2 inch
slices
1/2 cup flour
(Continued on next page)*

*1 egg, lightly beaten
1/2 tsp. salt
1/2 tsp. pepper
1/2 cup olive oil*

Flour eggplant slices and dip into egg, to which salt and pepper have been added. Fry in olive oil for 6 minutes on each side, or until slices are golden brown. *Serves 4.*

EGGPLANT CROQUETTES

2 large eggplants
3 Tbsp. grated Parmesan cheese
1 Tbsp. chopped parsley
1 Tbsp. chopped basil
3/4 tsp. salt
1/2 tsp. pepper

dash nutmeg
2 slices bread, soaked in
  water and squeezed dry
2 eggs
1/2 cup flour
1 cup olive oil

Cut eggplants into 4 parts each and boil for 20 minutes, or until tender. Drain well and chop fine. Mix together with the Parmesan cheese, parsley, basil, salt, pepper, nutmeg, bread, and eggs and shape as croquettes. Flour and fry in olive oil until golden brown on all sides. Serve with tomato sauce or plain. *Serves 4.*

EGGPLANT WITH CREAM

1 & 1/2 lbs. eggplant
salt to taste
1/4 cup butter
1/2 cup bouillon (optional)

lemon juice to taste
1/2 pt. sour cream
scant lb. each, tomatoes and
  mushrooms (optional)

Peel eggplants and cut into slices 1/4-inch thick. Sprinkle with salt and let stand for 1 hour. Squeeze out juice. Slowly simmer in hot butter until soft. If necessary, add a little bouillon. When soft, sprinkle with lemon juice and pour cream over. You may cook chopped tomatoes or mushrooms with them, or both. *Serves 6.*

EGGPLANT BAKED IN CHEESE SAUCE

2 & 1/2 lbs. eggplant
1/2 cup grated cheddar cheese
1 tablespoon flour
(Continued on next page)

1 cup milk
oil for frying
salt and pepper to taste
1 egg

Slice the unpeeled eggplant thick. Fry in very hot oil and remove before slices are soft. Put them into a casserole dish and dust each with flour. Mix the egg and milk, add the grated cheese and seasoning, and pour over the eggplant. Bake in a moderate oven until the eggplant is tender and set it in the sauce. Good hot or cold. *Serves 6 to 8.*

INDIAN EGGPLANT CURRY

3 Tbsp. ghee or peanut oil
1/2 tsp. cumin seed
1 tsp. salt
1 tsp. turmeric
1 tsp. cayenne
1 eggplant, chopped, skin and all

1 onion chopped
2 cups water
1 large ripe tomato, peeled
* and chopped (onion)*
1 cup yogurt

Heat the ghee or peanut oil and add the spices to it. When well heated, add the chopped eggplant and onion. Stir until well coated, then add the water and tomato. Cover and cook for 20 minutes, and add the yogurt. Stir well, continue to cook until heated. *Serves 4.*

RATATOUILLE

1 large onion, chopped
1/4 cup olive oil
2 zucchini, cut into 1/4-inch slices
2 medium-sized garlic cloves,
* finely chopped*
1 eggplant, peeled and cubed

salt and pepper to taste
2 large green peppers, cut
* into medium-sized slices*
4 tomatoes, peeled, seeded
* and coarsely chopped*

Sauté onion until transparent in olive oil in large skillet. (Do not brown.) Add remaining ingredients. Cover and cook over medium heat for 45 minutes, stirring occasionally. A little water may be added, if necessary. Garnish with chopped parsley.

Optional additions: 1/8 teaspoon basil and 1/8 teaspoon oregano. You may top the ratatouille with ripe olives cut in half, crumbled, crisp fresh bacon, or Parmesan cheese. However, this delicious mixture needs no "dressing up." Serve hot, or chill well and serve cold as a first course. *If you like a very strong garlic flavor, add 1 or 2 more cloves garlic. *Serves 8.*

EGYPTIAN EGGPLANT

1 large eggplant *3 eggs*
salt to taste *1/2 lb. dry pot cheese*
1/4 cup flour *1 tsp. minced parsley*
3/4 cup oil *1 Tbsp. lemon juice*

Cut unpared eggplant into 1/4-inch thick slices or rounds. Salt lightly and let stand approximately half an hour. Pat each slice dry, dust lightly with flour and fry in hot oil till browned on both sides. Pour off surplus oil, leaving the fried eggplant slices in bottom of frying pan. Remove half the fried eggplant to a plate. Beat 2 eggs, add dry cheese and 1 teaspoon minced parsley and spread over the eggplant slices in the pan. Cover with remaining fried eggplant, and cook over low heat for 3 to 5 minutes. Beat remaining egg till light and frothy. Lift cover and pour unbeaten egg over top layer of eggplant. Let cook uncovered until set. Garnish with parsley or a sprinkling of lemon juice. Serve hot. *Serves 4.*

There is also a small egg-shaped eggplant which the Italians love to stuff. You'll find it delicious.

ITALIAN STUFFED EGGPLANT

4 small eggplants *1 Tbsp. parsley flakes*
4 Tbsp. margarine or butter *1/2 tsp. salt*
1 small onion, sliced *1/2 tsp. oregano*
1 clove garlic, minced *2 tomatoes, sliced*
1/2 cup sliced mushrooms *1 Tbsp. salad oil*
1/2 cup grated Parmesan cheese

Cut eggplant in half lengthwise and remove pulp, leaving a shell 1/2 inch thick. Sauté onion, garlic and mushroom to margarine until tender. Chop eggplant pulp and add to onion mixture; cook

122

for 3 minutes. Stir in Parmesan cheese, parsley, salt, and oregano. Spoon mixture into eggplant shells. Top shells with tomato slices and brush lightly with oil. Place shells on baking sheet. Bake in a moderate oven, 350°, for 20 to 25 minutes. *Serves 8.*

This recipe for Eggplant a la Parmesan has been handed down from generation to generation in my family. It is excellent.

EGGPLANT A LA PARMESAN

2 medium-sized eggplant　　　　*Neapolitan Tomato Sauce*
grated Parmesan or Romano
*　cheese*

Peel eggplant; slice into 1/4-inch pieces, crosswise. Salt pieces and allow to stand until water reaches the surface. Wipe dry. Sauté in olive oil until slightly brown on both sides. Cover bottom of casserole with Neapolitan Tomato Sauce. Add layer of eggplant; cover with grated cheese. Add sauce and repeat alternately with eggplant, cheese, and sauce, until all of eggplant is covered. Bake for 45 minutes at 325°F to 350°F.

EGGPLANT BAKE

2 small eggplants　　　　*1 cup tomato sauce*
salt　　　　　　　　　　*1/2 cup bread crumbs*
flour　　　　　　　　　　*butter, to dot*
3 Tbsp. butter　　　　　　*salt and pepper*
1/2 cup cheese, grated

Peel eggplants and cut into 1/4-inch slices. Salt lightly, dip in flour, and fry lightly on both sides in butter. Grease a baking dish. Place slices in this and add part of the cheese, the tomato sauce, and seasoning. Sprinkle with bread crumbs, and again with cheese. Dot with butter. Bake in moderate (325°F) oven for 20 minutes, or until nicely browned. *Serves 2 to 4.*

Variation: Peel eggplant and hollow out. Soak 10 minutes in a marinade of olive oil and lemon juice. Remove from marinade. Stuff with chopped leftover meat, sprinkle with grated cheese, dot with butter, and bake in 350° oven until done, about 30 minutes. Serve with tomato sauce. The hollowed-out insides can be fried lightly, combined with stewed tomatoes and baked for a subsequent meal. *Serves 2 to 4.*

MOUSSAKA

4 medium eggplants (1 lb. ea)
salt
2 lbs. lean beef, ground
3 medium onion, chopped
1/2 cup butter or margarine,
*   divided*
1/2 cup dry red wine
2 tsp. salt
1/4 tsp. coarse black pepper
1 tsp. oregano
2 eggs, lightly beaten

1 cup grated sharp Cheddar
*   cheese, divided*
1/2 cup soft bread crumbs,
*   divided*
vegetable oil
2 lbs. tomatoes, drained
6 Tbsp. flour
3 cups milk
salt and pepper
dash nutmeg
4 egg yolks, lightly beaten

Peel eggplant, cut crosswise in 1/4-inch slices. Sprinkle lightly with salt; arrange in stacks; place heavy plate on top, let stand to drain.

Cook beef and onions in 2 tablespoons butter until beef is browned. Add wine, 2 teaspoons salt, 1/4 teaspoon pepper, and oregano. Simmer until liquid is absorbed. Stir in 2 beaten eggs, 3/4 cup grated cheese, and 1/4 cup bread crumbs.

Brown eggplant slices quickly on both sides in vegetable oil. Grease large casserole or baking dish (3 & 1/2 to 4 quart). Sprinkle bottom of casserole with remaining crumbs. Fill with alternate layers of eggplant, meat mixture and tomatoes, ending with eggplant, leaving 1 inch head space. Melt remaining butter; blend in flour, add milk slowly, stirring constantly. Season to taste with salt, pepper, and nutmeg. Pour a little hot milk mixture on egg yolks, return to remaining hot milk mixture. Cook for about 2 minutes over low heat, stirring constantly until thickened. Pour sauce into casserole. Sprinkle with remaining cheese. Bake at 350° for 45 to 60 minutes or until top is golden brown and eggplant is tender. *Makes 10 to 12 servings.*

BERRIES (Varietal)

Berries give us an easy way to stay healthy.
They are rich in vital nutrients and low in calories.
Different colors provide different anti-oxidant strength.
The darker the berry, the stronger the anti-oxidant.

BLACKBERRY: Not many around from a commercial standpoint, but often available wild. They have to be black to be ripe, and then they are as sweet as sugar.

BOYSENBERRY: When these are ready, they are absolutely loaded with juice. With a little sugar and a little cream, it just bleeds and bleeds the sweetest juice you've ever tasted. This has to be God's gift to berry lovers, and I am personally delighted they're making a comeback.

HUCKLEBERRY: People confuse it with the blueberry, but it's entirely different. It is a smaller berry and has ten large seeds. Blueberries are larger and have two or three times as many seeds, and that is a big difference when you eat them. The Huckleberry remains a wild berry and, unfortunately, these are scarce on the west coast.

LOGANBERRY: The people, at least the old-timers, really go for the loganberry, particularly for the wonderful jam and jelly. The minute the loganberry shows up, there is a good demand for it.

RASPBERRY: The production of the raspberry has gone down in the past few years. This is unfortunate because it has to be the easiest berry for the lady of the house to prepare because it is the only one without a stem or cap. They stay on the bush, so you just rinse them and serve.

OLLALIE BERRY: A member of the blackberry family, it is an improved type, about an inch and a half long and must be black to

126

be ripe. If there is red on it, it will be sour. It must be dead-black in color. The ollalie has tried to replace the boysenberry, but it hasn't succeeded. I'm pleased because the boysenberry is definitely making a comeback.

SAUCE FOR A SUMMERTIME SUNDAE

1/2 cup raspberry jelly
1 & 1/2 Tbsp. cornstarch
1/8 tsp. salt
1 cup orange juice
Red food color

2 Tbsp. orange-flavored
  liqueur
1 cup fresh nectarines, slices
1/2 cup raspberries
1/2 cup blueberries
vanilla ice cream

Melt jelly in pan over low heat; blend in cornstarch mixed with salt and juice. Cook and stir until mixture boils; boil gently for 3 minutes until clear. Stir in a few drops food color and liqueur. Add fruit; chill. Serve over ice cream. *Makes about 3 cups.*

PARADISE FRUIT SALAD

1 fresh pineapple
1 cup fresh raspberries
  or strawberries

1 cup blueberries
1 cup melon balls
Ginger Lime Dressing, below

Cut pineapple in half through crown. Remove core and chunk fruit. Toss lightly with raspberries, blueberries, and melon balls. Spoon into pineapple shells. Drizzle with Ginger Lime Dressing, recipe below. *Makes 4 to 6 servings.*

GINGER LIME DRESSING

1/4 cup honey
1/4 cup golden rum or orange
  juice
2 Tbsp. lime juice

1 Tbsp. chopped crystallized
  ginger
1 tsp. grated lime peel

Combine all ingredients well.

BLUEBERRIES

Blueberries dark color shows their powerful antioxidant strength.

There are few things tastier than ripe, delicious blueberries! People go absolutely wild over them. They have a very short season, so be sure to enjoy them as soon as they start arriving at in-season prices. Blueberries are now the second largest selling berry, right after strawberries. Look for those that are plump and full with a light, powdery, grayish blue bloom on them.

They are great by themselves, or with a little bit of milk, and of course, to bake in muffins, dumplings, and pies.

BLUEBERRY MUFFINS

2 cups sifted-all purpose flour	*1 egg beaten*
3 tsp. baking powder	*3/4 cup milk*
1/3 cup sugar	*1/4 cup shortening, melted*
3/4 tsp. salt	*1 cup blueberries*

Mix and sift the dry ingredients. Add the egg, milk, and melted shortening mixed together. Stir only enough to mix; add the blueberries. Fill greased muffin tins or greased gem pans two-thirds full. Bake at 425°F for 20 to 25 minutes.

BLUEBOTTOM ICE CREAM PIE-NO BAKE!

4 cups fresh blueberries	*1 graham cracker crust*
1 cup sugar	*1 qt. vanilla ice cream*
2 cups water	*2 Tbsp. orange juice*
1/4 cup cornstarch	

Combine blueberries and sugar. Mix water and cornstarch and stir into blueberries. Cook at a simmer until sauce is thickened. Reserve 1/2 cup of the mixture for decorating top. Cool. Spoon blueberry filling over crust. Spoon ice cream over blueberry filling. Beat orange juice into reserve blueberry filling. Drizzle over ice cream. Freeze. Remove pie 30 minutes before serving to thaw enough to cut. Cut into wedges to serve. *Makes one 9-inch pie.*

BLUEBERRY BUCKLE

1/2 cup shortening
1/2 cup sugar
1 egg, beaten
2 cups sifted all-purpose flour

1 tsp. salt
2 & 1/2 tsp. baking powder
1/2 cup milk

Cream the shortening and sugar. Add the beaten egg and mix well. Mix and sift the flour, salt, and baking powder together and add to the creamed mixture alternately with the milk. Spread this dough in a greased 8-inch square pan. Spread over the top of the dough 2 & 1/2 cups fresh blueberries. Mix and sift together 1/2 cup sugar, 1/2 cup flour, 3/4 teaspoon cinnamon; cut into this 1/3 cup butter or oleo. Spread this mixture over the top of the blueberries. Bake for 1 to 1 and 1/4 hours at 375°F. Serve warm as coffee cake or as a dessert. This may be rewarmed by placing in a paper bag and sprinkling the bag with water; place in a warm oven until the buckle is thoroughly heated.

BLUEBERRY DUMPLINGS

2 cups of sifted all-purpose
* flour*
1/2 tsp. salt
2 & 1/2 tsp. baking powder

1 & 1/2 Tbsp. sugar
1/2 cup shortening
1/2 cup milk

Mix and sift the flour, salt, baking powder, and sugar together. Cut in the shortening as for biscuits. Add the milk to make a biscuit dough -about 1/2 cup. Roll the dough to about 1/2 inch in thickness and fir into a greased 9 x 9-inch pan. Put 2 cups fresh blueberries on the dough. Do not add sugar at this time. Fold the dough like an envelope-bring each corner up toward the center-leaving a space in the center about 4 inches across. Bake at 425°F (hot oven) for about 25 minutes, until the dough is beginning to brown. Remove from the oven. Mix 3/4 cup sugar, 1/2 teaspoon cinnamon, and 1/2 cup melted butter together. Poke this mixture well inside the dumpling to mix with the blueberries. Return the dumpling to the oven from which the heat has been turned off, and leave for 15 minutes longer. Serve with whipped cream.

BLUEBERRY PIE

4 cups blueberries
1 cup sugar
2 Tbsp. flour
1/4 tsp. cinnamon

1/8 tsp. nutmeg
1/4 tsp. salt
2 Tbsp. butter

Line a pie tin with pastry. Wash the blueberries. Put the berries into the pastry lined tin. Mix the sugar, flour, spices, and salt and scatter over the berries. Dot the pie with the butter; add the top crust. Bake for 10 minutes at 425°F or until done.

CHERRIES

*Cherries are sweet and nutritious and are known to
have the ability to eliminate uric acid from the body. Because of
this, cherries are known to help those with arthritis and gout.*

Cherries talk to you by their color. They should be shiny and
almost black in color, which tells you they are ripe and just as
sweet as they can possibly be. Another way to tell for sure when
cherries are ripe is to watch for the birds. They won't touch it until
it's ready; but when it is, they'll strip a tree in no time. They will
be ripe in California in June, but we are going with July since that
is the month cherries come in season for the rest of the country.

RAINBOW SALAD

1 fresh pineapple
2 large peaches (2 cups sliced)
2 cups fresh cherries, pitted
1/2 cup orange juice

1/2 cup honey
1/4 cup lime juice
1 tsp. grated lime peel

Cut pineapple in half lengthwise. Remove fruit; core and cut into
bite-size pieces. In a 2 and 1/2-quart glass container or bowl, layer
half the pineapple, all the peaches and cherries and remaining
pineapple. Blend together orange juice, honey, and lime juice. Pour
over fruit. Top with lime peel. *Makes 6 to 8 servings.*

CHERRY PIE

3 cups pitted sour cherries
1 to 1 & 1/2 cups sugar
2 Tbsp. butter or margarine

1/4 cup enriched flour
dash salt
9-inch unbaked pastry shell

Combine cherries, sugar, flour, and salt. Fill pastry shell and dot
with butter or margarine. Make lattice top crust. Bake in hot oven
400°F for 45 minutes to 1 hour.

CHERRIES JUBILEE

1 lb. large black cherries
1/4 cup honey
1/4 cup claret or burgundy

1/4 cup marasquin or kirsch
3 Tbsp. dark rum
vanilla ice cream

Stem and pit the cherries. Put them in the chafing dish to marinate, for an hour before flaming, with the honey, wine, and one of the liqueurs. Have the ice cream on the plates when ready to serve. Heat the cherries. Add the rum, blaze, and spoon over the ice cream. *Serves 6 to 8.*

MELONS

Melons are a good source of pure water with many nutrients.
Most melons also have the ability to act
as an excellent diuretic.

Summertime is cantaloupe and watermelon time, and what could be a better dessert for picnics and barbecues? The kids love it, and melon is the easiest thing in the world to serve. Give them a treat and serve melon for breakfast. A little later, toward the end of summer and early fall, you will find a good supply of the varietal melons. There's a wide variety from which to choose.

ALFRESCO PEACHES IN MELON BOWL

1 watermelon
2 cups cantaloupe balls
1 cup honeydew melon balls

4 fresh peaches, peeled and
*   sliced*
Lime-Rum Marinade
Cream Fruit Dressing

Cut a thin horizontal slice off of watermelon to form base. On other side cut a thick horizontal slice; set aside. Form shell by scooping out watermelon with small ice cream scoop. Place watermelon balls, cantaloupe, honeydew balls and peaches in large bowl; mix lightly. Fill shell with fruits; pour marinade over. Replace lid and chill for 2 hours. Serve with Cream Fruit Dressing. *Serves 8.*

LIME-RUM MARINADE

2/3 cup sugar
1/2 cup water

1/3 cup fresh lime juice
1/2 cup light rum

In a saucepan, combine sugar and water; bring to boil. Reduce heat; simmer for 5 minutes. Remove from heat; add lime juice and rum. Cool before pouring over fruit. *Makes 1 and 1/4 cups.*

CREAM FRUIT DRESSING

1/2 cup mayonnaise
1/4 cup light corn syrup
1 Tbsp. orange rind
1 Tbsp. orange juice

1/4 tsp. nutmeg
1/2 cup whipping cream,
    whipped

Blend mayonnaise and corn syrup until smooth. Add rind, juice, and nutmeg; mix well. Fold in whipped cream. *Makes 1 and 1/4 cups.*

MELON RING BUFFET SALAD

1 honeydew, casaba or other
    melon
12 fresh plums, sliced
Coconut Cream Dressing

6 fresh peaches, peeled and
    sliced
walnut-coated cream cheese
    balls (optional)

Cut melon into 6 rings. Peel and scoop out each ring; place on 8 individual salad plates. Arrange plums and peaches in centers of melon. Garnish with cheese balls. Serve with Coconut Cream Dressing, recipe below. *Makes 6 servings.*

COCONUT CREAM DRESSING

1 cup dairy sour cream
1/2 cup flaked coconut

1/4 tsp. mace

Combine all ingredients; chill. *Makes 1 and 1/2 cups.*

HONEYDEW PLATTER

3 fresh nectarines
1/2 cup light corn syrup
1 Tbsp. coarsely grated fresh
    lime or lemon rind

1/4 cup lime or lemon juice
1 tsp. snipped fresh mint
1 honeydew melon
    (about 5 lbs.)

Finely chop enough nectarines to make 1 cup; mix with corn syrup, lime rind and juice, and mint. Chill along with remaining nectarines and melon. At serving time, cut 24 thick nectarine slices. Halve melon lengthwise; remove seeds. Cut each half into 4 wedges. Make 3 crosswise cuts, about 1 inch apart, in each wedge. Lightly press a nectarine slice into each cut. Arrange melon wedges petal-fashion on large round platter. Serve with sauce. *Makes 8 servings.*

SUMMER FRUIT SALAD
Contributed by Elaine Murphy

*Cantaloupe, peeled and either
  balled or cubed
Raspberries
Granny Smith apple or pippin
  (any tart apple) cored & cubed
Watermelon, balled or cubed,
  seedless if possible
Strawberries, hulled and
  quartered*

*Blueberries
Bananas, peeled and sliced
  into medallions
Mandarin orange segments,
  drained
Honeydew melon, peeled and
  either balled or cubed
Seedless grapes, green or red
Pineapple, cored, peeled &
  cubed, save juice if possible*

Use any or all of these ingredients. Dress with honey, fresh lemon or lime juice, a little bit of salt. If you don't have honey, a little sugar will do, but dissolve it in the lemon or lime juice before adding to fruit. Toss fruit in dressing and refrigerate for at least 1/2 hour (two hours would be better).

A variation on this is to use a small amount of balsamic vinegar mixed with water in place of the citrus juice; but be careful with this, since it can turn the salad dark and too tangy if too much is used. You can also add nuts to this – chopped walnuts, pecans, toasted almonds, pine nuts, toasted pumpkin seeds, etc. But, I recommend you sprinkle them on at the last minute, since they will get soggy if you mix them in the salad and leave them for any length of time.

PLUMS

The difference between plums and prunes has to do with sugar content. The very high sugar of prunes enables the fruit to dry without decay. Both are full of many vitamins and minerals, especially vitamins A and C, potassium, iron, and the wonderful soluble fiber, pectin.

The end of July and early August is peak season for fresh plums. There are many different varieties, but if they are fresh and ripe, they are all good now. We have a large group of wonderful recipes to share with you.

PLUM SAUCE

1 lb. fresh plums
3/4 cup sugar
2 Tbsp. cornstarch
1/4 tsp. cloves

1/4 tsp. cinnamon
1/4 tsp. allspice
1 & 1/2 cups water

Cut plums in half; remove pits and slice. Combine sugar, cornstarch, and spices. Gradually stir in water. Cook over medium heat until mixture begins to thicken. Add sliced plums, cover and simmer for 10 minutes. Serve with pancakes or waffles. *Makes 2 cups sauce.*

CHINESE PLUM SAUCE

1 medium onion, cut in wedges
1 Tbsp. vegetable oil
2 Tbsp. cornstarch
3/4 cup vinegar

3/4 cup sugar
2 lbs. fresh plums, quartered
1/2 tsp. salt
1/4 tsp. almond extract

In a saucepan, cook onion in oil until soft. Mix cornstarch with vinegar and sugar; add to onion. Cook, stirring until thickened. Add plums, salt and extract; continue cooking until fruit is tender. Spoon some sauce over partially-cooked spareribs. Grill, brushing frequently with sauce. Heat remaining sauce to serve with barbecued spareribs. *Makes about 2 and 1/2 cups.*

STUFFED PLUM SALAD WITH MOCK DEVONSHIRE CREAM

8 fresh plums, halved
crisp salad greens, chilled
1 pkg. (8 oz.) cream cheese,
  softened
1 cup dairy sour cream

2 Tbsp. sugar
2 tsp. grated lemon rind
1 tsp. vanilla extract
1/3 cup finely chopped
  crystallized ginger

Place plum halves cut-side up on bed of greens. Beat cream cheese until fluffy. Gradually beat in sour cream just until blended. Mix in sugar, lemon rind, and vanilla extract. Spoon mixture on plum halves and sprinkle with ginger. Chill until ready to serve. *Makes 8 servings.*

CHICKEN WITH PLUMS

3/4 cup butter
2 onions, finely chopped
1 cup chopped celery
6 slices stale bread, crumbled
8 fresh plums, diced
1 egg, lightly beaten

1 cup chicken broth
1 roasting chicken, about
  6 lbs.
salt and pepper
1 Tbsp. cornstarch
1/3 cup sugar
1 cup water

Preheat oven to 350°F. In a skillet, melt 1/2 cup butter; sauté onions and celery until golden. Add bread and half of plume; stir mixture together. Cool. Beat egg and broth together; pour over bread mixture. Toss to blend. Sprinkle chicken with salt and pepper. Stuff chicken; close opening with skewers. Rub with 2 tablespoons butter. Roast on rack for 2 hours or until leg moves easily. Mix cornstarch and sugar together; stir in water. Add remaining plums; cook, stirring constantly, until glaze bubbles and thickens. Simmer for 5 more minutes. Add remaining 2 tablespoons butter; stir until melted. Place chicken on platter. Spoon glaze over hot chicken. *Makes 6 servings.*

PLUM GOOD HAM

1 canned ham (5 lbs.)
1 tsp. dry mustard
1/2 tsp. cloves
2 Tbsp. cornstarch

1/3 cup lemon juice
1/2 cup water
1/3 cup sugar
8 fresh plums, diced

Preheat oven to 350°F. Cut ham in half, lengthwise; rub with mustard and cloves. Place half in baking pan. Mix cornstarch, lemon, water, and sugar. Cook, stirring until thickened. Add plums; simmer until tender. Spoon half of sauce on ham. Top with other half ham and rest of sauce. Bake for 1 hour. *Makes 12 to 15 servings.*

PLUM KUCHEN

2 cups flour
3 tsp. baking powder
1/2 tsp. salt
3/4 cup, plus 2 Tbsp. sugar
1 tsp. cinnamon

8 Tbsp. butter
1 egg
2/3 cup milk
4 cups fresh plums

Combine unsifted flour, baking powder, salt, and 2 tablespoons sugar, mix until well blended. Cut in 6 tablespoons butter until the mixture resembles coarse crumbs. Combine egg with milk and stir into the flour mixture until blended. Spread in a greased baking pan (about 8x12x2 inches).

Arrange plums, cut in eights, in rows, overlapping slightly; press into the dough. Spread 2 tablespoons melted or soft butter evenly over the plums. Sprinkle the top with 3/4 cup sugar, mixed with cinnamon. Bake in a hot oven at 400°F for about 30 minutes.

PLUM PIE

4 cups coarsely chopped ripe
  plums
1 cup sugar
1 Tbsp. firmly packed brown
  sugar
1/4 tsp. salt

pinch cinnamon
pastry for a 2-crust, 8-inch
  pie
3 & 1/2 Tbsp. quick-cooking
  tapioca
2 tsp. butter

In large mixing bowl, combine plums, sugar, tapioca, salt and cinnamon; mix well. Pour into unbaked pastry shell, sprinkle with brown sugar and dot with butter. Add top crust, crimp edges and pierce top with a fork. Bake in 400°F oven for 1 hour, or until crust is lightly browned.

FRESH PLUM SUNDAE

2 lbs. fresh plums
1 stick cinnamon
1/2 cup water
1 cup sugar
1 Tbsp. cornstarch

1/4 tsp. salt
1 Tbsp. butter or margarine
1 qt. vanilla ice cream or
  lemon sherbet

Cut plums into eighths; reserve 1 cup. Cook remaining plums, cinnamon stick, and water in covered saucepan over low heat for about 10 minutes. Mix sugar, cornstarch, and salt. Add to plums. Return to heat; cook, stirring until clear and thick, about 5 minutes. Remove cinnamon; stir in butter and rest of plums. Serve hot or cold over ice cream or sherbet. *Makes 8 servings.*

BELL PEPPERS

Green bell peppers are a good source of many
vitamins, including a high vitamin C content.
The red bell peppers are even more nutritious.
Red, orange, and yellow bells, as shown by their color,
possess a strong presence of vitamin A.
(Bell peppers are also members of the nightshade
family and may aggravate those with arthritis.)

This is one of my favorite subjects because I love bell peppers. The bell pepper is a tremendous source of vitamin C, and at the same time, is very, very low in calories. There are only 25 calories in 4 ounces of bell pepper.

A lot of people don't realize that the green bell pepper and the red bell pepper are one and the same. A red bell pepper is nothing more than a green bell pepper which has ripened. The fact that it is ripe means that it contains even more vitamin C and vitamin A.

My mother stuffed bell peppers when we were kids. A stuffed bell pepper is a one-dish meal, and you couldn't get stuffed with more nutrition. My mother really knew what she was doing, too.

Here is a recipe for red bell peppers that has been sent out individually to thousands of people who heard me talk about it on television and radio shows. If you haven't tried bell peppers, now is the time to do it.

JOE'S RED BELL PEPPER RECIPE

Put as many whole red bell peppers as you wish on a cookie sheet. Bake in a low 300°F oven for about an hour or until they blister and flatten out. Turn off the oven and cover the peppers with a dish towel and cover that with some heavy paper until cool. When cool, peel skin from the peppers and slice them into the size you desire. Put into glass containers to store.

To serve: Place in a baking dish and add olive oil, as desired. Add salt and pepper, and that's it! You may wish to add some garlic, or rosemary. Serve with meat dishes at a garnish-delicious!

JOE'S STUFFED BELL PEPPERS

4 fresh bell peppers
3 cups bread crumbs
1 cup Romano or Parmesan
  cheese, grated
6 Tbsp. chopped parsley

2 large tomatoes, cut into
  small pieces
2/3 cup olive oil
2 cloves garlic, minced

Cut the top off the bell peppers and save them to use as lids when cooking. Remove the seeds and center from the pepper. Combine all remaining ingredients, stuff peppers and replace top. Grease bottoms of peppers to prevent sticking and arrange in pan. Bake at 350°F for about 45 minutes.

NEW

VEGETABLE STUFFED PEPPERS
Contributed by Beatrice Johnson

2 bell peppers, any color
1 cup brown rice, cooked
1/2 cup walnuts, finely chopped
1 small yellow onion
1 teaspoon oregano or cilantro

1 cup corn, cut from the cob
4 carrots, shredded
2 tablespoons olive oil
1 clove garlic
A pinch of salt

Heat the olive in a skillet. Add the onion and garlic and sauté until brown. Add the corn, walnuts, oregano, and carrots and cook until thoroughly heated. Add the brown rice and mix. Remove from heat. Cut tops from peppers and scoop insides out. Add mixture to the bell peppers and bake in oven at 350 degrees for 30 minutes. Remove from oven, let cool and enjoy.

PEPPERS WITH CHEESE

6 large green peppers
1 & 1/4 lbs. sheep's cheese
2 eggs
vegetable oil

3 Tbsp. cottage cheese
3 Tbsp. sour cream
salt to taste

Remove stems, membrane, and seeds from peppers. Crumble cheese with fork, add eggs, and mix well. Stuff the peppers with this mixture. Oil a baking dish, put peppers upright in it, and top each pepper with cheese mixture. Bake in 475°F oven for about 15 minutes. Serve hot. *Serves 3 to 4.*

SPANISH SAUCE

1 & 1/2 cups peeled, sliced onions
4 Tbsp. fat
2 & 1/2 cups cooked tomatoes
1/2 cup diced green pepper
4 & 1/2 Tbsp. water

1 bay leaf
2 whole cloves
2 tsp. sugar
3 Tbsp. flour

Cook onions slowly in hot fat until tender. Add tomatoes, green pepper, bay leaf, cloves and sugar. Simmer for 15 minutes. Remove bay leaf and cloves, or strain if desired. Mix flour and water to a smooth paste. Stir into tomato mixture. Boil for 5 minutes. Makes 1 and 2/3 cups sauce. Serve on spaghetti, macaroni, croquettes, meat, or fish.

MUSHROOMS AND PEPPERS ITALIAN

1 lb. fresh mushrooms
2 large green peppers
1 medium onion, sliced
1/4 cup olive oil
2 large tomatoes, peeled and
  sliced

3/4 tsp. salt
1/8 tsp. ground black pepper
1/8 tsp. oregano leaves
1/8 tsp. basil leaves
1/16 tsp. garlic powder

Rinse, pat dry, and slice mushrooms (about 5 cups). Slice green peppers into 1/2-inch strips. In a large skillet, heat oil. Add mushrooms, peppers, and onion; sauté until mushrooms are golden. Add tomatoes and seasonings; stir gently. Cover and simmer for 20 minutes, stirring occasionally. Serve with meat or eggs. *Serves 6 to 8.*

GREEK STYLE SHISH KEBOB

1 & 1/2 lbs. boneless lamb cut
  in 1 & 1/2 inch cubes
12 bay leaves
12 slices lemon peel, 3 inches
  long

2 medium onions
2 green peppers
2 large tomatoes
olive oil
salt and pepper

Alternate lamb, bay leaves, and lemon peel on skewers. Cut each onion and green pepper and put on skewers. Arrange tomatoes on separate skewers. Brush all with oil. Broil or grill lamb, onion and green pepper kebabs 3 to 5 inches from heat for 8 to 10 minutes, on each side, or until lamb is at desired doneness, and onion and pepper are tender. Broil or grill tomatoes for about 3 minutes on each side. Baste lamb and vegetables frequently with oil. Season with salt and pepper to taste before serving. *Serves 6.*

MEAL-IN-A-PEPPER

1/2 lb. fresh mushrooms
6 medium green peppers
1/2 lb. ground lean beef
1/2 cup chopped onion
1 small tomato, diced

1 tsp. chili powder
3/4 tsp. salt
1/8 tsp. ground black pepper
1 can (10 1/2 oz.) condensed
  beef broth

Rinse, pat dry, and slice fresh mushrooms (makes about 2 and 1/2 cups) set aside. Cut a thin slice from stem ends of green peppers; remove stems, seeds, and membranes. Chop stems end of peppers (makes about 3/4 cup); set aside.

Drop green peppers shells onto boiling salted water. Cook for 5 minutes; drain. Place pepper shells upright in a 10 x 6 x 2 inch baking dish; set aside.

In a medium skillet, sauté ground beef until brown. Remove beef to mixing bowl. Add to skillet reserved mushrooms and chopped green pepper and the onion; sauté for 5 minutes, stirring. Add vegetables to ground beef along with tomato, chili powder, salt and black pepper; mix gently. Spoon mixture into green pepper shells. Pour beef broth into baking dish. Cover dish with foil. Bake in a preheated moderate oven (350°F) for 30 minutes.

STUFFED GREEN PEPPERS TURKISH STYLE
Contributed by Simla Somturk Wickless

This is one of my personal favorites; one of the dishes I beg my mom to make each time I go home to Turkey or they come visit us in SF. NOTE: The use of nightshade plants in this recipe can be avoided by omitting tomatoes from the stuffing and stuffing zucchinis rather than eggplants, tomatoes, or peppers.

Stuffed Green Peppers - Turkish Style

4 small green peppers
1 lb. leanest organic ground
  beef (ideally grass-fed)
1/2 cup chopped fresh mint,
  separated from stems
1/2 cup uncooked white rice
1 medium-large yellow
  onion, grated
1/3 cup extra virgin olive oil
1 flat tsp. sea salt

1 cup chopped fresh parsley,
  separated from stems
1/2 cup chopped fresh dill,
  separated from stems
3 medium, ripe tomatoes,
  peeled and grated
the juice from 1 lemon,
  fresh squeezed
4 cups filtered water or broth
1/2 tsp. ground black pepper,
  which is not really a pepper

Wash green peppers and cut tops off carefully (they will be placed back on). Carefully remove the seeds and spiny bits from inside the green peppers without damaging the structure of the pepper. Place green peppers, olive oil, and water/broth aside. Mix all the other ingredients well. Stuff the green peppers equally. Put their "hats" back on. Place stuffed peppers upright in a pot big/small enough to prop them all up. Pour the olive oil over the stuffed peppers. Cover with water or broth. Bring to a boil on high heat; then reduce to medium heat. Cook until done, about 40 to 45 minutes, when the rice is visibly cooked through. *Makes enough for 4 servings.*

Variations:

- Stuff small eggplants, medium tomatoes, or small zucchinis using the same recipe. These veggies need to be big enough to be able to carve out the insides in order to stuff them, but small enough to have a reasonable serving size (about 1 cup of food per stuffed veggie, or less).
- Use ground chicken or turkey instead of beef. Will be a bit Americanized, but hey - all in the name of health, right?
- Sprinkle hot red pepper flakes in the stuffing, to taste.
- Get creative with which veggies you stuff, and let me know!

BEETS

Beets are very nutritious, but the beet leaves are even more nutritious with higher calcium, iron, vitamin A, and vitamin C. Cook or steam the same as chard.

Right now, there should be a good supply of fresh beets, and they are tender and tasty. A beet is a root vegetable and may have some ridges, but it should be pretty smooth. Also, the leaves should be green and small. You know, you can take the leaves and cook and serve them just as you would spinach, and they're delicious. You may find you like them even better because the leaves of the beets have a nice soft feel in your mouth.

Of course, you can use the young leaves in salad, too, and the beet root when cooked and chilled makes a delicious addition to salad and adds color, also.

BEET TOPS

Wash leaves and stems thoroughly in cold water. Drain. Cut into inch pieces. Cook without additional water in a well-covered pot for 5 minutes. Add 1/8 teaspoon salt to each cupful, 1 tablespoon butter, oil, 2 tablespoons dry bread or cracker crumbs. Toss lightly. Serve hot.

Variation: Add 1 tablespoon brown sugar and 2 tablespoons mild vinegar to above. Cook 2 minutes over moderate heat. Garnish with diced hard-cooked egg.

ROASTED
BEET SALAD
Contributed by Beatrice Johnson

4 cups mesculin greens
1/4 cucumber, sliced
2 tablespoons olive oil
2 tablespoons balsamic vinegar

3 medium beets, greens
removed
2 tablespoons pine nuts
1/2 teaspoon salt

Preheat oven to 400 degrees F. Using a potato peeler, peel off the skins of the beets and discard. Cut each beet in half, and then into 4 wedges (eight wedges total per beet). Pour olive oil and salt into a large Ziplock bag. Add all beet wedges, seal Ziplock, and massage seasonings into beets until well coated. Wrap beets in heavy-duty foil, making sure it's sealed on all sides and place in a baking pan. Bake at 400 degrees F for 90 minutes, turning foil package over during midway point.

In a large bowl, combine beets, salad greens, sliced cucumbers, and pine nuts and toss. Sprinkle with balsamic vinegar.

CREAMED MASHED BEETS

3 cups cooked, mashed beets
1 Tbsp. lemon juice
1/2 cup heavy cream or
sour cream

2 tsp. salt
1/2 cup crumbs
1 Tbsp. butter

Drain cooked beets, put through ricer and add lemon juice and salt, fold in sour cream or stiffly beaten heavy cream. Top with crumbs and dot with butter. Slip under broiler flame to brown lightly and serve hot. *Serves 4.*

BEETS WITH ONIONS AND HERBS

12 medium-sized cooked beets	1 tsp. dried tarragon
6 Tbsp. butter	1 & 1/2 Tbsp. sugar
1/2 cup finely chopped green onions	1/4 cup vinegar
	salt and pepper to taste
1/4 cup chopped parsley	

Add all ingredients to beets and heat thoroughly. *Serves 12.*

ORANGE BEETS

In a sauce pan, mix:

1/2 tsp. salt	1/2 cup sugar
1/2 cup white vinegar	2 Tbsp. water
1 Tbsp. cornstarch	

Bring to a boil and stir until clear.

Stir in:

grated rind and juice of one large orange	3 & 1/2 cups small beets, cooked and drained

Heat gently. Stir in 3 Tbsp. butter just before serving. *Serves 6.*

HARVARD BEETS

8 medium beets	1/2 cup sugar
2 Tbsp. margarine	1/3 cup lemon juice
1 Tbsp. flour	salt and pepper to taste

Boil the beets in their skins until they can be pierced with a fork (30 to 60 minutes). Remove the skins and slice with a lattice or other fancy cutter. Melt the margarine and bring to bubbling. Add the flour. Add the sugar mixed with the lemon juice and cook until thick and transparent, stirring constantly. Add the beets, season to taste, and heat through. You can use a little water to dilute the lemon juice if you prefer it less piquant. *Serves 6 to 8.*

GINGER BEETS

1 Tbsp. flour
1 Tbsp. shortening
1/2 cup beet liquid
2 cups cooked beets, cut in
  strips
1/4 tsp. dry mustard (optional)

1 Tbsp. lemon juice or
  vinegar
2 Tbsp. brown sugar
1/4 tsp. salt
1 tsp. ground ginger

Blend flour and shortening and brown lightly. Add beet liquid and stir till smooth. Add the other ingredients. Cook for 3 to 5 minutes. *Serves 5 or 6.*

CARROTS

Carrots are the richest source of pro-vitamin A carotenes and full of many nutrients, as well.

The crisp and crunchy carrot is a true goodie from the ground. Carrots are generally available throughout the United States all year, but are in season in late summer. It is important that carrots be harvested while they are young and tender to enjoy their best flavor. From the outside appearance, it is difficult to tell if a carrot is young and tender, but you will notice a difference in the flavor.

You have to depend on the grower. If you happen to buy woody carrots, take them back to the produce department and tell the manager. In all probability, he is not aware of the condition, either, and the sooner he finds out, the better for everybody.

CARROT RAISIN NUT SALAD

4 large or 8 small carrots	*3/4 tsp. salt*
1/2 cup seedless raisins	*1 cup sour cream*
1/2 cup chopped pecans or	*2 tsp. grated lemon peel*
* peanuts*	*1 Tbsp. lemon juice*

Wash the carrots and place them on ice for an hour. Grate coarsely into a bowl. Add all the other ingredients, except the sour cream and mix together lightly. Place salad in a bowl and pour the sour cream over it. Toss salad lightly, if you desire.

CARROTS A LA NAPOLI

1 tsp. salt	*16 medium (2 lbs.) fresh*
1/2 tsp. sugar	* carrots*
1/4 cup olive or salad oil	*1/8 tsp. ground black pepper*
2 Tbsp. wine vinegar	*1/8 tsp. oregano leaves*
(Continued on next page)	

150

Wash all the carrots. Cut into slices 1/2-inch thick. Place in saucepan with boiling water and 1/2 teaspoon of salt. Cover and cook for 10 minutes or until tender. Drain well. Place in a bowl remaining ingredients. Marinate for 12 hours or overnight before serving. Serve hot or cold. *Yield: 5 cups.*

FRESH CARROTS AND PEAS-GERMAN STYLE

16 medium (2 lbs) fresh carrots   *1/2 tsp. salt*
2 Tbsp. butter or margarine   *2 Tbsp. flour*
2 Tbsp. hot water   *1 cup chicken stock*
1 tsp. sugar   *1/16 tsp. ground black*
1 cup shelled, fresh green peas   *pepper*
1 tsp. chopped fresh parsley

Wash carrots and cut them into julienne strips. Place in saucepan with butter, water, sugar, and 1/4 tsp. salt. Cover and cook slowly for 10 to 15 minutes or until carrots are crisp-tender. (Do not boil) Add peas 5 minutes before cooking time is up. Mix flour with 1/4 cup of the chicken stock to form a smooth paste in a small saucepan. Blend in remaining stock and salt. Stir and cook until of medium thickness, 3 minutes. Add carrot mixture, black pepper, and parsley. Serve hot. *Serves 6 to 8.*

TANGY CARROT CASSEROLE

1 lb. carrots   *1/4 cup flour*
1/2 tsp. sweet basil   *1 tsp. salt*
1/4 cup butter or margarine   *1/2 tsp. prepared mustard*
1 medium onion, minced   *2 cups milk*
1/4 lb. Cheddar cheese   *dash of pepper*
1 slice toast

Slice carrots diagonally; add basil and cook in salted water until tender. Drain. Sauté the onion in butter or margarine. Mix flour, salt, mustard, pepper, and milk and add to onion and cook, stirring over medium heat until thick. Grate the cheese. Place a layer of carrots in the casserole and cover with cheese. Alternate layers of carrots and cheese. Pour sauce over top. A slice of buttered toast, cut into cubes can be sprinkled over the top. Then bake in a 350°F oven for 15 minutes.

TART HERBED CARROTS

1 lb. carrots
1 cup broth (use 1 chicken
or vegetable bouillon cube
dissolved in 1 cup boiling
water)
2 Tbsp. cooking or salad oil
1/4 cup finely chopped onion
1 Tbsp. flour
1/2 tsp. salt

1/4 tsp. white pepper
1 tsp. parsley flakes
1/8 tsp. crushed savory
1/8 tsp. rosemary
1/8 tsp. crushed thyme
1/8 tsp. crushed marjoram
2 Tbsp. honey
2 Tbsp. cider vinegar or
lemon juice

Wash all the carrots; halve the larger carrots lengthwise. Put into a saucepan with the hot broth. Cover and bring to boiling. Reduce heat and cook until carrots are crisp-tender. Drain, reserving cooking liquid. Set carrots aside and keep warm.

Cook the onion in heated oil in a skillet for about 5 minutes. Stir in a blend of the flour, salt, pepper, and herbs, cook until bubbly. Gradually add the cooking liquid, stirring constantly and bring to boiling; cook for 1 to 2 minutes. Mix in the honey and vinegar. Add the drained carrots and heat thoroughly, spooning sauce over the carrots occasionally.

Turn into a heated serving dish. Sprinkle with chopped parsley and, if desired, sprinkle with crumbled bacon. *Yield: 5 to 6 servings.*

ROAST-CHICKEN AND CARROTS

1 roasting chicken (about
  5 lbs.)
salt and pepper
2 Tbsp. each butter and water
8 medium-sized carrots, sliced
1 tsp. grated lemon peel

6 green onions, white parts
  only, sliced
3/4 tsp. whole thyme,
  crumbled
3 slices bacon
2 Tbsp. lemon juice

Season chicken lightly inside cavities with salt and pepper. In a pan, heat butter and water. Add carrots, onions, 1/2 teaspoon of the thyme, and lemon peel; cover and cook until carrots are just tender, 5 to 7 minutes.

Spoon vegetables into body cavity of chicken; close opening. Place chicken on a rack in a shallow pan with breast up. Roast in a 325°F oven for 30 minutes, arrange bacon over breast and legs, and sprinkle with remaining 1/4 teaspoon thyme. Continue roasting for 1 to 1 and 1/2 hours, or until the breast meat is fork tender. Drizzle with lemon juice just before removing from oven. Serve chicken surrounded with carrot stuffing; sprinkle with bacon. The vegetable stuffing helps flavor the chicken as it roasts and vice versa. *Serves 4 to 6.*

CARROT PIE

3/4 cup sugar
2 Tbsp. honey
1/2 tsp. salt
1 tsp. cinnamon
1 tsp. pumpkin pie spice

1/2 tsp. nutmeg
2 eggs, lightly beaten
2 cups cooked, sieved carrots
1 cup evaporated milk
1 unbaked 9-inch pie shell

Combine sugar, salt spices; add remaining ingredients, mixing well. Pour into pastry-lined pie plate. Bake in preheated oven at 400°F for about 45 minutes or until filling is firm. *Yield: 6 servings.*

FRESH CARROT BREAD

2/3 cup butter or margarine
1 cup sugar
2 eggs
1 & 1/2 cups sifted all-purpose
2 tsp. double-acting baking
　powder

1 tsp. ground cinnamon
1/2 tsp. salt
1 cup finely grated carrots
1 cup seedless raisins
1/2 cup chopped nuts

Place butter or margarine in a mixing bowl. Gradually blend in sugar. Beat in eggs. Sift together flour, baking powder, cinnamon, and salt and gradually add to the mixture. Mix carrots, raisins, and nuts and stir into the batter. Turn into a well-greased, lightly floured 9 x 5 x 3 inch loaf pan. Bake in a preheated moderate oven (350°F) for 1 hour. Cool in pan for 10 minutes. Turn out onto wire rack to finish cooling. (Make the bread the day before it is to be served.) Store in a tightly closed box. Delicious with cream cheese, butter, or margarine. *Yield: 1 loaf.*

RAISIN-CARROT CAKE

1/2 cup shortening
1 cup sugar
1/2 tsp. grated orange peel
2 eggs
2 cups sifted water
1 & 1/2 tsp. baking powder
1 & 1/2 tsp. soda

1/4 tsp. nutmeg
1/4 tsp. cloves
1 & 1/2 cups chopped raisins
2 cups finely shredded, raw
　carrots
1/3 cup water
1 tsp. salt

Blend shortening with sugar and orange peel until fluffy. Beat in eggs, one at a time. Add half of flour resifted with baking powder, soda, salt and spices. Mix in raisins, carrots, and water. Blend in remaining flour. Turn into 2 greased and floured 8-inch layer cake pans. Bake in moderate oven (350°F) for about 35 minutes. Let stand for 5 minutes, turn out onto racks to cool. Put layers together and frost. *Makes one 8-inch cake.*

CARROT PANCAKES

1 cup cooked carrots *1/2 cup milk*
2 Tbsp. butter *1 egg*
1 cup flour *1 tsp. baking powder*
1/2 tsp. salt

Mash and heat 1 cup cooked carrots and while hot, stir in 2 tablespoons of butter. Sift together flour with baking powder and salt and make into a batter with milk mixed with well-beaten egg. To this, add the hot carrot pulp, beat until smooth and cook like pancakes in hot frying pan. Serve with crisp bacon.

CELERY

Celery is rich in potassium and sodium. Celery is great for replacing electrolyte loss. It is also known for its calming effect on the nervous system and its ability to lower blood pressure.

There is an easy way to prepare celery. Most people take it stalk by stalk to clean and slice. Try keeping it intact and slice the entire bunch as you slice bread or salami. Cut one-inch lengths or smaller for use in salads and cooking, and always slice some three or four-inch lengths for dips and spread. Drop them all in a colander and rinse with cold water. Celery is an ideal food for dieters, just 17 calories in 3 and 1/2 ounces.

Try your favorite spreads by filling the cavity of celery for a delicious snack. Cream cheese with chives and onion, or chopped nuts, yellow cheese spreads, and peanut butter go well on celery.

CELERY AND SHRIMP SALAD ORIENTAL

3 cups thinly sliced celery
1 lb. cooked, peeled and
   deveined shrimp, diced
1 cup bean sprouts
1/2 cup coarsely chopped
   green pepper
1/4 cup chopped scallions
1/2 cup French dressing
2 Tbsp. toasted sesame seed

In a large bowl, combine celery, shrimp, bean sprouts, green pepper, and scallions. Toss with dressing; chill. Serve sprinkled with sesame seed. *Serves 6.*

CELERY AND MUSHROOM SAUTE

4 Tbsp. butter or margarine,
2 1/2 cups sliced fresh mushrooms
1/2 tsp. onion powder
4 cups thinly sliced celery
1/4 cup water
1/2 tsp. salt
1/16 tsp. ground black
   pepper

In a large skillet, melt 2 tablespoons of the butter. Add mushrooms; sauté until golden. Remove from skillet; set aside.

Melt remaining 2 tablespoons butter. Add celery; sauté for 5 minutes. Stir in water, salt, onion powder, and black pepper. Cover and simmer for 10 minutes or until celery is just crisp-tender. Stir in reserved mushrooms. Garnish with diced pimiento, if desired. *Serves 6.*

CELERY AU GRATIN

1 large stalk celery
1 can (10 1/2 oz.) condensed
chicken broth
1/4 cup butter or margarine

1/4 tsp. ground nutmeg
1/8 tsp. ground black pepper
2 cups soft bread crumbs
1 cup shredded Swiss cheese

Trim stem end of celery. Cut celery stalk crosswise, about 7 inches from base (save tops for soups, stews, etc.) Cut stalk, lengthwise into 6 wedges. Place in a large skillet. Add chicken broth; bring to boiling point. Reduce heat; cover and simmer for 8 minutes or until celery is crisp-tender. Remove celery to a buttered 12 x 8 x 2 inch baking dish; cover to keep warm.

In a medium saucepan, melt butter; remove from heat; stir in nutmeg and black pepper. Add bread crumbs; stir until butter and crumbs are mixed. Blend in cheese. Spoon over celery wedges.

Bake uncovered in a preheated moderate oven (375°F) for 12 minutes or until cheese melts and crumbs brown. *Serves 6.*

CELERY STEAK ROLL-UPS

6 "cube" steaks (about 2 lbs.)
2 & 1/2 tsp. salt, divided
1/4 tsp. ground black pepper
1 & 1/2 dill pickles, cut lengthwise into quarters
6 strips celery, about 4 inches
long
5 Tbsp. flour

1/4 cup salad oil
1 cup minced onions
1 lb. tomatoes, broken up
2 tsp. original Worcestershire
sauce
4 cups sliced celery
2 cups sliced carrots

Sprinkle steak with 1 and 1/2 teaspoons of the salt and the black pepper. Place a dill pickle slice and a celery strip on each steak; roll up and fasten with wooden toothpicks. Dust with flour. In a large skillet or Dutch oven, heat oil. Add beef rolls; brown on all sides. Remove beef rolls; set aside. Add onions; sauté for 1 minute. Blend in tomatoes, Worcestershire sauce, and remaining 1 teaspoon salt. Return beef rolls to skillet. Bring to boiling point; reduce heat; cover and simmer for 1 hour. Add sliced celery and carrots. Return to boiling point; reduce heat; cover and simmer for 30 minutes longer. Serve with boiled parsley potatoes, if desired. *Serves 6.*

CREAMED CELERY ALMONDINE

3 & 1/2 cups thinly sliced celery
1 & 1/2 cups chicken broth,
divided
1/2 tsp. salt
1/3 cup toasted, slivered almonds
4 tsp. flour

1 egg yolk
2 Tbsp. cream
1/16 tsp. ground white
pepper
1 & 1/2 Tbsp. butter or
margarine, softened

Place celery, 1 cup of the chicken broth, and salt in a saucepan. Cover and cook for 5 minutes or until celery is crisp-tender. Combine flour with celery mixture. Mix egg yolk with cream and white pepper; blend into celery mixture. Cook and stir over low heat for 2 to 3 minutes or until the sauce is of medium thickness. Serve sprinkled with almonds. *Serves 6.*

MEATBALL CELERY RAGOUT

1 & 1/2 lbs. ground lean beef
3/4 cup fine dry bread crumbs
1 clove garlic, minced
1 egg, lightly beaten
1/4 cup milk
1 & 3/4 tsp. salt, divided
1/8 tsp. ground black pepper
4 Tbsp. salad oil, divided
6 cups sliced celery

2 Tbsp. flour
1 beef bouillon cube
3/4 cup boiling water
1 & 1/2 lbs. tomatoes,
broken up
4 cups uncooked, small
potato chunks
2 cups cut fresh green beans
1 & 1/2 tsp. basil leaves

In a medium bowl, combine beef, bread crumbs, garlic, egg, milk, 3/4 teaspoon of the salt, and black pepper. Shape into 2 dozen meatballs; set aside. In a Dutch oven or large saucepan, heat 2 tablespoons of the oil. Add celery; sauté for 2 minutes; remove celery to a large bowl; set aside. In the same Dutch oven, heat remaining 2 tablespoons oil. Add meatballs; brown on all sides, about 5 minutes. Remove meatballs to bowl with celery. To drippings in Dutch oven, add flour; cook and stir for 1 minute. Dissolve bouillon cube in water. Add to Dutch oven with tomatoes. Bring to boiling point, stirring and scraping drippings from Dutch oven. Add potatoes. Cover and simmer for 20 minutes, stirring occasionally. Add reserved meatballs and celery, remaining 1 teaspoon salt, green beans, and basil leaves; stir gently. Cover and simmer for 10 minutes longer or until meatballs and vegetables are cooked. *Serves 6.*

NECTARINES

Nectarines were only grown with white flesh until they were cross bred with the yellow peach in the central valley in the 1940's. Both are full of many nutrients, natural sugars, and vitamin A and C.

A nectarine is a nectarine...It is not a fuzzless peach, nor is it a cross between a peach and a plum. Nectarines have been around for a long, long time. This delicious fruit wasn't named nectarine without reason. In Greek and Roman mythology, the definition of nectar is the drink of the gods, delicious and invigorating.

Prior to 1940, almost all nectarines were of the white flesh variety, and although they were delicious, they were so tender and delicate they could not be shipped. Nectarines had to be consumed in the area where they were grown as soon as they became ripe. All of the commercial varieties which we know today have been developed since World War II and have a wonderful red-gold color. They are much heartier, can be shipped successfully throughout the United States, and are available in tremendous numbers at very reasonable prices.

WALNUT NECTARINE CHUTNEY

3 or 4 fresh nectarines
1/3 cup walnuts
3/4 cup dried currants
1/4 cup onion
1/2 tsp. ginger

1/4 tsp. cayenne
1/2 tsp. salt
1 and 1/2 cups cider vinegar
1 cup brown sugar, firmly
*   packed*

Chop nectarines to measure 2 cups. Put walnuts, currants, and onion through food chopper, using fine blade. Combine in saucepan with nectarines and all remaining ingredients. Bring to boil; simmer for 1 hour or until dark brown in color. *Makes about 2 cups.*

BAKED BEANS SAN JOAQUIN

1 or 2 fresh nectarines
1 lb. baked beans
2 Tbsp. chili sauce
1 Tbsp. chopped onion
1/4 tsp. liquid smoke

1 pkg. (5 & 1/2 oz.) cocktail
  wieners or 3 to 4 regular
  franks, halved
1 Tbsp. butter or margarine
1/4 tsp. prepared mustard

Dice nectarines to measure 1 cup. Combine with beans, sauce, onion, and liquid smoke in 1-quart casserole dish; top with wieners. Blend butter with mustard; dot over casserole. Bake at 375°F for 25 minutes until hot. *Makes 3 or 4 servings.*

CHICKEN AND NOODLES NECTARINE

2 broiler-fryers, halved
  (about 2 lb. each)
1/4 cup catsup
1/4 cup water
1/4 cup melted butter
1/4 cup dry sherry or apple
  juice
2 Tbsp. tarragon vinegar

2 tsp. soy sauce
3 or 4 fresh nectarines
1/2 lb. spinach noodles
1 can (5 oz.) water chestnuts,
  drained
1/2 cup chopped green onion
salt and pepper

Wash chicken; pat dry. Arrange in 13 x 9 x 2 baking pan. Mix catsup, water, butter, sherry, vinegar, and soy; pour over chicken. Marinate several hours, turning often. Bake skin-side down at 425°F for 25 minutes, basting often with sauce. Turn and baste; bake for 35 minutes longer until tender. Meanwhile, dice nectarines to measure 2 and 1/2 cups. Cook noodles as package directs; drain. Spoon sauce from chicken over noodles; fold in nectarines, chestnuts, onion, salt and pepper. Heat through. Turn onto hot platter; arrange chicken on top. Serve at once. *Makes 4 servings.*

SUMPTUOUS SUMMER SUPPER

1 slice ready-to-eat ham
(1 to 1 & 1/2 lb.)
2 medium white onions,
* peeled*
1 medium green pepper, cut
* in strips*
1 cup chicken stock or
* bouillon*

1 Tbsp. molasses
1 tsp. Worcestershire
1/4 tsp. ginger
10 oz. fresh green peas
3 or 4 fresh nectarines, sliced
2 tsp. cornstarch
1 Tbsp. water

Trim some fat from ham; melt in large skillet. Cut ham into 1-inch cubes; brown lightly in melted fat. Cut onions lengthwise into 6 or 8 slices. Combine chicken stock, molasses, Worcestershire, and ginger; pour over ham. Add onions, green pepper, and peas. Cook until vegetables are just tender. Add nectarines. When hot, mix cornstarch with water and stir in. Cook and stir until thick and clear. Serve at once over rice or noodles. *Makes 6 servings.*

NECTARINE TARTS

2 eggs, separated
6 Tbsp. powdered sugar
2 Tbsp. soft butter
1 tsp. grated orange rind
pinch of salt
1 Tbsp. sherry or orange juice
1/2 tsp. vanilla

1/2 cup whipping cream,
* whipped*
3 Tbsp. very dry macaroon
* crumbs*
8 baked tart shells
8 fresh nectarines, peeled
* and sliced*

Beat egg whites foamy. Beat in 4 tablespoons sugar, one at a time, until stiff peaks form. Cream butter, rest of sugar, and rind. Add egg yolks, salt; beat until fluffy. Gradually beat in sherry and vanilla. Fold in cream and meringue. Sprinkle crumbs in tart shells; top with nectarines. Cover with sauce. *Makes 8 servings.*

NECTARINE BETTY

4 cups fresh nectarines, sliced
1/2 cup brown sugar, firmly
  packed
1/4 cup margarine or butter

1 qt. day-old bread cubes
1/4 cup granulated sugar
1/4 tsp. cinnamon

Combine nectarines and brown sugar in 1 and 1/2-quart baking dish. Melt margarine in large saucepan; mix in bread cubes, granulated sugar and cinnamon until coated. Spread over fruit. Bake in a preheated 350°F oven for 25 minutes or until heated through. *Makes 6 servings.*

NECTARINE 'N NUT DESSERT

3 cups fresh nectarines, sliced
1 cup granulated sugar
2 Tbsp. flour
4 eggs
2 Tbsp. powdered sugar

1/4 tsp. salt
1 cup finely chopped walnuts
  or pecans
1/2 tsp. vanilla

Arrange nectarines in 1 and 1/2-quart casserole dish. Sprinkle with 1/2 cup granulated sugar mixed with flour. Beat eggs until thick; beat in remaining granulated sugar and salt. Add nuts and vanilla. Spoon over nectarines. Bake at 375°F for 30 to 35 minutes until topping is browned. Sprinkle with powdered sugar. *Makes 6 servings.*

NECTARINE CHEESECAKE-PIE

2 & 1/2 cups sliced fresh
  nectarines
Unbaked 9-inch pastry shell
3 eggs
1/2 cup whipping cream

1 & 1/4 cups powdered sugar
2 pkgs. (3 oz. each) cream
  cheese, softened
1 tsp. grated lemon rind
1 tsp. lemon juice

Arrange 1 and 1/2 cups nectarine slices in bottom of pastry shell. Beat 2 eggs lightly with cream and 1 cup sugar; pour over fruit. Beat cheese with 1 egg, 1/4 cup sugar, lemon rind and juice; gently turn into pastry shell. Bake at 375°F for 30 minutes. Chill. Garnish with 1 cup nectarine slices and, if you wish, a dollop of softened cream cheese. *Serves 6 to 8.*

PEACHES

Peaches and nectarines are virtually fat and sodium free, making them an ideal food for those with cholesterol and blood pressure problems. "

Georgia and California may have been enjoying peaches earlier, but for the rest of the country, they are coming in now. That bright rosy blush on a peach is lovely to look at, but don't let it fool you. Red is not necessarily ripe in selecting peaches, and the blush depends on variety. Look for a fresh creamy yellow skin and a golden undercolor. Avoid those with too much green on their skins. The best sign of all is that they smell absolutely peachy.

Peaches are a good source of vitamins A and C and are low in both calories and sodium. They will keep best in the refrigerator and stay fresh several days, but you'll have better, peachier flavor if you serve them at room temperature.

Most peaches are washed and defuzzed before they are shipped to market. However, some of our recipes here are fruit salads or desserts, so you may wish to remove the skin. Dip the fresh peach in boiling water for just a few seconds and you will find the skin slips off easy and clean-as-a-whistle.

PEACH SLAW

Make your next slaw a green and gold delight. Lightly toss sliced, fresh peaches and Spanish peanuts with shredded cabbage. Add enough sharp French or coleslaw dressing to moisten.

PEACH SALAD COMPOTE

6 cups cut-up fresh fruit
(peaches, grapes, melon,
strawberries, etc.)
lemon juice or ascorbic acid
mixture
1/2 cup whipping cream, whipped

1 cup mayonnaise
2 Tbsp. lemon juice
1 tsp. grated lemon peel
1 tsp. allspice
crisp salad greens

Toss fruit with lemon and chill. Fold cream into mayonnaise; blend in juice, peel, and allspice. Serve fruit on greens. Pass dressing. *Makes 6 servings.*

PEACHES A LA GARDEN COURT

1 egg
1 Tbsp. lemon juice
1 & 1/2 tsp. wine vinegar
1/2 tsp. salt
3/4 cup oil

1 pt. fresh raspberries or
strawberries
6 fresh peaches, peeled and
halved
crisp salad greens

In blender, combine egg, lemon juice, vinegar, and salt. Blend at high speed for 30 seconds. On medium-low speed, gradually drip in the oil; blend until thick and smooth. Blend in half of berries. Transfer to bowl and fold in remaining berries. Place peach halves on greens; spoon sauce over. *Makes 6 servings.*

SHOULDER LAMB STEAKS WITH PEACHES

6 shoulder lamb steaks
2 Tbsp. vegetable oil
1 onion, minced
1 & 1/2 cups tomato sauce
1/2 cup vinegar
1/4 cup water

3 Tbsp. light brown sugar,
firmly packed
1 Tbsp. Worcestershire sauce
2 tsp. salt
6 fresh peaches, peeled and
sliced

In large skillet, brown steaks on both sides in oil. Remove. Add onion and cook until soft. Add tomato sauce, vinegar, water, brown sugar, Worcestershire, and salt. Stir to blend. Return steaks to skillet; spoon some sauce over. Cover pan. Simmer over low heat, turning occasionally, about 1 hour, or until steaks are tender. Add peaches and simmer for 5 minutes more. Serve at once with cooked rice. *Makes 6 servings.*

ZESTY CINNAMON PEACHES

8 large fresh peaches, peeled   *1/2 cup sugar*
1 cup water   *2 Tbsp red cinnamon candies*
1 cup orange juice   *12 whole cloves*
1/3 cup lemon juice

Halve peaches and remove pits. In large saucepan, combine remaining ingredients. Add half peaches; simmer until tender, about 10 minutes. Remove with slotted spoon; set aside. Simmer remaining peaches until tender. Chill all peaches in syrup. *Makes 8 servings.*

PEACHES 'N' CREAM PIE

Pastry:
2 cups sifted flour   *6 Tbsp. shortening*
1 tsp. salt   *4 to 6 Tbsp. ice water*
6 Tbsp. butter

Filling:
6 fresh peaches, peeled and   *dash salt*
*   sliced*   *1/2 tsp. nutmeg*
1/2 cup sugar   *1/2 cup whipping cream*
3 Tbsp. flour   *1/2 tsp. vanilla*

In a mixing bowl, combine flour and salt. Cut in butter and shortening with pastry blender. Add ice water and stir with fork until dough forms a ball. Chill. Preheat oven to 450°F. Roll out 1/2 pastry to line a 9-inch pie plate. Fill shell with peaches. In a small bowl, combine remaining ingredients; pour over peaches. Roll out remaining pastry; put over top of pie and crimp edges. Slash top;

bake for 10 minutes. Reduce heat to 350°F and continue baking for additional 45 to 50 minutes. Serve warm or cool with ice cream, if desired. *Makes 6 servings.*

FRESH PEACH MERINGUE PIE

One 9-inch baked pastry crust

1/4 cup cornstarch

1/4 cup sugar

1/4 tsp. salt

2 cups peach puree

2 Tbsp. butter or margarine

3 egg whites

1/4 tsp. salt

1/4 cup sugar

Combine cornstarch, 1/4 cup sugar, and 1/4 teaspoon salt in saucepan. Gradually stir in peach puree. Stir over medium heat until thick and bubbly. Remove from heat. Save 1/2 cup. Add butter to rest of peach mixture. Stir until melted. Pour into baked crust. Cool for 15 minutes. Add salt to egg whites; beat until frothy. Beat in 1/4 cup sugar, a little at a time, until stiff. Stir the 1/2 cup reserved filling mixture until smooth. Gently fold into egg whites. Pile lightly on filling, carefully covering to edges. Bake at 350°F for about 25 minutes. Cool completely away from drafts.

AUTUMN

AUTUMN

Labor Day is coming, and it's time to get together with friends and have a barbecue with corn on the cob, a big, fresh tossed salad, and watermelon for dessert.

Most families look forward to Labor Day weekend and the coming of autumn as a new beginning. It signals the start of the new school year and the household resumes a definite routine once again, particularly with regard to regularly scheduled meals. It is also the season when fresh fruits and vegetable are at their most abundant—harvest time best.

The first hint that autumn is on its way is when you see the pomegranates and cranberries starting to arrive. And when the first ornamental Indian corn, gourds, and pumpkins of the year appear, you know autumn's just around the corner. There's another tip. Green bell peppers have turned into red bell peppers, and if that isn't a sign of fall, I don't know what is.

After the pomegranates and ornamental corn and gourds, there is no question about the fact that the persimmons have to follow. They come about the time of the Jewish New Year. Your fruit bowl should feature lots of apples, grapes, and pears. National Apple Week is in mid-October, and this is a good time to make some of your favorite apple recipes, in addition to keeping apples for the fruit bowl. There will also be a plentiful supply of fresh broccoli and Brussels sprouts for fall dinners.

As the days get shorter, you'll see lots of pumpkins on the market for Jack O'Lanterns and pumpkin pie. Halloween is always a big holiday at our house. On top of being invaded by all the witches and hob-goblins, Halloween is also my birthday, so that's when I celebrate and, of course, get all my favorite foods for a birthday dinner.

Then, it's November and election time and our big American holiday of Thanksgiving, when we celebrate and give thanks for the harvest. That is a time when we really make use of all the fresh fruits and vegetables with which we are blessed.

PEARS

*Pears contain a good amount of the soluble fiber pectin,
known to help clean the veins and arteries of cholesterol.*

On those warm days you want something juicy and succulent, pears are something you can really enjoy. When you bite into a fresh, ripe Bartlett pear, it just bursts with juice.

When they are ripe, pears are definitely one of the most popular items in produce. Most people will not buy green pears and ripen them themselves. In fact, the sale of ripe pears to green ones is about ten to one. But don't wait until the pear develops a deep yellow color, or it is going to be over ripe, and that is one thing you don't want in a Bartlett pear. The fruit should be firm, but tender, and of course, filled with juice.

You will also see what we call 'apple pears' in the market. The little apple pear is a bit rounder and it may be quite firm, but it is tasty and it's sweet, and you'll enjoy it. It has that singular something that some pears don't have, and it is also very good for baking.

The Bosc pear is the ugly duckling in the pear family. It is brownish in color, with some russeting, and it has a gooseneck. But it's a delicious pear and it, too, is very good for baking.

Pears have a wonderful delicate taste which blends beautifully with the others.

ZIPPY PEAR SALAD

2 fresh Bartlett pears, halved
and cored
Iceberg lettuce cups, chilled
3 Tbsp. Roquefort cheese

3 Tbsp. cream cheese
3 Tbsp. butter or margarine
1 tsp. prepared horseradish
dash Tabasco and dash salt

On 4 salad plates, arrange pear halves on lettuce. Blend other ingredients; spoon into pear centers. Garnish with cress, if desired. *Makes 4 servings.*

SUMMER BUFFET SALAD

4 fresh pears
2 fresh plums, quartered
2 cups fresh blueberries
1 fresh nectarine, sliced
3/4 cup sugar
1/3 cup white vinegar

2 Tbsp. chopped onion
1 & 1/2 tsp. dry mustard
1 tsp. salt
1 cup salad oil
Romaine lettuce, chilled

Prepare dressing by combining sugar, vinegar, onion, mustard and salt in electric blender; whirl until smooth, gradually adding oil. Chill. At serving time, line large plate with lettuce. Pare, halve, and core pears; place cored sides down in spoke arrangements on lettuce, alternating necks out, necks in. Quickly spoon some dressing over pears to prevent browning. Place plums between pears, skin up; group blueberries at edge of plate; center with nectarines. Serve at once with remaining dressing. *Makes 8 servings.*

SAVORY PEAR SAUTÉ

Sauté thick wedges of fresh pears in a mixture of butter, finely chopped onion and marjoram or thyme. Serve as an accompaniment to broiled fish or chicken.

MINT-SAUCE PEAR DESSERT

2 fresh pears
1/2 cup mint jelly
1 Tbsp. cornstarch
1/3 cup water
1 & 1/2 tsp. grated orange rind

1/4 cup crème de menthe
  liqueur
dash salt
6 servings vanilla ice cream,
  meringue shells or rice
  pudding

Pare, halve, and core pears. Cut each half lengthwise into 4 slices. Melt jelly; blend in cornstarch mixed with water. Cook and stir until thickened. Add rind, liqueur and salt; mix well. Add pear slices; heat 2 or 3 minutes. Spoon over ice cream, meringues, or pudding. *Makes 6 servings.*

BARTLETT BREAD PUDDING

3 or 4 fresh pears
1/4 cup lemon juice
2 cups dry bread cubes
1/3 cup melted butter or
  margarine

1/4 cup sugar
1/2 tsp. salt
1/4 tsp. allspice
1/4 tsp. cinnamon
1/2 cup raisins

Pare, halve, and core pears; dice to measure 3 cups. Mix with lemon. Mix bread, butter, sugar, salt, and spices. Place 1/2 of the combination in buttered 1 and 1/2 quart casserole; top with pears, raisins and remaining bread. Bake covered at 350°F for 15 minutes. Uncover; bake 20 minutes longer. Serve with whipped cream or vanilla ice cream, if desired. *Makes 4 or 5 servings.*

PEAR-PEANUT BUTTER SQUARES

1 fresh pear
1/3 cup granulated sugar
1/3 cup brown sugar, firmly
*   packed*
1/3 cup butter or margarine
1/3 cup peanut butter

1 egg
3/4 cup sifted all-purpose
*   flour*
1/4 tsp. baking powder
1/2 tsp. soda
1/4 tsp. salt

Pare, halve, core, and mash pear; cream with sugars, butter, peanut butter, and egg. Sift remaining ingredients together into creamed mixture; mix well. Pour into greased 9 x 9 inch pan. Bake at 350°F for 24 minutes. Cool. Cut into 2 and 1/4-inch squares.

PEAR CARAMEL CRUNCH PIE

5 fresh pears
1 unbaked pastry for 9-inch pie
*   shell*
1 Tbsp. flour
1 Tbsp. lemon juice
1 tsp. cinnamon

1 cup brown sugar, firmly
*   packed*
1 & 1/2 cups crushed corn
*   flakes*
1/3 cup butter or margarine

Pare, halve, core, and slice pears. Line a 9-inch pie plate with pastry; flute edges. Sprinkle flour on pie shell. Arrange pears over and sprinkle with lemon juice.

With pastry blender or 2 knives, mix all remaining ingredients; spread over pears. Bake at 375°F for 45 to 50 minutes, until pears are fork tender and top is crisp and lightly browned. Serve warm. *Makes 6 servings.*

PROSCIUTTO PEAR BITES

Contributed by Zuzy Martin Lynch

2 pears
2 Tbsp. freshly squeezed lemon
juice
2 Tbsp. water

3 ounces prosciutto, very
thinly sliced
Freshly ground pepper

Combine lemon juice and water in a small mixing bowl (acidulated water). Peel and core (remove core) the pears and cut each into bite-sized chunks, about 40 pieces total, and place in the acidulated water. Slice the prosciutto into thin strips and fold into little square packets. Use toothpick to pierce through the prosciutto and into pear chunk. Place on a serving plate and top with a sprinkling of freshly ground black pepper. *Yields 6 to 8 servings.*

GRAPES

Grapes are known to clean, nourish,
and strengthen the body.

September is the month for grapes, and you'll find many varieties available. Right now, they have all their sugar because they have ripened on the vine. At this time of year, they also contain maximum nutrition. This is when you get the best of the crop at the lowest price, and that is the best time to enjoy them. They'll be around for a couple of months, but in October, they will not all be fresh picked. Absolutely, the month of September is Grape Month.

Be sure to look for grapes with a green stem, because that's a sign of freshness. Put them in the refrigerator as soon as you get home, and they'll keep for a week, at least.

Grapes are not very high in vitamin C, only 4 milligrams per 3 and 1/2 ounces, but they contain 100 units of vitamin A, 158 units of potassium, and they are low in sodium, containing only 3 milligrams, and there are only 69 calories in 3 and 1/2 ounces of grapes.

Seedless grapes outsell all other varieties, and they are delicious, but do try some of the variety grapes for a change. If you want to give your kids a treat, put some fresh, sweet grapes in the freezer, or better yet, put a whole pan of them in the freezer for four or five hours. Let the kids chew on something that's good for them. They are delicious, and the kids will love them. They're much better to feed your kids than candy.

At our house, we generally eat fresh grapes, but we also have some fine recipes using grapes:

WALDORF GRAPE SALAD

1 cup seedless grapes
1 cup diced apple
1 cup sliced celery
1 cup chopped walnuts
1 cup diced Swiss cheese

1/2 cup heavy cream
1/2 cup mayonnaise
1 Tbsp. sugar
1 tsp. lemon juice
lettuce cups

Gently toss together first five ingredients in large salad bowl. In another bowl, whip cream, add remaining ingredients, except lettuce, and blend well. Fold dressing into salad. Serve cold on lettuce cups. *Makes 6 to 8 servings.*

LEMON SOLE IN WHITE WINE HOLLANDAISE

3/4 cup halved white seedless
  grapes
3 sprigs of parsley, chopped
3 tomatoes, peeled, seeded
  and chopped

6 filets of sole
3 shallots, chopped
3 cups dry white wine
salt and pepper
Hollandaise sauce

In a shallow pan, place grapes, tomatoes, shallots, and parsley. Over this, lay filets of sole and cover with wine. Simmer fish gently for about 10 to 12 minutes, until cooked. Remove filets carefully to a hot serving dish and keep hot. Strain sauce, press tomatoes and grapes through sieve, and season lightly with salt and pepper.

Stir tomato-and-grape sauce gently into Hollandaise sauce. Pour sauce over the sole and garnish with a small bunch of seedless grapes and with parsley or grape leaves. Serve at once.

CHICKEN VERONIQUE

6 whole broiler-fryer chicken
  breasts, halved
salt
paprika
3/4 cup butter, divided
1/2 lb. mushrooms, sliced

1/2 cup flour
2 tsp. sugar
4 cups chicken broth
1/4 cup lemon juice
2 cups seedless green grapes
seedless green grape clusters

Bone chicken breasts, if desired. Sprinkle chicken with salt and paprika. Melt 1/2 cup of the butter in a large skillet. Add chicken, skin side down. Brown well on both sides; remove. Melt remaining 1/4 cup butter in skillet, add onion and mushrooms. Cook over low heat for 5 minutes. Blend in flour and sugar. Stir in chicken broth and lemon juice. Bring to a boil, stirring constantly. Add chicken; cover and simmer 30 minutes, or until tender. Add grapes in the last 5 minutes of cooking time. To serve, place chicken breasts on Tarragon Biscuits" on serving platter; spoon a small amount of sauce over each. Garnish with grape clusters and serve remaining sauce.

*NOTE: Tarragon Biscuits are made by preparing 12 of your favorite flaky biscuits. Then blend together 1/4 cup of soft butter with 1/2 teaspoon dried leaf tarragon. Split the biscuits; spread with butter mixture. Lightly brown in broiler.

PASTRY CREAM

6 tart shells
5 egg yolks
2/3 cup sugar
1/3 cup all-purpose flour

2 cups hot milk
1 tsp. vanilla extract
grapes

Beat yolks until thick and gradually beat in sugar. Continue beating until mixture forms a ribbon when you lift the beater. This can be done with an electric mixer. Beat in flour. When well blended, add hot milk in a thin stream, beating constantly. Put mixture in top part of double boiler over simmering water. Stir

179

with a wire whisk until mixture is smooth and flour is cooked. Remove from heat and beat in vanilla, or any other flavoring you choose. Cool cream slightly. Spoon a layer into bottom of tart shells. Any leftover cream can be stored in refrigerator and used for other tarts or cakes. Top cream with grapes. Glaze with Grape Glaze, recipe below.

GRAPE GLAZE

3/4 cup honey
1 Tbsp. grated lemon peel
2 Tbsp. lemon juice

2 Tbsp. orange juice
1/3 to 1/2 cup sherry

Combine all ingredients in small saucepan. Cook, stirring constantly, over low heat for 5 minutes. Remove from heat, cool slightly; pour over sliced grapes. Allow grapes to marinate in syrup several hours before serving. Garnish with fresh mint leaves for color and flavor, if desired.

ZABAGLIONE DELLA ROBBIA

1 lb. grapes, halved and
* seeded (about 3 cups)*
2 red apples, slices
2 oranges, sliced
1 cup melon balls (optional)

8 egg yolks
3 Tbsp. sugar
1 cup dry white wine
1 tsp. nutmeg

Beat yolks and sugar together in the top of a double boiler. When frothy, place over boiling water and continue beating for 5 to 8 minutes. Slowly add wine; beat until mixture is thick and light. Pour into individual dessert dishes and sprinkle with nutmeg. Surround with fruit. Dip fruit into warm zabaglione.

POMEGRANATES

The deep red color shows the presence of the
strong anti-oxidant, vitamin A.

The only real way to learn about pomegranates is to buy one because they certainly have a personality all their own. Grenadine is made from pomegranate juice, and the seeds make a nice addition to fruit cups or fruit salads.

Kids absolutely love pomegranates, and most will chew and eat the seeds right along with the sweet pulp surrounding them. But beware, pomegranate juice is also used as a permanent dye and everything within splatter distance can be permanently ruined. Probably the safest method is to roll the pomegranate on a table, as you would a lemon, until the kernels break down from solid pulp to juice. Then, stick a hole in the side with a sharp knife or cut a little round hole with a vegetable parer and let the kids suck the juice out. And even then, be prepared for red polka-dots.

GINGERY POMEGRANATE, CARROT, BEET, AND PECAN SLAW
Contributed by Kristin Hoppe

3 cups shredded carrots	*3 cups shredded beets*
3/4 cup chopped raw pecans	*3/4 cup pomegranate seeds*
1/4 cup minced shallot	*2 Tbsp. minced fresh ginger*
1 garlic clove, minced	*1/4 cup apple cider vinegar*
1 Tbsp. Tamari	*2 tsp. cold pressed sesame oil*
dash red pepper flakes to taste	*1/3 cup cold pressed olive oil*

In blender, puree shallot, ginger, garlic, vinegar, tamari, sesame oil and red pepper. With motor running, add olive oil in a stream and blend until smooth. Add vinaigrette to carrots, beets, chopped

pecans, and pomegranate seeds. Toss to combine and serve!
Servings: 8

POMEGRANATE SALAD DRESSING
Contributed by
Simla Somturk Wickless

*2 Tbsp. pomegranate syrup
or molasses(bought or
homemade, below)*

*1 Tbsp. olive oil
Sea salt, to taste
Optional: squeeze of lemon,
to taste*

Combine and whip (with a fork) the dressing ingredients until blended well. Toss salad of choice with dressing, and enjoy!

To make your own pomegranate syrup or molasses:

Pour 2 cups of 100% organic pomegranate juice into a small saucepan. Simmer on low heat until juice is reduced to a syrupy consistency. Use what you need for the recipe and store the remainder in a glass jar in the fridge. May be used as a marinade, salad dressing, colorful tangy-sweet drizzle over desserts, cheeses, or cut-up fruit. *Serves 2 in a large salad.*

PERSIMMONS

There are 2 types of persimmons: The Hychia, which must
be soft to use (mostly for cooking), and the Fuyu, which is to
be eaten firm like an apple, or sliced in a salad.
A deep orange color shows strong presence of Vitamin A.

It's only natural that after the pomegranates, you'll see persimmons arrive. They'll be a little expensive at first, and I'd be a little hesitant about buying the first ones. They usually don't have all their sugar and they aren't quite ripe, so I'd be a little cagey about them. Let someone else buy the first ones.

Persimmons are one of the few fruits that should be really soft, but, of course, not bruised or decayed. If you buy them too firm, they will really pucker in your mouth. Let them ripen at room temperature inside a closed plastic bag for a couple of days.

One writer described the experience of eating an unripe persimmon as "your mouth feels like it's trying to turn itself inside out" and that is true. But when it is ripe and sweet, it is delicious. Either peel and eat it like a banana, or cut it in half and eat it like a melon with a spoon. They are good with sweet cream or ice cream. Or, try these recipes for tasty persimmon desserts:

PERSIMMON PIE

2 eggs, slightly beaten
2 cups persimmon pulp
  (may be mixed in any pro-
  portion with pumpkin or
  squash pulp)
3/4 cups sugar (white)
(Continued on next page)

1/2 tsp. cinnamon
1/4 tsp. ginger
1/4 cloves
1 &2/3 cups evaporated milk,
  top milk or light cream
One 9" unbaked pastry shell
1/2 tsp. salt

Mix in order, pour in shell. Bake for 15 minutes at 425°F. Reduce heat to 350°F and continue for 45 minutes. Serve plain or with whipped cream.

PERSIMMON COOKIES

1 cup persimmon pulp
1 cup chopped nuts
1 cup chopped raisins
1 cup sugar
1/2 cup butter

1 egg
1 tsp. soda dissolved in pulp
2 cups flour
1/2 tsp. each cloves,
    cinnamon, and nutmeg

Cream shortening and sugar, add nuts and raisins to flour, beat egg and add to pulp. Add to dry ingredients. Drop from teaspoon on greased baking sheet. Bake in moderate oven.

PERSIMMON CHEESECAKE
Contributed by Marisa Riparbelli

Boxed graham cracker crumbs
2 – 8 oz. pkgs. cream cheese,
  softened
1/2 cup sugar
2 eggs

1 cup sour cream
1 tsp. vanilla

1 to 2 large persimmons'
  worth of persimmon pulp
  (use only the soft
  persimmons)
1/2 tsp. cinnamon

1/4 cup sugar

Using an 8" spring form pan, follow directions for the crust on box of graham cracker crumbs. Press into pan and bake at 350 for 10 min. Cool. Mix together first group of ingredients with electric mixer until smooth. Pour into cooled crust and bake at 350 for an hour. Cool for 20 minutes. While it's cooling, mix together next group of ingredients (sour cream, sugar, vanilla). After the cake has cooled for 20 minutes, top with the sour cream mixture and bake another 7 minutes.

PERSIMMON PUDDING
WITH HARD SAUCE
Contributed by Marisa Riparbelli

1 & 1/2 cups sugar
3 Tbsp. butter melted
2 eggs, well beaten
1 tsp. cinnamon
1 & 1/2 cups flour
3/4 cup <u>whole</u> milk

1 & 1/2 cups persimmon pulp
(3 to 4 very ripe)
3/4 tsp. salt
1/4 tsp. nutmeg
3 tsp. baking soda

You will need a steamed pudding mold for this recipe. It must have a lid that snaps shut.

Mix dry ingredients together. In a separate bowl, mix all wet ingredients together with electric mixer. Pour into greased pudding mold. Cover with wax paper, then put lid on and snap shut. Place an inverted pie tin with holes punched in it in the bottom of a pot. Place pudding mold on inverted tin and fill with water about one third of the way up the pudding mold. Cover pot. Bring to a boil. Once boiling, steam/simmer for 2 and 1/2 hours. Let cool for 5 minutes uncovered and with wax paper removed. Invert. Serve while still warm or at room temperature. Do not make too far ahead.

Hard Sauce

1/2 cup softened butter
1 Jigger brandy

1 cup powdered sugar

Using an electric beater, blend butter and sugar first, then add brandy and blend. I usually double this. It can be done a couple of hours ahead and kept in a Tupperware container unrefrigerated.

CAULIFLOWER

Cauliflower is a member of the cabbage family, possessing sulfur compounds, plus many nutrients making it a great cancer fighter.

A head of cauliflower should be firm and very compact; the florets should be white and any remaining leaves should be green and look fresh. Although cauliflower isn't as nutritionally valuable as most green vegetables, it does contain an excellent amount of vitamin C and some Iron. It is very low in calories, about 27 per cupful of raw flowerets.

Cauliflower has gained tremendous popularity as a raw vegetable dipper. Try this one with cauliflower, carrot sticks, celery sticks, and other vegetable dippers:

1/2 lb. Roquefort cheese	*1 cup heavy cream*
1/4 lb. cream cheese	*dash of Tabasco sauce*

Thoroughly blend the two cheeses together with the heavy cream until it reaches "dip" consistency. Add a dash of Tabasco sauce and mix well. Refrigerate to allow ingredients to infuse about 1/2 hour before serving.

CAULIFLOWER WITH HAM

1 head of fresh cauliflower	*3 egg yolks, slightly beaten*
1/2 cup chopped ham	*1 Tbsp. flour*
1/2 cup grated cheese	*1/2 tsp. salt*
1 cup light cream	

Break cauliflower into flowerets and cook in slightly salted water until almost tender. Arrange layers of cauliflower, ham, and cheese alternately in buttered baking dish, reserving some cheese for top. Blend egg yolks, flour, salt, and cream and pour over layers.

Sprinkle with remaining cheese. Bake at 325°F until egg mixture thickens, about 25 minutes. *Serves 6.*

CALIFORNIA MORNAY

1 head fresh cauliflower
1 & 1/2 cups medium rich cream
sauce (recipe below)

1 cup grated cheddar cheese
2/3 cups buttered bread
crumbs

Wash cauliflower, remove outer leaves, break into flowerets and steam in 1 inch of boiling, salted water. Cook until crispy-tender. Drain thoroughly.

Transfer flowerets to a shallow baking dish. Cover with 1/2 cup cheese sauce, then remainder of cheese. Top with bread crumbs. Heat in 350°F oven until hot and bubbly. *Serves 6 to 8.*

To make cream sauce:
3 Tbsp. butter
3 Tbsp. flour
1/2 tsp. salt

3/4 cup milk
3/4 cup light cream

Melt butter. Add flour and salt. Then add milk and cream. Cook until thick.

TEMPURA OR DEEP-FRIED VEGETABLES

Wash and break fresh cauliflower into small flowerets. Dry. Wash ten artichoke hearts, cut in half, and dry very thoroughly on paper towel. Wash parsley and snip in large sprigs. Dry on paper toweling. Wash and slice fresh mushrooms. Dry.

Prepare a batter of:
1 cup flour
1 cup ice water
1 slightly beaten egg
(Continued on next page)

2 Tbsp. salad oil
1/2 tsp. sugar
1/2 tsp. salt

Keep batter cool with one or two ice cubes in it. Dip vegetables in batter; cook in deep hot fat (360°F to 365°F) till browned. Drain on paper towel. Dash with salt or use a dip made of 1 and 1/2 tablespoons soy sauce mixed with 1/4 cup prepared mustard.

CAULIFLOWER CREOLE

1 medium head cauliflower
1/2 cup chopped onion
6 Tbsp. butter or margarine
salt and pepper to taste
1 Tbsp. chopped parsley

3 Tbsp. flour
1 or 2 green peppers,
*   chopped fine*
3 cups chopped tomatoes

Divide the cauliflower into flowerets and boil in plain water. Meanwhile, brown the onion in some of the butter, add the tomatoes, and stew for about 1/2 hour to make a smooth sauce. Mix the flour with the remaining margarine to thicken. Add to the sauce. Put in the green pepper and stew a few minutes. Season and add the cauliflower, heat through for 5 minutes. Garnish with the chopped parsley. *Serves 4 to 6.*

CAULIFLOWER CUSTARD

1 medium cauliflower,
*   separated into flowerets*
2 Tbsp. butter
3 Tbsp. flour
1 tsp. salt

1 Tbsp. minced parsley
2 cups milk
3 eggs
1/4 tsp. white pepper

Cook the cauliflower until tender-crisp in salted water to cover. Drain. Arrange in a buttered 1 and 1/2 quart casserole.

Melt the butter in a pan, add the flour, 1/2 teaspoon of the salt, and the parsley, stirring until smooth. Slowly add 1 cup of the milk and cook until thickened, then pour over the cauliflower. Beat the eggs in a bowl, add the remaining 1/2 teaspoon salt, the pepper, and the rest of the milk. Pour over the creamed cauliflower in the casserole and bake in a moderate oven (350°F) for 30 to 35 minutes or until the custard is set. Serve hot. *Serves 4 to 6.*

AUTUMN SALAD

2 cups sliced fresh cauli-
flowerets
20 cherry tomatoes, halved
1/4 cup diced green pepper
salt and pepper to taste

3 cups torn salad greens
2 cups sliced fresh nectarines
1/2 cup bottled Italian
dressing

Combine all ingredients, except dressing, salt, and pepper, in salad bowl. Cover and chill. Add dressing, salt and pepper. Toss gently. *Makes 6 to 8 servings.*

SWEET POTATOES AND YAMS

There are red and blonde sweet potatoes.
The red is the most nutritious. It exhibits orange flesh,
showing that it has a strong presence of the key
anti-oxidant vitamin A. This sweet potato, for generations,
has been known as the yam. But, the only yam is called
NAME, grown primarily in Mexico and South America.
It has white flesh and a gray exterior and possesses many vitamins
and minerals, but not the strong vitamin A.

In September, we begin to see beautiful sweet potatoes and yams at very reasonable prices. They'll be in plentiful supply right through Thanksgiving, although one variety or another is available almost all year around. I would recommend that you try them because you don't even need any sugar, molasses, or honey on fresh sweet potatoes or yams. Once cooked, they are sweet. Just add a little butter and you will find they are delicious. The sweet potato versus yam controversy seems to go on forever, but all sweet potatoes and yams that are sold in the United States today are basically sweet potatoes. There are varieties of sweet potatoes which are also known as yams because they are copper skinned and are a deep orange color inside. The sweet potato has a tan tone or color on the outside and is a light, creamy yellow on the inside. In the produce business, the sweet potato that is sold as a sweet potato is called a choker because it's so dry; whereas the sweet potato that is sold as a yam is sweet and juicy. That is why the sweet potato that is known as a yam is sold in preference to the actual sweet potato.

Sweet potatoes became a staple for the early settlers in America, and the south practically survived on them during the Civil War and during the Reconstruction. They are high in nutritional value, though the amounts vary greatly according to the variety, growing location, and season.

Following, you will find a surprising number of recipes for sweet potatoes and yams. Their flavor blends well with many fruits such as oranges, apples, and pineapple; and they are a natural with lamb or pork chops, veal, and best of all with ham. This is also the season when we look for ways to use leftover turkey, and we've included a very good yam and turkey recipe.

Because of their natural sweetness, they are ideal in desserts, and you'll find recipes for pudding, cookies, cakes, and pies, and last, but not least, a recipe for Louisiana Yam Cajun Candy.

BAKED YAMS

Wash and trim yams. Dry well. Arrange on baking sheet. Bake yams for 15 minutes at 400°F. Reduce temperature to 375°F, and bake medium size for 45 minutes and large ones for 60 minutes.

YAMS DE LUXE

6 yams
Marshmallows

1/2 cup crushed pineapple or
1/2 cup chopped pecans

Boil yams and drain. Peel and mash. Moisten with hot milk or fruit juice and beat until light. Add salt and butter to taste, pineapple or nuts. Put into buttered casserole dish, top with marshmallows, bake at 375°F until marshmallows melt and brown.

CANDIED YAMS

4 medium yams, cooked and
  peeled
1 tsp. grated lemon rind

1/2 cup light corn syrup
1 Tbsp. lemon juice
3 Tbsp. melted butter or
  or margarine

Cut yams into crosswise slices 1/2 inch thick; place in greased 1 quart casserole. Combine remaining ingredients; mix well and pour over yams. Bake in moderately hot oven (375°F) 30 minutes. *Serves 4.*

ROASTED SWEET POTATOES (YAMS)
Contributed by Zuzy Martin Lynch

4 medium sweet potatoes
  (yams), peeled
3 Tbsp. melted unsalted butter
Pepper

1 Tbsp. lemon juice
1/2 cup brown sugar
1 tsp. grated lemon rind
Kosher salt

Cut sweet potatoes (yams) into crosswise slices 1/2-inch thick; place in 1-quart casserole dish (coat dish with thin layer of butter or olive oil). Combine remaining ingredients; mix well and pour over sweet potatoes. Bake in moderately hot oven (375°F) for 30 minutes. Salt and pepper to taste. *Serves 4.*

ORANGE CANDIED YAMS

6 medium-sized yams
1 cup orange juice
1/2 tsp. grated orange rind
1 cup sugar

1/4 cup butter
1/2 tsp. salt
1 cup water

Peel and slice uncooked potatoes in 1/4 inch slices; arrange in buttered baking dish. Make a syrup of the next 6 ingredients and pour over potatoes. Cover, bake in a moderate oven until tender. Baste occasionally. Remove lid for last 10 minutes to brown. If you use boiled potatoes, reduce the amount of water and bake uncovered for shorter time.

SUNDAY-SUPPER

1 broiler-fryer chicken, cut in
  serving pieces
1/4 cup butter or margarine,
  melted
salt and pepper
(Continued on next page)

1/3 cup orange juice
1/4 to 1/2 tsp. ground ginger
dash ground allspice
4 medium yams, cooked,
  peeled and halved
1/2 cup apricot preserves

Place chicken, skin-side down, on foil-covered broiler rack. Brush with some of the butter and sprinkle with salt and pepper. Broil 6 to 7 inches from source of heat 20 minutes or until golden brown. Turn chicken and broil 10 to 15 minutes longer.

Meanwhile, add preserves, juice, spices, and a dash of salt to remaining melted butter in small saucepan. Heat until blended. Place yams on broiler rack with chicken; brush all with apricot sauce. Broil 1 minute, turn yams and chicken and brush again with sauce. Broil about 1 minute longer. Serve remaining sauce with the yams and chicken. *Serves 4.*

HAM AND YAM DINNER

2 Tbsp. cornstarch
1/2 tsp. ground ginger
2 cups apple juice
1 Tbsp. cider vinegar
1 cup dark corn syrup
1 tsp. grated lemon peel

1/4 cup butter or margarine
1/2 cup dark, seedless raisins
2 cups cubed cooked (or left-
  over) ham
6 medium yams, cooked,
  peeled and quartered

Blend cornstarch and ginger in large skillet; gradually blend in apple juice. Add all remaining ingredients, except ham and yams. Bring to a boil; simmer 30 seconds. Add ham and yams; simmer about 5 minutes, stirring occasionally, or until ingredients are heated through. Turn into serving dish and garnish with lemon twists, if desired. *Serves 6.*

LAMB CHOPS WITH STREUSEL YAMS

4 medium yams, cooked,
  peeled and halved lengthwise
salt and pepper

4 shoulder lamb chops, 1
  inch thick
Streusel Topping

If desired, remove a small slice from the bottom of each yam to level. Sprinkle yams on both sides with salt and pepper. Place, bottom side up, on broiler pan with chops. Broil 3 to 4 inches from source of heat for 14 to 16 minutes, turning chops and yams midway through broiling. Sprinkle yams with Streusel Topping* about 4 minutes before end of broiling time. Watch carefully and remove yams when topping has browned. Sprinkle chops on both sides with salt and pepper before serving. *Serves 4.*

*Streusel Topping: Mix together 1/3 cup firmly packed light brown sugar, 1 tablespoon flour and 1/2 teaspoon salt. Cut in 3 tablespoons butter until crumbly. Stir in 1/3 cup chopped pecans.

TURKEY AND YAMS IN CHEESE SAUCE

1/4 cup butter or margarine
1/4 cup flour
1 tsp. salt
dash white pepper
2 cups milk
8 oz. grated sharp Cheddar
* cheese*

3/4 tsp. dry mustard
10 oz. asparagus, cooked
* and cut*
4 medium yams, cooked,
* peeled and sliced*
12 slices cooked turkey
* about 3/4 lb.)*

In saucepan, melt butter; quickly add flour, salt and pepper, stirring constantly. Gradually stir in milk and continue cooking until sauce thickens and comes to a boil, stirring constantly. Add cheese and mustard; stir until cheese melts. In 2-quart casserole dish, arrange asparagus, yams, and turkey; add sauce and bake in 350°F (moderate) oven for 20 to 25 minutes or until sauce is bubbling. Garnish with parsley, if desired. *Serves 6.*

YAM PORK CHOP SKILLET

1 Tbsp. shortening
4 shoulder pork chops
4 medium yams, peeled and
* thinly sliced*
1 large onion, thinly sliced
2 & 1/2 cups fresh diced tomatoes
(Continued on next page)

1 medium green pepper,
* cut into rings*
salt and pepper
1/4 tsp. thyme
1/4 tsp. marjoram

Melt shortening over medium heat; brown porn chops. Arrange yam slices, onion slices, and green pepper rings over pork chops. Sprinkle with salt and pepper, thyme, and marjoram. Top with tomatoes. Cover and cook over low heat for 1 hour, or until chops and yams are tender. *Serves 4.*

YAM 'N' SAUSAGE DINNER

6 medium yams, cooked,
  peeled and mashed
1 cup apple sauce
2 eggs, slightly beaten
1/2 tsp. salt

1/2 tsp. cinnamon
1/4 tsp. nutmeg
12 link sausages
2 & 1/2 cups sauerkraut

Combine yams, applesauce, eggs, salt, cinnamon, and nutmeg; mix well and turn into greased 1 and 1/2 quart casserole. Fry sausages until browned. Arrange sausages over yam mixture. Bake in moderate over (350°F) for 30 minutes. Heat kraut to serving temperature; drain and serve with yam casserole. *Serves 6.*

VEAL AND YAMS

2 lbs. veal cutlet, 1/2 inch thick
2 Tbsp. all-purpose flour
3/4 tsp. salt
3 Tbsp. shortening
3/4 cup finely chopped parsley

2 tsp. prepared mustard
1 chicken bouillon cube
1 & 1/2 cups boiling water
6 medium yams, peeled and
1 cup sour cream
1 tsp. paprika

Pound veal with wooden mallet or edge of saucer until it is about 1/4 inch thick. Cut into 6 pieces. Combine flour and salt; dredge veal in flour mixture. Melt fat over medium heat; add veal and brown well on both sides. Add onion and cook until tender. Add parsley, paprika, and mustard. Dissolve bouillon cube in water; add bouillon to meat mixture. Cover and cook over low heat for 25 minutes. Add yams. Cover and cook for additional 20 minutes, or until veal and yams are tender. Remove veal and yams from skillet. Add sour cream to liquid in skillet; mix well and heat to serving temperature. Pour sour cream sauce over veal and yams to serve. *Serves 6.*

YAM BUTTERSCOTCH COOKIES

1/2 cup butter or margarine
2/3 cup brown sugar, firmly
packed
1 & 1/4 cups mashed cooked yams
2 & 1/2 tsp. baking powder
1 tsp. vanilla

2 cups sifted all-purpose
flour
1 tsp. cinnamon
1 tsp. salt
1 egg, beaten
walnut halves

Cream butter or margarine; gradually add sugar and beat until light and fluffy. Add yams, egg, and vanilla and beat until well mixed.

Sift flour, cinnamon, salt, and baking powder together. Add to yam mixture and mix until all ingredients are blended. Shape dough into roll about 2 inches in diameter. Wrap in wax paper and chill until firm enough to slice. Slice 1/8 inch thick and place on greased baking sheets. Top with walnut halves. Bake in hot oven (425°F) for 10 to 12 minutes, or until done. *Makes 6 dozen cookies.*

YAM SPICE CAKE

4 cups sifted cake flour
1 & 1/2 tsp. salt
4 tsp. baking powder
1/2 tsp. baking soda
2 tsp. cinnamon
2 tsp. nutmeg
1/4 tsp. cloves

1 cup shortening
1 & 1/2 cups sugar
4 eggs
2 & 1/2 cups mashed, cooked
yams
1 cup milk

Sift flour, salt, baking powder, baking soda, and spices together. Cream shortening. Gradually add sugar and beat until light and fluffy. Add eggs, one at a time, beating well after each addition. Add yams and mix thoroughly. Add sifted ingredients alternately with milk to a creamed mixture. Mix well after each addition. Turn into two greased 8-inch square pans. Bake in moderate oven

(350°F) 1 hour and 20 minutes, or until done. Cool 5 minutes in pans. Turn out on cooling racks and cool thoroughly. Cover with your favorite simple frosting mix. *Makes two 8-inch squares layers.*

LOUISIANA YAM PIE

2 cups mashed cooked yams
1 cup firmly-packed brown
   sugar
1 cup light cream
3 eggs
1/2 tsp. salt
1 tsp. cinnamon

1 tsp. ground nutmeg
1/2 tsp. ground ginger
10-inch unbaked pastry shell
2 cups dairy sour cream
1/4 cup sifted confectioners
1/2 tsp. vanilla

In large mixing bowl, combine yams, brown sugar, cream, milk, eggs, salt, cinnamon, nutmeg, and ginger. Pour into pastry shell. Bake in 350°F (moderate) oven for 1 hour or until knife inserted in center comes out clean. Cool. Mix together sour cream, confectioners sugar and vanilla. Serve with yam pie.

LOUISIANA YAM CAJUN CANDY

2 cups sugar
1 & 1/2 cups packed, light or
   dark brown sugar
1/2 tsp. salt
1 & 1/3 cups milk

1/4 cup light corn syrup
1/4 cup butter or margarine
3/4 cup pecan halves
1 & 1/2 tsp. vanilla extract
1 cup mashed yams (about 2
   medium yams, cooked,
   peeled and mashed)

In heavy, 4-quart saucepan or Dutch oven, combine sugar, salt, milk, yams and corn syrup, stir until well combined. Cook over medium heat, stirring constantly, until all sugar is dissolved and mixture begins to boil. Reduce heat to low and cook, stirring occasionally, until mixture reaches 224°F on candy thermometer or forms soft ball when a small spoonful is dropped in cold water.

Remove pan from heat; add butter but do not stir. Cool mixture to 110°F on candy thermometer. Meanwhile, reserve 1/4 cup pecan halves; chop remaining pecans and set aside. Grease a 9 x 9 inch pan. Add vanilla to cooled mixture. Beat until candy seems to stiffen and loses its gloss. Stir in chopped nuts and spread candy in greased pan; top with reserved pecan halves. When cooled, cut into squares. Store in tightly covered container in refrigerator up to one week. *Makes about 2 lbs.* – DO NOT DOUBLE RECIPE.

CURRIED ROASTED YAMS
Contributed by Elaine Murphy

2 peeled yams, cut into
* 1 & 1/2 to 2-inch pieces*
Salt

2 Tbsp. curry powder
1/4 cup Canola or peanut oil

Preheat oven to 475 degrees. Put all ingredients except salt in a bowl and toss until yam pieces are coated with the curry and oil. *Note: Some brands of curry powder include salt, which is not recommended.* These should not be salted until they come out of the oven, and may not need to be salted at all. Spread the pieces on a baking sheet with a 1/2" edge, and roast for 20 to 25 minutes. These yams have a heavenly scent, flavor, and color. Even people who don't like yams say they like these.

Note about buying yams: Usually you will see two kinds of sweet potatoes or yams in the grocery store – one with a light brown skin and one with a purplish, darker skin. For this recipe, use the darker ones, which are generally sweeter and moister. Be sure to coat them with the oil and curry if they are not going to be cooked immediately, otherwise they will turn dark from exposure to air.

COCONUT YAM SOUP
Contributed by
Simla Somturk Wickless

This recipe is simple, soothing, warming, and perfect for winter. The healthy fats help lift your mood and support your stress hormones, the intense vitamin A from the yams help strengthen your immune system plus your eyes, for those quiet days spent reading indoors. Three ingredients. Make it tonight!

2 large or 4 small yams,
  peeled & cut in chunks
  (you can also use sweet
  potatoes)
Sea salt and black pepper
  to taste

1 can coconut milk
  (regular, not light)
2 cups chicken or
  vegetable stock, or filtered
  water, more for
  consistency, if desired

Place chunked yams into pot with can of coconut milk and water or stock. Let simmer until the yams are soft and can easily be pierced by a fork. The smaller you cut the pieces of yam, the quicker they will cook. Process yams and coconut milk in blender or food processor to desired consistency, or use your hand blender to do so. *Makes about 4 to 6 servings. You can always freeze extras for another day.*

Variations:
- Toast pumpkin seeds, sunflower seeds, or sliced almonds for garnish.
- Sweeten further using a few dashes of cinnamon, nutmeg, and coriander.
- Squeeze juice from 1 lime and add hot pepper or favorite hot spicy sauce for a kick.

APPLES

"An apple a day keeps the doctor away." Why?
Because of their many vitamins and minerals,
plus the wonderful soluble fiber called pectin,
which helps clean the blood of cholesterol.

Since Eve made her initial selection in the garden...there have been more than 7,000 named apple varieties recorded. Now, 10 or 12 varieties account for an annual average U.S. production of over 6 billion pounds. Because of the number of varieties and the influence of changing weather conditions, it is best for the consumer to become familiar with those particularly suiting his needs and available in his area.

They say an apple a day keeps the doctor away. They certainly provide good quantities of vitamins A and C and are rich in pectin and fruit acids, as well as minerals. Raw apples help in combating intestinal disorders since they have properties which aid the digestive juices. Apples are called nature's toothbrush since no other food has its combination of crisp, crunchy texture and bright, mouth-stimulating flavor, which enables it to perform this service for dental health. Maybe we should say, "An apple a day keeps the dentist away."

You'll find green apples are good for baking in pies and cakes since they are generally a bit more tart. Delicious apples are probably the most popular for eating out of hand. In my book, the Gravenstein is the finest eating apple grown, and I would like to see its popularity increase.

At any rate, we have some wonderful recipes to suit every taste.

POACHED GOLDEN APPLES

6 apples
1 cup sugar
1 cup water

1/2 tsp. vanilla
1/2 tsp. salt

Pare, core, and cut apples in half lengthwise or into quarters or slices. Boil sugar and water together for 5 minutes. Add vanilla and salt. Poach apples gently in syrup, covered, turning occasionally until apples are cooked. Makes about 6 cups of slices. Serves as meat garnish, dessert, or breakfast fruit.

APPLE-BANANA WALDORF SALAD

1 3-oz. pkg. orange-flavored
  gelatin
1 & 1/2 cups boiling water
1 Golden Delicious apple
1/2 cup mayonnaise
1 small banana

1-2 apples, pared, cored and
  diced to measure 1 cup
1 tablespoon lemon juice
1/4 cup celery, diced
1/4 cup walnuts, chopped

Dissolve gelatin in water; chill until syrupy. Spoon a 1/2-inch layer into bottom of a 6-cup mold.

Core, but do not pare, one apple. Cut in thin wedges; arrange wedges in gelatin in mold; chill until almost set.

Blend mayonnaise a little at a time with remaining gelatin; beat with rotary beater until foamy. Chill until it begins to set around edges. Fold apples, lemon juice, celery, and nuts into gelatin. Cut banana in half lengthwise, cut into chunks, and slice into gelatin. Spoon over first layer of gelatin. Chill until firm; unmold onto a serving dish. Garnish with lettuce and additional apple crescents (unpared), if you wish.

RACK OF LAMB AUX POMMES

Rack of lamb, French cut
4 medium apples
1 cup water
1 cup sugar
1/4 tsp. mint flavoring

1/2 cup light corn syrup
2 tsp. lemon juice
6 to 8 drops green food
coloring

Allow at least 2 ribs per serving when purchasing rack of lamb. Season lamb to taste with salt and pepper. Roast, rib-side down, in a shallow roasting pan, at 300°F for about 30 minutes per pound.

One-half hour before lamb is done, wash, peel and core apples. Cut into 3/8-inch thick rings. Blend remaining ingredients in a 10-inch skillet; simmer for 5 minutes. Slide apple rings into skillet; simmer until apples are just tender, turning once.

Lift rack of lamb to serving platter, placing frills on rib ends. With a flat spatula, gently place apple rings around lamb. *Approximately 5 to 6 servings.*

GOLDEN APPLE RINGS

3 medium-sized apples
1/4 cup butter (or margarine)
1/4 cup brown sugar, firmly
* packed*

1 tsp. cinnamon
1/8 tsp. cloves
1/8 tsp. ginger
1/4 tsp. salt

Core and cut apples in 1/2-inch crosswise slices. Melt butter in a skillet. Stir in brown sugar, spices, and salt. Sauté apple rings in butter mixture over low heat, turning occasionally until tender. Serve with scrambled eggs and sausage or bacon. *Makes approximately 12 apple rings.*

HERB-BAKED APPLES WITH
CRISP-BAKED CHICKEN

3/4 cup orange juice	*1 tsp. lemon juice*
2 Tbsp. brown sugar (packed)	*1/4 tsp. marjoram, crumbled*
1 small bay leaf	*6 medium-sized apples*

Combine orange juice, sugar, bay leaf, lemon juice, and marjoram in a small saucepan.

Cut tops from apples, and core, if desired, using small end of a melon ball cutter or apple corer. Arrange in baking dish.

Heat first mixture to boiling, and pour over apples. Cover, using foil if dish does not have a lid. Bake in moderate oven (350°F) for about 35 minutes, basting several times. Uncover, baste again and continue to bake for 10 minutes longer, or until apples are tender. Serve warm or cold. *Makes 6 servings.*

1/2 cup wheat germ	*3/4 cup buttermilk*
1/2 cup cornflake crumbs	*2 & 1/2 to 3 lbs. frying*
2 tsp. onion salt	*chicken pieces*
1/4 tsp. dill weed	*3 Tbsp. melted butter or*
1/4 tsp. pepper	*margarine*

Combine wheat germ, cornflake crumbs, onion salt, dill weed, and pepper on a sheet of waxed paper; mix well. Turn buttermilk into a shallow dish. Dip chicken pieces first in buttermilk, then in crumb mixture, coating on all sides. Arrange in a single layer in a flat baking pan. Drizzle melted butter over chicken pieces. Bake in a moderate oven (350°F) for about 45 minutes, until chicken is tender. *Makes 6 servings.*

GOLDEN-HAM SANDWICH

4 slices buttered toast
4 slices cooked ham
1/2 cup mayonnaise
1/2 cup chopped celery
1 tsp. chopped parsley

1/2 tsp. curry powder
1/4 tsp. salt
2 apples
1/2 cup grated Cheddar
*   cheese*

Line ovenproof dish or cookie sheet with toast and arrange ham slices on toast. Combine mayonnaise, celery, parsley, and spices. Spread over ham. Wash, core, and pare apples; cut into very thin slices. Arrange apple slices on top of mayonnaise mixture and sprinkle with the grated cheese. Broil just until cheese melts. Serve hot. *Makes 2 luncheon-size, open-faced sandwiches.*

McINTOSH SANDWICH

12 slices raisin bread
1/2 cup mayonnaise
prepared mustard
6 thin slices boiled ham

1 red apple, unpeeled
6 slices American cheese
butter, softened (optional)

Spread raisin bread with mayonnaise and a little mustard. Cover half the slices with ham. Core apple, slice 6 thin rings and place on ham. Place cheese slice on apple. Cover with remaining bread. Brush with butter, if desired. Broil (or grill) sandwiches until golden. Cut in half and serve at once. *Makes 6 servings.*

APPLE RICE CREAM

1 & 3/4 cups milk
1/3 cup raw regular rice
1/4 tsp. salt
1 egg beaten
3/4 cup sugar

1 tsp. vanilla
1/4 tsp. mace
1/2 cup whipping cream
2 medium-sized apples

Combine milk, rice, and salt in top of double boiler. Bring to boiling over direct heat, stirring often. Set over boiling water and cover. Simmer for 45 minutes, stirring once or twice. Stir a little of the hot mixture into the beaten egg, then stir into the remaining rice. Add sugar and cook, stirring constantly for 2 to 3 minutes until egg thickens. Remove from heat; stir in vanilla and mace. Cool. Beat cream to soft peaks. Fold into cooled rice. Core apples, and cut in matchstick pieces. Fold into pudding. *Serves 6.*

CINNAMON APPLES

1 cup red cinnamon candies
2 cups water
1 stick cinnamon

3 whole cloves
2 Tbsp. lemon juice
6 to 8 apples

Combine cinnamon candies, water, and spices in deep kettle. Simmer, stirring often, until candies dissolve. Add lemon juice. Pare and core apples. Place half the apples in hot syrup, spoon syrup over them, and simmer covered for 5 minutes. Turn apples carefully, cover, and cook for 5 minutes longer. Uncover and cook until tender, about 3 to 4 minutes, basting frequently. Remove apples with a slotted spoon. Cook remaining apples. When all apples are cooked, boil syrup down until reduced to 3/4 cup. Spoon over apples. Service warm or chill. *Makes 6 to 8 servings.*

SPICY APPLE MUFFINS

1 medium-sized apple
1 & 3/4 cups sifted all-purpose
  flour
1/2 cup sugar
3 tsp. baking powder

1 tsp. salt
1/2 tsp. apple pie spice
1 egg, beaten lightly
1/2 cup milk
1/3 cup melted shortening

Pare and core apple; chop finely to measure 1 cup. Resift flour with sugar, baking powder, salt, and spice. Combine egg, milk and shortening. Stir into dry mixture, mixing just until all of flour is moistened. Fold in apples. Spoon into greased muffin pans, filling about 2/3 full. Bake in moderately hot oven (375°F) for 25 to 30 minutes, until nicely browned. Let stand for 5 minutes, then turn out. Serve warm. *Makes 12 (2 and 1/2 inch muffins).*

Variation: For a spicy-sugar topping, blend 3 tablespoons sugar with 1/4 teaspoon apple pie spice. Melt 2 tablespoons butter or margarine. Dip warm muffin tops first in butter, then in spicy-sugar mixture.

JOE'S APPLESAUCE RECIPE

Peel and slice apples and put them in a pot with a very small amount of water. Cover and cook over a low fire until apples soften enough to mash easily. Add a little sugar to taste if you think the apples require it, and cook a little longer (very little), and then mash and cool. Dust with cinnamon or nutmeg, if you like.

TINY RAISIN-APPLE LOAVES

1/3 cup butter or margarine, softened	*2 cups sifted flour*
	1 tsp. baking powder
2/3 cup sugar	*1 tsp. salt*
2 eggs	*1/2 tsp. baking soda*
3 Tbsp. milk	*1 cup grated raw apple*
1 tsp. lemon juice	*1 cup chopped raisins*

Cream together butter, sugar, and eggs until light and fluffy. Beat in milk and lemon juice. Sift together dry ingredients; stir into creamed mixture just until moistened. Stir in apple and raisins. Spoon batter into 3 greased 6x3 inch loaf pans. Bake at 350°F for 40 to 45 minutes or until toothpick inserted in center comes out clean. *Makes 3 loaves.*

NOTE: Batter may be baked in 1 (9x5x3 inch) loaf pan. Increase baking time to 1 hour.

MOLASSES APPLE PAN DOWDY

5 or 6 tart apples
1/2 cup water
1 & 1/2 cup molasses
3/4 cup sugar
3 Tbsp. butter
3 Tbsp. corn starch
2/3 cup milk

1/2 tsp. mace
1/2 tsp. salt
2 cups sifted all-purpose
  flour
4 tsp. baking powder
1/2 tsp. salt
1/3 cup shortening

Pare, core, and slice the apples in wedged into a buttered baking dish 8x13x2 inches. Add the water and cook in the oven for a few minutes until the apples are soft.

In a saucepan, mix the molasses, sugar, butter, corn starch, mace, and salt. Boil together until thoroughly blended. Pour this mixture over the apples.

Mix and sift the flour, baking powder, and salt into a bowl; cut in the fat as for biscuits. Add the milk and mix. Roll this dough to 1/4 inch thickness and cut with 2 and 1/2 inch biscuit cutter. Place the biscuits over the molasses mixture. Bake in a hot oven (425°F) until the biscuits are brown. The biscuits must be thin to bake quickly so as not to burn the molasses. Serve a biscuit with the apple and molasses mixture over it.

ROYAL BREAD PUDDING

3 cups Joe's applesauce
1 tsp. lemon juice
5 Tbsp. butter or margarine

1/4 cup marmalade
1 & 1/2 tsp. cinnamon
2 Tbsp. sugar

Combine applesauce and lemon juice; place half the mixture in small casserole.

Spread bread slices with butter or margarine and marmalade. Cut 4 slices into cubes, cut remaining slice in 4 triangles. Place cubes on applesauce in casserole, combine cinnamon and sugar, sprinkling

207

1/2 over cubes, top with remaining applesauce. Arrange triangles in a pattern to top casserole, sprinkle with remaining cinnamon and sugar. Bake in moderate oven (350°F) for 1/2 hour. *Serves 6.*

APPLESAUCE CAKE

3 cups Joe's applesauce
2 cups sugar
1 & 1/4 cups butter or other
* shortening*
2 eggs
3 cups flour (cake flour) sifted
1/2 tsp. salt

2 tsp. soda
1 tsp. cinnamon
1 tsp. nutmeg
1 tsp. cloves
1 tsp. cocoa
2 cups raisins (golden)
1 cup chopped walnuts

Cream butter and sugar until light and fluffy; add eggs, and continue beating. Sift flour, salt, soda, cocoa, and spices together 3 times. Add dry ingredients alternately with applesauce, blending in thoroughly. Fold in nuts and raisins thoroughly. Pour into a greased and floured 9x13 inch baking pan. Bake for 45 minutes to 1 hour in a 350°F oven. Delicious served with whipped cream, or you may serve it just plain or with your favorite icing.

APPLE PIE

1 recipe plain pastry
6 to 8 tart apples
3/4 cup granulated or brown
* sugar*

1/2 tsp. salt
1/4 tsp. cinnamon or nutmeg,
* or both*
2 Tbsp. butter

Line a pie plate (9 inch) with pastry. Fill with pared and thinly sliced apples. Dot with butter. Moisten edge of crust, cover with top crust and press edges together. Brush crust with milk or cream and bake in hot oven (450°F) for 10 minutes, then reduce heat to moderate (350°F) and bake for 40 to 50 minutes longer.

NEW TWIST ON
WALDORF SALAD
Contributed by
Alexandra I. Lopez

1/4 cup Greek style yogurt
1 tsp. light agave nectar
or 1/2 tsp. honey

1 Tbsp. fresh lemon juice
2 Tbsp. olive oil
Salt and fresh pepper to taste

2 pink apples, cored, unpeeled
and cut into small dice
1 medium English cucumber,
peeled, seeded, and cut into
small dice
1 Tbsp. fresh chives,
finely minced

1 small celery root, peeled
and cut into small dice
4 radishes, thinly sliced
1/4 cup toasted pepitas
(pumpkin seeds)

In a small bowl, whisk together yogurt, lemon juice, and agave nectar with salt and pepper. Drizzle in the olive oil and continue to whisk until incorporated. Set aside.

In a large bowl, combine apples, celery root, cucumber, radish, pepitas, and chives. Stir in the dressing and combine well to coat. Refrigerate for 20 minutes before serving. Garnish with more pepitas and chives. *Serves 4.*

BROCCOLI

Broccoli has it all, vitamins A, C, and E, the key anti-oxidants, plus it is a member of the cabbage family, making it a great infection and cancer fighter.

Broccoli is one vegetable that has been increasing in sales by leaps and bounds, and with good reason. Fresh broccoli is very easy to prepare and it has a very pleasant, mild flavor. Broccoli is actually a storehouse of nutrition with vitamins A and C, minerals, and protein. It is very low in sodium, which makes it great for people who have to watch their salt intake.

Be sure it's fresh. Broccoli should have a nice green color. The buds on the head of the broccoli must be nice and compact. Another thing to look for is a large number of small stems or shoots, instead of just a few heavy stalks. When you buy broccoli with young and tender shoots, they will be full of flavor and both the heads and the stems will cook in the same amount of time. Should the stalks seem too heavy, slice them lengthwise part way so the heads and stalks will cook evenly.

Raw broccoli will keep in a plastic bag in your refrigerator for three or four days. When you cook it, cook enough for two meals. You can serve it hot as a vegetable with dinner, and the next day, you can serve it cold in a salad. It's great with just a little olive oil, a little minced garlic, and some lemon juice.

One thing is very important: when you cook broccoli (or most vegetables, in fact), don't overcook them. We have a special word for it in Italian, *al dente*. It means to cook just until tender so that it has firmness and a little resistance. When you overcook, not only do you lose much of the natural flavor of fresh vegetables, but you also lose a lot of the nutrition. Aside from that, it is not very appetizing—because it is overcooked, it becomes dull, discolored, and soggy. Cook in a small amount of water or steam for ten to

210

twelve minutes, *al dente* and it will be nice and firm, and will retain that beautiful green color. It will be delicious the next day, too.

Everybody has a weakness they say, and I guess garlic is mine. Garlic certainly does something for broccoli; it brings out the flavor and it tastes like a million dollars. My wife either places the garlic in with the broccoli while it's cooking or sometimes she minces the garlic very fine and stirs it into the broccoli after it's cooked. Then, she puts the lid back on and lets it stand for five or ten minutes so the flavor of the garlic permeates completely through the broccoli. It's delicious!

BOILED BROCCOLI

8 oz. fresh broccoli for each portion
(5 cups) of water

2 to 3 tsp. salt to each quart water

Rinse the fresh broccoli and put into boiling salted water. Cook until it is just tender, for 15 to 20 minutes. Serve with butter, Hollandaise, mushroom, or Neapolitan tomato sauce.

BROCCOLI SOUR

1 bunch fresh broccoli
1/4 cup olive oil
1/2 tsp. salt

1/2 tsp. pepper
juice of 1 lemon

Wash and clean broccoli thoroughly. Cook in 2 quarts boiling water for 15 minutes, taking care not to overcook, and drain. Place broccoli on serving dish, sprinkle with oil, salt, pepper, and lemon juice, and serve. *Serves 4.*

CREAMED BROCCOLI

1 bunch fresh broccoli	3/4 cup water
1/2 tsp. salt	2 Tbsp. sherry or sauterne
4 Tbsp. flour	2 Tbsp. lemon juice
4 Tbsp. butter	1/4 cup Parmesan cheese
1 cup cream	1/4 cup slivered almonds,
1 bouillon cube	(optional)

Cook broccoli until just tender, drain. Put in shallow pan. Prepare white sauce with balance of ingredients. Pour sauce over broccoli. Sprinkle with cheese and almonds. Bake for 20 minutes at 350°F.

BROCCOLI FLOWERETS

1 onion	3 lbs. fresh broccoli
1 clove garlic	1 tsp. salt
2 Tbsp. oil or vegetable	2 Tbsp. lemon juice
shortening	1 cup water

Use tender parts of stems with the flower or head. Cut stems into 1/4 inch rounds, and separate the heads into flowerets. Brown diced onion and garlic in shortening. Remove the garlic. Add broccoli, salt, lemon juice, and water. Cover and simmer for 15 to 20 minutes. *Serves 6 to 8.*

BROCCOLI ROMAN STYLE

1 small bunch fresh broccoli	1/2 tsp. salt
3 Tbsp. olive oil	1/2 tsp. pepper
2 cloves garlic, sliced	1 & 1/2 cups dry red wine

Trim and cut broccoli into small flowerets, wash well and drain. Place olive oil and garlic in large skillet and brown garlic. Add broccoli, salt, and pepper and cook for 5 minutes. Add wine, cover skillet and cook over very low flame for 20 minutes, or until broccoli is tender, stirring gently. *Serves 4.*

WALNUT BROCCOLI

2 lbs. fresh broccoli
1/2 cup butter
4 Tbsp. flour
1 & 1/2 tsp. powdered chicken
stock base
2/3 cup chopped walnuts

2 cups milk
2/3 cups water
6 Tbsp. butter
2 cups seasoned bread
stuffing

Cook broccoli until just tender. Drain, chop, and put in a flat, greased 2-quart casserole dish.

Melt the 1/2 cup butter, blend in flour and cook gently over low heat. Add chicken stock base. Gradually add 2 cups milk. Cook until thickened and smooth, then pour over broccoli.

Heat water and 6 tablespoons butter until melted. Pour over stuffing and toss. Add nuts. Top the broccoli and sauce with the stuffing. Bake at 350°F for 30 minutes. *Serves 12.*

SAUTÉED BROCCOLI WITH GARLIC
Contributed by Deborah Dal Fovo

2 bunches fresh broccoli,
about 2 pounds
1/4 cup extra virgin olive oil,
plus more if needed
Kosher salt to taste

2 garlic cloves, peeled and
and very thinly sliced
Dash of hot red pepper
flakes, optional
Freshly ground black pepper
to taste

Rinse the broccoli under cold, running water and drain. Lay each broccoli bunch horizontally on a cutting board and cut the entire head of florets from the stalk with a large knife. Separate the florets and set aside. Cut 1 inch off the bottom of each broccoli stalk and discard. Stand the stalks upside down on a cutting board with the bottom end facing up. Using a sharp knife cut away the tough, dark green exterior peel of each stalk and to reveal the tender white core using the white center visible on the bottom of the stalk as a guide. Discard the green peel, chop the white core into bite-size pieces and set aside with the florets.

Bring one inch of water to a boil over medium-high heat in a skillet or sauté pan large enough to comfortably hold all the broccoli pieces. Season the water lightly with salt and return to a boil. Add the broccoli pieces and cover the pan. Steam over medium heat until tender, about 6 to 7 minutes. Drain the broccoli then refresh in an ice water bath for a couple of minutes if a bright green color if desired. Otherwise, drain and set aside.

Pour off any cooking water remaining in the skillet and dry with kitchen paper. Add the olive oil, garlic and hot pepper flakes to the skillet and place over medium heat. When the oil is hot and the garlic begins to sizzle, add the steamed broccoli and season lightly with salt and pepper.

Sauté for 4 to 5 minutes, tossing or stirring constantly, until the broccoli has softened slightly and is very savory. Serve hot or warm. *Serves 6.*

BRUSSELS SPROUTS

Brussels sprouts are another member of the cabbage family with its sulfur compound strength. It has a strong presence of vitamin C, potassium, iron, and calcium, making it a strong cancer fighter.

Brussels sprouts should be small and compact with fresh, green leaves. The best way to cook them is to either steam or boil them in a small amount of water for about six to eight minutes. Cook them al dente. That means to cook them just until tender, not overcooked. When you bite into the sprout, it should be nice and tender, but firm.

When they are cooked al dente, there is not too much of an aroma. Some people object to the smell when cooking Brussels sprouts or any member of the cabbage family. I've been told that if you put a piece of celery or some celery leaves in with them while they are cooking, there will be no odor, and it doesn't change the taste at all. Be sure to try fresh Brussels sprouts cooked al dente in Neapolitan tomato sauce.

Here is a tasty and very attractive salad:

BRUSSELS SPROUTS AND CHERRY TOMATOES

1/2 lb. fresh Brussels sprouts, cooked
4 to 6 large lettuce leaves

1/2 pt. fresh cherry tomatoes
1/2 cup oil and vinegar dressing

Pour dressing over hot Brussels sprouts, turning each to coat thoroughly. Cover and refrigerate for at least 3 hours. Cut tomatoes in half and toss with Brussels sprouts. Serve in individual salad bowls lined with lettuce leaves. *Serves 4 to 6.*

BRUSSELS SPROUTS MILANESE

2 lbs. fresh Brussels sprouts,
cooked
3/4 cup (3 ozs.) each: grated
Swiss and Parmesan cheese,
combined

2 Tbsp. butter, melted
1/4 tsp. salt
dash pepper
1 tsp. lemon juice

Heap sprouts into buttered 1-quart baking dish; sprinkle with cheese. Blend butter with salt, pepper, and lemon juice and pour over sprouts. Bake in 350°F (moderate) oven for 20 minutes until lightly browned. *Makes 6 to 8 servings.*

BRUSSELS SPROUTS WITH HERB BUTTER

1 cup butter
1/4 cup chopped parsley
1/2 tsp. oregano leaves
1/8 tsp. pepper

1/4 tsp. each: tarragon
leaves, ground thyme
2 lbs. fresh Brussels sprouts
cooked

Cream butter; mix in seasonings. Chill for 1 hour or longer. Let herb butter soften before using. Serve over the Brussels sprouts. *Makes 6 to 8 servings.*

BRUSSELS SPROUTS SIMMERED IN CREAM

2 lbs. fresh Brussels sprouts,
partially cooked and
coarsely chopped
3 Tbsp. butter
1/8 tsp. white pepper

3/4 cup heavy cream
2 Tbsp. butter
1 tsp. lemon juice
2 Tbsp. minced parsley

Sauté chopped Brussels sprouts in butter for 3 to 5 minutes; season with salt and pepper. Stir in cream; cover and simmer for 8 to 10 minutes until cream is almost completely absorbed. Toss with 2 tablespoons butter and lemon juice. Turn into heated serving dish; sprinkle with parsley. *Approx. 6 to 8 servings.*

BRUSSELS SPROUTS
WITH WINE AND RAISINS

2/3 cup golden seedless raisins
2/3 cup dry white wine
2 lbs. fresh Brussels sprouts,
   partially cooked

dash each: pepper, nutmeg
2 Tbsp. butter

Combine raisins and wine. Let stand 1 hour; then combine Brussels sprouts, seasoning with butter and finish cooking over very low heat for 5 minutes. *Serves 6 to 8.*

SPRING SPROUTS AND ONIONS

1 & 1/2 lbs. fresh Brussels
   sprouts, cooked
1/2 cup butter (1 stick)
1 tsp. chervil

2 lbs. fresh white onions,
   cooked and drained
1/2 cup chopped parsley

Melt butter in large skillet. Mix in remaining ingredients and heat to serving temperature. *Serves 6 to 8.*

BRUSSELS SPROUTS SOUFFLE

1/2 lb. fresh Brussels sprouts,
   cooked and chopped fine
3 Tbsp. butter
1/4 cup flour
1/2 tsp. salt

1 cup milk
4 eggs separated
1 cup grated cheddar cheese
   (about 4 ozs.)

Melt butter in large saucepan. Blend in flour and salt. Gradually add milk and stir over low heat until mixture boils, about 1 minute. Beat egg yolks until thick and lemon-colored and stir into sauce. Mix in cheese and sprouts. Beat egg whites until stiff, but not dry, and fold in. Turn into ungreased 2-quart soufflé dish or casserole. Bake in 300°F (slow) oven for 1 and 1/2 hours. *Serves 6 to 8.*

SIMPLE BRUSSELS SPROUTS WITH MUSHROOMS
Contributed by Elaine Murphy

15 to 20 Brussels sprouts
15 to 20 Crimini mushrooms
1/4 cup olive oil

3 to 4 cloves garlic
1/2 stick butter
Salt and pepper to taste

Either buy the sprouts on the stalk, if available, or choose small, tight sprouts with light-colored stem ends (if the stem ends are dark brown, the sprouts will be bitter). Trim sprouts of any loose leaves and mushroom stems, and slice each in half. Preheat the pan with butter and olive oil, and add sprouts and mushrooms until slightly browned on one side. Crush or mince garlic, add salt, stir into vegetables, and immediately lower heat to lowest setting. Cover pan and let the natural juices of the mushrooms and sprouts slowly steam them (about 15 to 20 minutes). Don't overcook or the sprouts won't be green; but you don't want them to be crunchy. Add freshly ground pepper before serving. *This can be served as an entrée for 4 or a side dish for 6 or 8 people.*

This can be made without the mushrooms, and still be delicious and attractive. It looks beautiful and goes well with roasted or baked yams, and is excellent with pork.

SHREDDED BRUSSELS SPROUTS WITH BACON AND PARMESAN
Contributed by Patti McKenna

1 lb. fresh Brussels sprouts
1/2 cup chicken broth
3 to 4 strips bacon, cooked
1 to 2 Tbsp. olive oil

1/2 white onion, chopped
1/4 tsp. salt
1 tsp. fresh thyme, chopped
Grated Parmesan cheese

Fry bacon strips until crisp; drain, crumble and set aside. Trim, halve, and very thinly slice Brussels sprouts. In a frying pan, sauté chopped onion in just enough olive oil to prevent sticking. When tender, add salt and thyme. Simmer for two minutes, then add chicken broth and Brussels sprouts. Stirring frequently, cook over medium heat for five to six minutes, or until Brussels sprouts are tender, but not soggy. Top with crumbled bacon, followed by grated Parmesan cheese.

MASALA MIX
BRUSSELS SPROUTS
Contributed by Connie Umbenhower

1 pound Brussels sprouts
1 small red onion, chopped
1/2 tsp. mustard seeds
1/4 tsp. cumin powder
1/2 red bell pepper, chopped
2 Tbsp. tomato paste
Salt to taste (celery salt is
* also a delicious option)*

2 Tbsp. canola oil
2 cloves garlic, minced
1/2 tsp. coriander powder
1/4 tsp. turmeric
1/4 tsp. cayenne pepper
1 tsp. tamarind paste (can
* substitute with 2 Tbsp.*
* white wine vinegar)*

Wash Brussels sprouts thoroughly, cut off the ends, remove any leaves that are discolored and cut them into quarters.

Heat oil. Add mustard seeds and let them pop, then add onions and garlic and fry over medium heat until golden brown. Add coriander, cumin, and turmeric, mix thoroughly with the onions and let spice mixture cook for a couple of minutes. Add chopped bell peppers, continuing to stir until ingredients are completely saturated into each other. Stir in the cayenne pepper, tomato paste and tamarind paste. Mix well, then add in the Brussels sprouts and salt to taste.

Cook for another 10 to 12 minutes, stirring occasionally until the Brussels sprouts are cooked, but not soggy (depending on the size of the Brussels sprouts, you might want to sprinkle with water while cooking if mixture gets too dry). Serve with jasmine rice.

BRUSSELS SPROUTS
WITH CRISPY PANCETTA
Contributed by Kristin Hoppe

1 lb. Brussels sprouts,
washed & cut in quarters,
lengthwise
2 Tbsp. rice wine vinegar
Salt and pepper

1/4 lb. Pancetta – cubed
2 Tbsp. olive oil
2 garlic cloves
1/3 cup chicken broth

In a large skillet over high medium-high heat, add Pancetta and cook until brown. Remove pancetta from pan and drain on paper towel. In the same skillet over high heat, add olive oil. Once oil shimmers, add garlic cloves. Add Brussels sprouts and sauté for 30 seconds without tossing, in order to give it a light golden char. Add rice vinegar and chicken broth. Using a wooden spoon, scrape the browned bits from the bottom of the skillet. Reduce heat to low and place lid on skillet. Let Brussels sprouts cook for another 2 to 3 minutes or until tender. Remove from heat and throw in pancetta and toss. Add salt and fresh ground pepper to taste. *Servings: 4 as a side.*

PUMPKIN

Pumpkins are one of the winter squashes, giving us edible flesh and seeds. Its orange color shows the presence of the key anti-oxidant, vitamin A. They also provide us with a good amount of vitamin B and potassium.

It's getting close to Halloween, and all the kids look forward to that. It's a challenge for Mother and Dad to see what they can come up with insofar as frightening Jack O'Lantern faces are concerned. The important thing is to look for one with a nice shape so it will stand up nice and straight.

In spirit with the harvest season, when carving a pumpkin, I always reserve the seeds. Some people find it difficult to remove and clean the seeds of the pumpkin, but if you take out the entire cluster, put a colander under the faucet and run cold water through it, the seeds will fall right out into the colander. Dry them off on a towel and spread them out on a cookie sheet, sprinkle with salt, and bake them in the oven for about twenty minutes, and they're really good. You have to be careful that you don't burn them, though, because they can burn in a hurry. They are full of vitamins and protein, and they're really tasty.

Pumpkin is very good just sliced into sections, with a little butter, salt, and pepper and baked, just as you would serve squash.

To prepare pumpkin for use in breads, pies, and puddings, it is generally easier to boil it in sections; or, slice off the top, remove the seeds and invert it on a cookie sheet and bake until tender. It can then be easily removed and mashed or pureed in a blender.

PUMPKIN WITH SOUR CREAM

4 lbs. pumpkin, peeled and
diced (about 5 cups)
1/4 cup water
1 & 1/2 tsp. salt

1/4 cup brown sugar or
honey
1/4 cup butter
1 cup sour cream

Cook pumpkin in boiling salted water over low heat until tender. Drain pumpkin and mash, stir in sugar, butter, and sour cream. Serve at once. *Makes 6 servings.*

PUMPKIN BREAD

3 & 1/2 cups unsifted flour
2 & 1/2 cups sugar
2 tsp. baking soda
1 tsp. ground cinnamon
1 tsp. ground nutmeg

2 cups pureed cooked
pumpkin
1 cup corn oil
2/3 cup water

Grease and flour 2 (9 x 5 x 3 inch) loaf pans. In a large bowl, stir together flour, sugar, baking soda, salt, cinnamon, and nutmeg. Stir together pumpkin, corn oil, and water. Add eggs, one at a time, beating well after each addition. Make a well in center of flour mixture. Add pumpkin mixture and stir just until flour is moistened. Pour into prepared pans. Bake in 350°F oven for 1 hour or until cake tester inserted in center comes out clean. Remove from oven. Cool for 10 minutes before removing from pans. Cool on rack. When completely cool, wrap in plastic film or foil and store overnight. Serve with Golden Spread. *Makes 2 loaves.*

Golden Spread: Stir 1/2 cup margarine until smooth and fluffy. Gradually add 1/2 cup dark corn syrup, beating well. *Makes 1 cup.*

PUMPKIN PIE

*1 unbaked (9 inch) pastry
shell with high fluted edge
1/3 cup firmly packed brown
sugar
1 tsp. ground cinnamon
1/2 tsp. salt
1/2 tsp. ground ginger*

*1/8 tsp. ground clove
3 eggs
1/2 cup dark corn syrup
1 & 1/2 cups undiluted
evaporated milk
1 & 1/2 cups pureed cooked
pumpkin*

In a large bowl, stir together brown sugar, cinnamon, salt, ginger, and clove. Beat in eggs and corn syrup until thoroughly blended. Mix in evaporated milk and pumpkin. Pour into unbaked pastry shell, pouring in last portion after pie has been placed on rack. Bake in 425°F oven for 15 minutes. Reduce heat to 350°F and continue baking for 1 hour or until knife inserted halfway between center and edge comes out clean. *Makes 6 servings.*

STEAMED WALNUT-PUMPKIN PUDDING

*1/2 cup shortening
1 cup brown sugar
1/4 cup granulated sugar
1/2 tsp. each cinnamon,
nutmeg, ginger
2 eggs, well beaten
1 cup chopped walnuts
2 cups sifted flour*

*1 & 1/2 tsp. baking powder
1/4 tsp. baking soda
1 & 1/2 tsp. salt
1 cup mashed or pureed
pumpkin
1/2 cup sour cream
Brandy Whipped Cream
Sauce*

Cream shortening, brown and white sugar, and spices together until light and fluffy. Beat in eggs; stir in walnuts. Resift flour with baking powder, soda, and salt. Add to creamed mixture alternately with pumpkin and sour cream. Turn into a well-greased 1 and 1/2 to 2-quart mold. Cover tightly. Set mold in pan of hot water. Water should come halfway up sides of mold (replenish water, if necessary, during steaming). Cover pan and steam pudding for about 2 hours in continuously boiling water. Remove mold from water; let stand for 5 minutes before removing pudding. Serve hot with Brandy Whipped Cream Sauce. *Makes 8 servings.*

To make sauce, beat one egg until light and fluffy. Beat in 1/3 cup melted butter, 1 and 1/2 cups sifted powdered sugar, pinch of salt, and one tablespoon brandy flavoring. Cover and chill until ready to serve. Stir before spooning on pudding. *Makes 2 cups sauce.*

PUMPKIN COOKIES

1/2 cup shortening
1 cup sugar
2 eggs, well beaten
1 cup pureed pumpkin
1 tsp. soda

1 tsp. salt
1 tsp. baking powder
2 tsp. cinnamon
3 cups sifted flour
1 cup raisins

Sift dry ingredients. Cream sugar and shortening. Add eggs and pumpkin. Add dry ingredients. Mix well, stir in raisins. Bake for 10 minutes at 375°F.

PUMPKIN CAKE

3 cups unsifted cake flour
2 cups pureed cooked pumpkin
2 tsp. ground cinnamon
1 tsp. salt
2 cups sugar

1 cup corn oil
1 Tbsp. baking powder
1 cup chopped walnuts
4 eggs
1 recipe Glaze (next page)

Sift together flour, baking powder, cinnamon, and salt. In large mixing bowl with electric mixer at high speed, beat eggs until light and frothy. Gradually add sugar, beating until thick and ivory colored. Slowly pour in corn oil, beating constantly. With mixer at low speed, add dry ingredients alternately with pumpkin, beginning and ending with dry ingredients. Beat until smooth after each addition. Stir in nuts. Pour into ungreased 10x4 inch tube pan. Bake in 325°F oven for 60 to 70 minutes or until cake tester inserted in center comes out clean. Cool in pan 1/2 hour, remove and cool completely on wire rack. Brush with Glaze when cool. *Makes 1 (10 inch) tube cake.*

Glaze: In small saucepan, stir together 1/2 cup light corn syrup, 1/2 teaspoon grated lemon rind, and 1/2 teaspoon ground ginger. Bring to boil over medium heat. Remove from heat. *Makes 1/2 cup.*

ROASTED PUMPKIN DESSERT
Contributed by
Simla Somturk Wickless

This is a healthier variation of a favorite seasonal dessert from Turkey. Easy to make, with a beautiful presentation, it can replace traditional pumpkin pie as a more nutritious, lower glycemic dessert with heart-healthy fats from the nuts. It can also take the place of yams or sweet potatoes with marshmallows as a side dish. No refined anything here, and only 3 ingredients!

1 small pumpkin, about
12 – 16" in diameter

1/4 cup agave nectar
1/2 cup chopped walnuts

Preheat oven to 375 degrees. Wash the pumpkin. Prep your workspace – you may want to lay out some newspaper or towels under the pumpkin to make cleanup easier. Using a sturdy knife, cut the pumpkin in half. Use a large spoon to scrape out the seeds and stringy bits. Put seeds aside if you want to roast them for later. Cut pumpkin into 2" thick slices (like a melon slice). Cut these in half as well, across the middle, so that you have two triangular shapes (easier to cook and serve). Place in oven-safe baking dish. Drizzle all the pumpkin slices with the agave nectar. Beware: agave nectar is sweeter-tasting than sugar, so don't overdo it. Bake until fork pierces easily through the pumpkin, indicating it's cooked. Serve warm, topped with 2 tablespoons of crumbled nuts per slice of pumpkin. *Yield: Depends on the size of the pumpkin. Usually about 12 servings.*

Variations:

- When we were in Florida over Thanksgiving, I got a Kabocha squash (a Japanese pumpkin) for my mom to try right before we left. She couldn't reach me in time to ask what to do with it, so she treated it like a regular pumpkin and made this traditional Turkish dessert – brilliant, mom! I love creative and intuitive cooking.

- Try kabocha squash (Japanese pumpkin) instead of a regular pumpkin. With kabocha squash, you can eat the skin when cooked as well, for the added fiber.

- Save and clean off the seeds from the pumpkin and roast separately for a healthy snack.

- Use crumbled pecans, pistachios, or almonds for the nut topping instead.

- Great for breakfast: Add some toasted oats and enjoy with a glass of your favorite milk beverage or alternative.

SQUASH

There is winter squash, or hard squash, and summer squash,
such as zucchini. Summer squash contains a decent amount of
vitamins and minerals, but the hard squash with the orange flesh is
best because of the strength of the key anti-oxidant, vitamin A.

Instead of baking a potato, why not bake a squash? It is absolutely packed with vitamin A, so it's real good for you and provides a nice change of pace.

The banana squash is a huge squash. Some grow to as big as 100 pounds or more. They look like big torpedoes or zeppelins. You don't realize how big or what shape they really are because in stores you see them cut in pieces. But also try some of the immature squash that are produced all year long in the United States, such as the Italian squash, which is known as zucchini, yellow, acorn, and summer squash. You'll find they have a lot of flavor and nutrition.

BAKED SQUASH

3 lbs. squash　　　　　　　　*2 eggs*
1 green onion, chopped　　　 *1/4 cup butter*
*　(including top)*　　　　　　 *2 Tbsp. cream*
1 tsp. salt　　　　　　　　　 *buttered corn flakes*

Steam squash in small amount of water; drain and mash. Add salt, onion, butter, well-beaten eggs, and cream. Put in buttered casserole dish and spread with buttered corn flakes. Bake in slow oven for about 30 minutes. *Serves 4 to 6.*

CUP OF GOLD
ACORN SQUASH

3 acorn or table queen squash
6 Tbsp. brown sugar
3 Tbsp. butter or margarine

1 Tbsp. fresh grated orange peel
3 oranges, peeled, sectioned, seeded (1 & 1/2 cups)

Cut squash in half; scoop out seeds. Place cut-side down in shallow baking pan filled with 1/4 inch water. Bake at 357°F for 40 minutes. Turn squash; fill each center with 1 tablespoon brown sugar, 1/2 tablespoon butter, 1/2 teaspoon grated peel and 4 to 5 orange sections. Add more water to pan, if necessary. Continue baking until tender, about 20 to 25 minutes. Baste occasionally as butter melts and juice forms.

BAKED SQUASH
WITH FRESH PEACHES

2 small acorn squash or
  1 butternut or hubbard
  squash
2 fresh peaches, pureed
  (about 1 cup)

1 tsp. lemon juice
2 Tbsp. brown sugar
salt
pepper
butter

Wash, cut in half, and seed the squash. Puree the peaches by gutting them in blender (leave skin on, if desired). Mix puree and lemon juice. Place squash in a baking dish, pour pureed peaches over squash, then salt, pepper, and dot with butter. Cover and bake at 350°F for about an hour or until tender when pierced with a fork. *Serves 4.*

SPAGHETTI SQUASH

Here's something new under the sun. At first glance, it looks like a little golden watermelon from its outside appearance. It is called spaghetti squash, and I couldn't figure out what it had in common with spaghetti. You steam or boil it whole, and it becomes soft, like a yam. Cut it in half across the width and take a fork and loosen the fibers, which are wrapped circular on the inside and come out just like spaghetti. It's amazing. Be sure to let the kids watch because they will love to see it.

At first, I thought it would only be a passing fancy—that people would try it and then sales would drop off. But that isn't happening. People love it. As in any squash, you can flavor it with tomato sauce, pesto sauce, butter sauce, cheese sauce, or just plain butter or even honey, and it is absolutely delicious.

Trader Vic's is so impressed with this squash they have perfected recipes to use it as a vegetable, a salad, and even a pudding, and we are including them here for you to try.

1/2 spaghetti squash, cooked
1 & 1/2 cup sour cream
1 tsp. fresh, chopped ginger

salt and pepper to taste
1/2 cup grated Parmesan cheese

Loosen spaghetti squash and place in a heavy pan. Add sour cream and place over high heat. Mix well with a fork. Add chopped ginger. Appoint with salt and pepper. Place it in an au gratin dish. Sprinkle with grated Parmesan cheese and place under a broiler until golden brown. *Serves 4 to 6 people.*

SHRIMP AND SPAGHETTI SQUASH SALAD

1 & 1/2 spaghetti squash, cooked　　*2 tsp. apple cider vinegar*
1 cup shrimps, cooked　　　　　　　　*juice of 1 lemon*
1/2 cup chopped celery　　　　　　　　*salt and pepper to taste*
2 Tbsp. vegetable oil

Loosen spaghetti squash and place in a bowl. Add all other ingredients. Mix well with two forks. Appoint with salt and pepper. Serve as a small salad. On a salad plate, arrange lettuce leaves and a slice of tomato about 1/2 inch thick. Loosely build up the salad mixture on top, garnish with parsley or watercress. *Serves 4 to 6 people.*

SPAGHETTI SQUASH PUDDING

1/4 spaghetti squash, cooked　　　　*2 Tbsp. bread crumbs*
2 eggs　　　　　　　　　　　　　　　　*salt, pepper, nutmeg to taste*
1 & 1/4 cup white sauce

Cook the vegetable spaghetti in manner outlined.

Make Pudding Mix: Put cream sauce into adequate mixing bowl and stir. Add egg yolks and seasoning, and bread crumbs after mixing in "Spaghetti." Whip egg whites until not entirely stiff and fold that into mixture. Place in pre-buttered baking dish, or individual cups. Bake at 375°F for approximately 20 minutes, or until done and puffed up. If you use individual cups or molds, invert them on a serving dish. *Serves 6 to 8 people.*

Naturally, my favorite member of the squash family is the Italian squash, or zucchini. You can steam it, boil it, bake it, even fry it, and it's great in casseroles or stuffed. We have many recipes for it, including cookies and bread.

CHEESY ZUCCHINI SALAD

2 hard boiled eggs, grated
2 medium zucchini, grated
1 cup shredded lettuce
Basic Salad Dressing, below

1 small onion, thinly sliced
1 cup cheese, grated
salt, pepper, dill weed

Combine all ingredients, adding the seasonings to taste. Toss lightly.

Basic Salad Dressing:

6 Tbsp. oil
3 Tbsp. lemon juice or wine
    vinegar
salt, pepper, garlic salt

herbs and seeds
    (select from oregano, basil
    tarragon, thyme, curry
    powder, caraway, dill,
    sesame seeds)

MARINATED ZUCCHINI

6 raw zucchini, thinly sliced
2/3 cup cider vinegar
1/8 cup wine vinegar
4 tsp. sugar

1/2 cup each: celery & green
    pepper (chopped fine)
1 Tbsp. minced onion
salt and pepper to taste

Marinate overnight.

BAKED ZUCCHINI

Cut zucchini lengthwise into 1/4-inch slices. Place on oiled baking sheet or foil. Brush top side with salad oil. Salt and pepper. Sprinkle with Parmesan cheese. Bake at 350°F for 30 to 45 minutes, until soft.

FRIED ZUCCHINI

Cut zucchini lengthwise into thin slices. Bread in egg and seasoned bread crumbs. Fry in oil. Brown on both sides. Drain on paper towels.

STIR-FRIED SQUASH

1 lb. zucchini squash
2 Tbsp. oil
1 Tbsp. water

1/2 tsp. salt
1/4 tsp. pepper
1 Tbsp. soy sauce

Scrub squash and slice into 1/2-inch pieces. Heat oil in skillet, add squash and stir for 1 minute. Add soy sauce, water, salt, and pepper. Stir and cover. Cook over medium heat for 4 to 6 minutes or until crisp-tender. *Makes 6 servings.*

STUFFED ZUCCHINI

1 & 1/2 cups bread crumbs
1/2 cup Romano or Parmesan
  cheese (grated)
1/3 cup oil (olive oil, usually)

1 good-sized tomato (cut into
  small pieces)
1 clove garlic, minced
3 Tbsp. chopped parsley
salt and pepper to taste

Pick out medium-size straight zucchini and cut in half, lengthwise. Hollow out the halves like little boats. Chop the pulp, or the insides of the zucchini, fine and add it to the above ingredients and mix well. Fill hollowed-out zucchini with mixture and put into an oiled casserole and bake at 350°F for about 45 minutes. Cover casserole for first 30 minutes, and uncover for last 15 minutes to brown slightly.

FRESH ZUCCHINI FRITTATA

2 Tbsp. butter or margarine
1/4 cup thinly sliced green onion
2 cups thinly sliced fresh
  zucchini
8 eggs

1/2 cup water
1 & 1/4 tsp. seasoned salt
1/8 tsp. Tabasco
1/2 cup finely diced fresh
  tomato

Melt butter in an ovenproof skillet. Add onion and zucchini and sauté quickly until just crispy tender. Beat eggs just enough to blend white and yolks, stir in water and Tabasco. Pour over zucchini in skillet; sprinkle tomato on top. Let cook on medium heat for about 5 minutes, then bake in 350°F oven for 20 minutes or until eggs are set and top is dry. *Makes 4 generous servings.*

ZUCCHINI AND CHEESE CASSEROLE

3 cups finely grated zucchini
1 cup cracker crumbs
1 cup grated Cheddar cheese

2 beaten eggs
2 Tbsp. chopped onions

Combine the above ingredients and put in a well-buttered casserole. Bake for 1 hour at 350°F. *Serves 6.*

ZUCCHINI DROP COOKIES

1 cup zucchini, peeled and grated
1 tsp. soda
1 cup sugar
1/2 cup shortening (part butter
  or margarine)
1 egg, beaten
1 cup raisins

2 cups flour
1 tsp. cinnamon
1/2 tsp. cloves
1/2 tsp. nutmeg
1/2 tsp. salt
1 cup nuts, chopped

Beat thoroughly the zucchini pulp, soda, sugar, and shortening. Add egg. Beat well. Sift flour and spices. Add dry ingredients with nuts and raisins. Drop by teaspoonful on greased baking sheet. Bake at 375°F for 12 to 15 minutes. *Makes about 3 dozen cookies.*

ZUCCHINI BREAD

3 eggs
1 cup oil
1 & 2/3 cups sugar

1 cup brown sugar
2 tsp. vanilla
2 cups peeled, drained,
  grated zucchini

In separate bowl, mix:
3 cups flour
1/4 tsp. baking powder
1 tsp. salt

1 tsp. soda
3 tsp. cinnamon
1/2 cup chopped walnuts

Beat eggs until light and foamy. Add next 5 ingredients and mix lightly. Add flour mixture and blend. Add nuts. Bake at 325°F for 1 hour or until done in a greased loaf pan.

STUFFED ACORN SQUASH
Contributed by
Simla Somturk Wickless

This is such a versatile and fun recipe to make, and it's seasonal and beautiful to boot! A great addition to your Thanksgiving or holiday dinner spread. Packed *full* of antioxidants, fiber, and vitamins (A, B, C, E), as well as an appropriate amount of healthy fats. Fantastic served with a black bean dish, marinated tempeh, roasted poultry, stir-fried garlic beef, or lamb chops, and a side of your favorite greens or salad.

2 small acorn squashes
1/3 cup organic dried
 cherries, whole
1 and 3/4 cups organic
 chicken broth (use
 vegetable broth if vegan)
1 Tbsp organic butter or
 unrefined coconut butter
 (optional–to replace 1 Tbsp
 of the olive oil in the rice)

1 cup wild rice-brown
 rice mix
1/3 cup pecans, chopped
 roughly
1/4 cup organic orange juice
3 Tbsp extra virgin olive oil
1 tsp sea salt and 1/2 tsp
 ground black pepper for
 the rice
Addl. sea salt and ground
 black pepper to taste

NOTE: if using coconut butter, add to the rice in step 6; do not heat it up along with the olive oil in step 5 – it burns easily.

Preheat oven to 450 degrees. Wash and prep the acorn squash, cut in half through the middle, cut flat on both "bottoms", and clean out – with seeds and stringy, fibrous bits carved out using a spoon.

You'll end up with 4 halves. Rub the insides and outside edges with some of the olive oil.

Place acorn squash on cookie sheet lined with oven-safe wax paper and bake in oven for 1 hour while you prep the rest of the dish. Rinse the rice in a fine mesh strainer for at least 30 seconds. Heat remaining olive oil in a 3-quart pot with lid on low-medium heat for 1 to 2 minutes. Do not let it burn. Stir in rinsed rice; increase to medium heat; stir until coated with olive oil and keep stirring for 2 to 3 minutes. You're "toasting" the rice for better flavor and digestibility. Stir in the cherries and dried pecans. Stir for another 1 to 2 minutes. Add chicken broth and orange juice to the rice. Stir to dislodge any rice stuck to the bottom and bring to a boil. Add sea salt and ground black pepper. Lower the heat to low-medium or lower, maintaining a brisk, but low, simmer. Cover and do not remove cover for 40 minutes. At 40 minutes, check the liquid level and doneness of the rice. If necessary, add 1/3 more cup of liquid, bring back to a boil, and cover again. Check again in 10 to 15 minutes. At about the 1 hour mark, check the doneness of the acorn squash. Use a fork. The fork should pierce the inside of the acorn squash smoothly. If not done yet, that's okay! See the next step. Once the rice is cooked through (al dente, with a light bite to it, is great, too), spoon the rice evenly into all 4 acorn squash halves. Place stuffed acorn squash back into oven at 450 minutes for 10 minutes. Check doneness again. If not done, reduce heat to 300 degrees and leave in oven for another 10 minutes. *Makes 4 servings.*

Variations

- Top with finely chopped green onions, fresh parsley or mint before serving.

- Use other nuts or seeds in place of pecans, such as: pine nuts, walnuts, almonds, pistachios, sunflower, or pumpkin seeds.

- Add ground chicken, turkey, or beef to the stuffing – sauté in separate pan with 1 medium onion before doing so.

- Use other types of dried fruit, such as: dried apricots, raisins, prunes, dates, shredded coconut.

- Add additional spices, such as: cinnamon, nutmeg, cardamom, turmeric, sage.

- Use quinoa or a quinoa-millet mix instead of the wild rice mix.

- Add some fruit! Apples, pears, or persimmons will work great with this recipe.

- Use coconut oil to rub the squash.

ZUCCHINI HUMMUS SPREAD
Contributed by Beatrice Johnson

2 zucchini
2 tablespoons olive oil
1/4 cup pine nuts
1 teaspoon salt
Pinch of paprika

1/2 cup tahini
2 tablespoons lemon juice
1/2 clove garlic
1 teaspoon cumin

Peel the zucchini until all skin is removed. Chop zucchini into smaller pieces and put in food processor. Add all remaining ingredients except for pine nuts and blend until smooth. Add pine nuts, 1 tablespoon at a time, until right taste and consistency is achieved. Sprinkle with pinch of paprika.

CRANBERRIES

Their red color shows a strong presence of vitamin A.
They have also been known to be beneficial
in treating bladder infection.

As Thanksgiving and the Christmas holiday approach, you'll see more and more colorful cranberries on the market.

We seem to associate this bright red cranberry with the festivities of the holidays. There are many, many ways to use them.

10-MINUTE CRANBERRY SAUCE

4 cups fresh cranberries   *1 to 2 cups water*
2 cups sugar

Combine cranberries, sugar, and water in saucepan. Heat to boiling point, stirring until sugar dissolves; then boil rapidly until berries pop open (about 5 minutes). *Makes 1 quart of cranberry sauce.*

For a thicker sauce: Continue cooking until berries are mushy and liquid is somewhat reduced. Sauce will become jelly-like when chilled.

For a spicy sauce: Stir in a few whole cloves and a cinnamon stick while berries are cooking.

Tangy sauce: Add 1 teaspoon or more grated lemon peel after removing from heat.

Wine: Reduce liquid to 1 and 1/2 cups and cook as directed. When cooled to room temperature, stir in 1/4 cup or more wine. Serve on pancakes with a sprinkle of brown sugar or drizzle of maple syrup.

CHICKEN RUBY

1 broiler, cut in quarters
1 tsp. salt
1/4 cup butter (margarine)
1/2 medium onion (chopped)
1/4 tsp. cinnamon
1/4 tsp. ginger

1 tsp. grated orange rind
3/4 cup orange juice
1 1/2 cups fresh cranberries
1/2 cup chopped walnuts
3/4 cup sugar

Sprinkle chicken with salt. Brown in butter in skillet. Add onion, spices, orange rind, and orange juice. Simmer covered for 20 minutes. Add cranberries and walnuts. Sprinkle with sugar. Simmer uncovered for 10 minutes longer.

CRANBERRY CREAM DESSERT SALAD

3 cups miniature marshmallows
2 cups crushed pineapple,
  well drained

3 oz. pkg. of cream cheese
1/2 pt. whipping cream
4 cups fresh cranberries,
  chopped

Combine 1 and 1/2 cups miniature marshmallows with well-drained crushed pineapple. Break cream cheese into small pieces and mix with whipping cream and remaining 1 and 1/2 cups miniature marshmallows. Place both the pineapple-marshmallow mixture and marshmallow-cream mixture in the refrigerator for several hours or overnight until marshmallows are well softened. Shortly before serving, beat marshmallow-cream mixture until like whipped cream. Fold in the pineapple-marshmallow mixture and 4 cups chopped, fresh cranberries. Place in serving dish or dishes and refrigerate until served.

CRISSCROSS CRANBERRY PIE

2 cups sugar
1 Tbsp. flour
1/4 tsp. salt
1/3 cup water

4 cups fresh cranberries
grated rind of 1/2 lemon
2 Tbsp. butter
pie pastry

Mix dry ingredients together; add water and heat until sugar is melted. Add cranberries; cook slowly until all the skins pop open. Add lemon rind and butter. Cool, but do not stir. Pour into a pastry lined 9-inch pie plate. Cover with crisscross pastry strips; brush top with milk. Bake in hot oven (425°F) for 30 minutes.

CRANBERRY MUFFINS

3/4 cup fresh cranberries,
  halved
1/2 cup powdered sugar
2 cups flour
3 tsp. baking powder

1/2 tsp. salt
1/4 cup sugar
1 egg, well beaten
1 cup milk
4 Tbsp. shortening, melted

Mix cranberry halves with powdered sugar and let stand while preparing muffin mixture. Sift dry ingredients. Add egg, milk, and melted shortening all at once; mix until dry ingredients are dampened; do not heat. Fold in sugared cranberries. Fill muffin tins 2/3 full. Bake in moderate oven 350°F for 20 minutes. *Makes 1 dozen.*

CRANBERRY PUDDING

1 cup fresh cranberries
1/4 cup sugar
1/4 cup chopped walnuts or pecans
1/4 cup melted butter or margarine

1/2 cup sugar
1/2 cup flour
1 egg
2 Tbsp. shortening, melted

Grease well an 8-inch pie plate. Spread cranberries over the bottom of the plate. Sprinkle with 1/4 cup sugar and nuts. Beat egg well. Gradually add 1/2 cup sugar and beat until thoroughly mixed. Add flour, melted butter, and shortening to egg and sugar mixture. Beat well. Pour batter over top of cranberries. Bake in a slow oven (325°F) for 45 minutes or until crust is golden brown. Cut like pie. Serve either warm or cold with generous scoops of vanilla ice cream.

CRANBERRY KISSEL

4 cups fresh cranberries　　　*1 & 1/2 Tbsp. cornstarch*
2 cups water　　　　　　　　*1/2 cup soured cream*
1 cup sugar

Cook cranberries in water until soft. Sieve into bowl. Mix sugar and cornstarch in saucepan; add cranberry mixture slowly, stirring to smooth. Cook over medium heat, stirring constantly, till mixture thickens. Cool. Serve with sour cream. *Serves 6.*

CRANBERRY COFFEE CAKE

2 cups sifted all-purpose flour　　*5 Tbsp. butter*
3 tsp. double-acting baking　　　*1 egg, beaten*
*　powder*　　　　　　　　　　　*1/2 cup milk*
3/4 tsp. salt　　　　　　　　　*2 & 1/2 cups fresh*
1/2 cup sugar　　　　　　　　　*　cranberries, coarsely*
　　　　　　　　　　　　　　　　*　chopped*

TOPPING

1/4 cup all-purpose flour　　　*3 Tbsp. butter*
1/2 cup sugar

Sift flour, baking powder, salt, and sugar together. Cut in butter with pastry blender until crumbly.

Mix beaten egg and milk. Add to flour mixture. Stir slowly to mix, then beat until blended well. Spread batter evenly into 8x8x2 inch buttered baking dish. Sprinkle halved cranberries evenly over top. For topping, mix flour and sugar together. Cut in butter. Sprinkle over cranberries. Bake in 375°F oven for 30 to 35 minutes. *Makes 9 coffee cake squares.*

CRANBERRY REFRIGERATOR COOKIES

3 & 1/4 cups all-purpose flour
1 tsp. baking powder
1/4 tsp. baking soda
1 tsp. salt
2/3 cup granulated sugar
1 cup brown sugar
1 & 1/4 cups shortening

2 eggs
1 & 1/2 tsp. vanilla or
almond extract
1 cup walnuts, chopped
2 cups fresh cranberries,
chopped

Sift through flour, baking powder, soda, and salt. With electric mixer at medium speed, gradually add both sugars to shortening. Cream until fluffy. Add eggs and vanilla. Beat at high speed until mixed (1 minute). Add walnuts. Mix at low speed. Then add flour mixture. Blend well. Work in chopped, fresh berries with fingers. Press and shape dough into 3 loaves 2 inches square. Wrap tightly in waxed paper, plastic, or aluminum foil. Store in refrigerator or freezer. To bake, cut with sharp knife into slices 1/8 to 1/4 inches thick. Place 1 inch apart on ungreased baking sheet. Bake at 375°F for 10 to 12 minutes or until golden brown.

TURNIPS AND RUTABAGAS

These two are members of the cabbage family.
They were both very popular before potato acceptance.

Turnips and rutabagas have long been regarded as winter staples. They are available all year round but are particularly plentiful during the fall and winter.

A half cup of cooked rutabagas provide almost half the vitamin C required daily, while containing only 35 calories. Turnips contain some vitamin C, one third the daily adult requirement for ascorbic acid, and one-half cup contains only 23 calories. Turnip greens, which can be prepared like spinach, are very rich in vitamin A.

Enjoy turnips and rutabagas fixed simply like mashed potatoes or add them to soups and stews. If you haven't tried them raw as finger foods, you're missing something. Simply peel and cut into 1/4 inch slices. Sprinkle with salt and allow to chill in refrigerator about 10 minutes before serving.

TURNIPS WITH OLIVE OIL

1 lb. small turnips
10 small white boiling onions
1/4 cup olive oil
salt and freshly ground black
  pepper to taste
1 tsp. sugar

1 & 1/2 cups water
3 Tbsp. each: finely chopped
  parsley and fresh dill or
  4 Tbsp. finely chopped
  fresh mint leaves
lemon slices (optional)

Pare and quarter the turnips. Combine with the onions, olive oil, salt and pepper, sugar, and water in a heavy saucepan. Cover and cook over moderate heat for about 45 minutes or until tender.

Transfer to a heated serving platter, sprinkle with the parsley and dill, and serve, accompanied by the lemon slices, as a side dish with lamb, poultry, or game. To serve cold: Remove from the heat and allow to cool. Transfer to a serving platter lined with lettuce leaves, cover with clear plastic film, and chill. Just before serving, sprinkle with the parsley and dill. Garnish with the lemon slices. Serve as an appetizer. *Serves 4.*

TURNIP CASSEROLE

3 & 1/2 cups turnips, pared
  and diced
2 Tbsp. butter
2 Tbsp. flour
1/2 tsp. salt

dash pepper
1 & 1/2 cups milk
2/3 cups shredded Cheddar
  cheese

Cook turnips in boiling salted water until tender. Drain thoroughly. Melt butter in saucepan, add flour, salt, and pepper. Add milk and cook, stirring constantly until the mixture thickens.

Combine sauce and turnips, pour into a casserole. Top with cheese and bake in 350°F oven until hot and bubbly.

GLAZED TURNIPS

6 medium turnips
3 Tbsp. hot, melted butter
1 tsp. paprika
1 Tbsp. brown sugar

1 cube beef bouillon
salt and pepper
1 Tbsp. chopped parsley

Steam or boil turnips until tender. Drain and dry on absorbent paper. Brown in hot melted butter and sprinkle with paprika and sugar. Dissolve beef cube in small amount of water and pour over turnips. Salt and pepper to taste. Sprinkle with chopped parsley and serve at once.

RUTABAGA CASSEROLE

2 medium rutabagas, peeled   *1/2 tsp. nutmeg*
and diced (about 6 cups)   *1 tsp. salt*
1/4 cup fine dry bread crumbs   *2 eggs, beaten*
1/4 cup cream   *3 Tbsp. butter*

Cook the rutabagas until soft (about 20 minutes) in salted water to cover. Drain and mash. Soak the bread crumbs in the cream and stir in the nutmeg, salt, and beaten eggs. Combine with the smashed rutabagas. Turn into a buttered 2 and 1/2 quart casserole dish, dot the top with butter, and bake in a moderate oven (350°F) for 1 hour or until lightly browned on the top. *Serves 6 to 8.*

VEGETABLE MEDLEY

6 medium turnips, cubed   *1 cup carrots, cubed*
(3 cups)   *2 Tbsp. butter or margarine*
1 cup fresh peas   *salt and pepper*

Cook turnips in boiling, salted water until tender, about 15 minutes. Cook peas and carrots together in small amount of boiling, salted water – 8 minutes. Drain vegetables and combine. Add butter and seasonings. *Makes 6 servings.*

BROWNED RUTABAGA CUBES

1/4 cup butter   *1 tsp. salt*
4 cups raw rutabaga   *2 Tbsp. dark, brown sugar*

Melt the butter in a frying pan. Add the rutabaga cubes and cover. Cook over low heat, stirring frequently until all sides are browned. Add salt and sugar, stirring well so they are evenly distributed. Continue to cook over low heat (covered) until the rutabaga is fork-tender (about 20 minutes). Serve hot. *Makes 4 to 6 servings.*

RUTABAGA PUDDING

1 cup cooked rice
2 cups cooked and mashed
  rutabaga
1 Tbsp. butter
1/2 cup milk

1/4 cup sugar
1 tsp. salt
dash of pepper
dash of nutmeg

Combine above ingredients.

Fold in: *2 beaten egg yolks,* then beat egg whites. Bake in 1 & 1/2 to 2-quart buttered casserole dish for 1 hour at 350°F.

WINTER VEGETABLE MEDLEY
Contributed by Elaine Murphy

1 rutabaga, cubed
1/2 head cabbage, sliced
4 Tbsp. chopped fresh parsley
2 to 3 cloves fresh garlic, grated

1 turnip, cubed
1 large yellow or white
  onion, coarsely chopped
4 to 6 Tbsp. extra virgin olive
  oil

Spices to taste:
Bay leaves
Red pepper, ground or
  flakes, or spicy paprika

Basil
Sea Salt
Black Pepper

Sauté all vegetables, except garlic, in a chef's pan or large sauté pan until they begin to soften and create broth in the pan. Add garlic and spices, mix well, cover, and reduce heat to low. Cook for about 20 minutes. This is very good with pork, chicken, or turkey, although it can be served with beef (especially corned beef). Mustard greens or kale give this a nice flavor, as well as adding a contrasting color. These would be added at the same time as the other veggies.

WINTER

WINTER

The holiday season is fast approaching, and although many fruits and vegetables are available on the produce counters, they are at premium prices. Of course, at this time of the year, people don't seem to pay quite as much attention to the prices of food. They're spending money buying gifts and planning holiday parties, and if the fresh fruit and vegetables they want to serve are higher, they seem to buy them, anyway.

This is the time of year that the beautiful tropical fruits come into the United States, and they are coming down in price a little each year. Some of these are considered strange and exotic, particularly to people who do not live in the coastal states.

Papayas are a fairly new item in the Midwest and Eastern states. This is the time to be looking for them, and you'll find many wonderful recipes in the chapter on exotic fresh fruits and vegetables.

Although almost everyone is familiar with pineapple, a lot of people are still reaching for the can when there is beautiful pineapple—bright, gold, and just bursting with flavor—right in their produce department. How about a pineapple centerpiece for your Christmas table this year? Or, if you have family coming to stay for the holidays, surprise them with a Christmas breakfast consisting of a fresh papaya with a wedge of lemon along with their sweet rolls and breads.

Tangerines, preferably with a few leaves still attached, make a nice addition to the fruit bowls, and the kids will love them because they are easy to peel. Grapefruit, lemons, and limes are also plentiful now.

There are still plenty of fresh cranberries, so when you are doing your Christmas baking, try a cranberry nut bread. The taste is great, not too sweet, but a little tart, and those bright, red cranberries make it a perfect Christmas bread.

Check the index for recipes for that leftover turkey; you'll find quite a few, some of which I'm sure you'll find unusual.

GRAPEFRUIT

Grapefruit are very high in Vitamin C, potassium, folic acid.

I like to eat grapefruit fresh and keep things simple, but I know some people like to make things fancy, so we are including some recipes here for grapefruit toppings, glaze for ham, and even a recipe for a grapefruit pie so you can take full advantage of the tart and tangy grapefruit flavor.

It's important to keep the moisture in, so store grapefruit in a big plastic bag in the refrigerator, so it will be both temperature and moisture controlled and will keep for almost a month.

GRAPEFRUIT TOPPINGS

For each grapefruit half, use one of the following:

1 tablespoon maple syrup and a dash of cinnamon and nutmeg

Mixture of 1 tablespoon each of apricot jam and peanut butter

Mixture of 1 tablespoon each of honey and peanut butter

1 tablespoon molasses or honey

2 teaspoons coffee liqueur

2 tablespoons brown sugar

1 tablespoon sherry

1 & 1/2 teaspoons each of brown sugar and Kirsch

GLAZED BAKED HAM STEAK
WITH FRESH GRAPEFRUIT SAUCE

1 center cut ham steak
(1 & 1/2 inches thick)
1/3 cup sugar
1/4 cup honey

1 Tbsp. fresh grated
grapefruit peel
1/4 cup fresh squeezed grape-
fruit juice
Fresh Grapefruit Sauce

Score ham slice 1/8 inch deep in diamond pattern on both sides; place in shallow baking pan. In saucepan, combine sugar, honey, grapefruit peel, and juice. Bring to a boil and cook for 2 to 3 minutes or until slightly thickened.

Pour glaze over ham; cover pan with aluminum foil and bake at 325°F for 30 minutes. Remove foil; continue baking for 25 minutes. Serve with Fresh Grapefruit Sauce.

FRESH GRAPEFRUIT SAUCE

1/2 cup sugar
2 Tbsp. cornstarch
dash of salt
3/4 cup water
1 tsp. fresh grated grapefruit
* peel*

1 & 3/4 cups fresh squeezed
grapefruit juice
few drops of red food
coloring (optional)
1 grapefruit, peeled,
sectioned, and seeded

In saucepan, thoroughly combine sugar, cornstarch, and salt. Add water, blending until smooth. Stir in grated peel and juice. Bring to a boil over medium heat, stirring constantly. Cook for 2 minutes. Add food coloring, if desired. Just before serving, add grapefruit sections and heat until warm. *Makes 1 and 1/2 cups.*

PINK AND PRETTY GRAPEFRUIT PIE

1 pkg. (3 ozs.) raspberry
flavored gelatin
1 cup boiling water

2 large grapefruits
1 baked 9-inch pastry shell
Instant Cream Filling (recipe below)

Dissolve gelatin in boiling water. Grate 2 teaspoons grapefruit peel; reserve for filling. Measure grapefruit juice from 1 grapefruit and, if necessary, add enough cold water to yield 3/4 cup liquid; stir into gelatin mixture. Chill half of mixture until syrupy; pour into a baked pie shell and refrigerate. Peel and section remaining grapefruit, draining well; set aside. Prepare Instant Cream Filling. Pour prepared filling over chilled gelatin layer, spreading to form a smooth top. Add layer of remaining gelatin that is slightly thick, but not set. Arrange drained grapefruit sections on top in spiral design; chill until set.

Instant Cream Filling:

1 pkg. (3 ozs.) softened
cream cheese
1 cup milk
1 cup dairy sour cream

1 pkg. (3 & 3/4 oz.) instant
vanilla pudding mix
2 tsp. fresh grated grapefruit
peel

Beat cream cheese until fluffy; gradually beat in 1/4 cup milk until smooth. Add rest of milk and remaining ingredients, including reserved peel; beat until smooth, about 1 minute.

LEMONS

*Lemons have a very strong presence of the key
anti-oxidant Vitamin C. It is used in many industrial
products as a cleaning agent.*

Lemons really add zip to your other foods. We see both lemons and limes, usually in wedges, beside fish, seafood, salad, vegetables, etc. But they don't have to be used only as a garnish; there are some delicious recipes which we will share with you.

I do want to mention that lemons have to be cured for a few days after they are picked. This is to allow them to soften just a little bit. You can cure them yourself by giving them four or five days to ripen in your own kitchen. Just before you use a lemon, place it in warm water for a few minutes, then dry it off and roll it on the kitchen table. That way you are going to get all of the lemon juice that's in the lemon, maybe about twice the amount you will get from a hard lemon.

Here is a recipe for lemon barbecue sauce which comes from many, many years back in my family. It's easy to make and is excellent as a salad dressing or with cooked vegetables, also. This delicate sauce combines the tart flavor of fresh lemons with fine Italian seasonings to enhance any cut of meat, fish, or chicken prepared for barbecuing.

ITALIAN BARBECUE SAUCE

6 fresh lemons	*chopped sprig of parsley*
1/4 cup olive or salad oil	*small chopped garlic clove*
1/4 tsp. dried oregano	*salt and pepper*

To the juice of 6 fresh lemons, add olive or salad oil, oregano, garlic, and parsley. Season with salt and pepper to taste. Stir ingredients thoroughly and set sauce aside for 1 hour. Brush sauce on chicken, steak, fish, or hamburger before barbecuing. Baste

253

while cooking and baste again before serving. Any remaining sauce may be stored in refrigerator for later use.

BARBECUE SAUCE

1/2 cup catsup
1/2 tsp. fresh grated lemon
  peel
2 tsp. fresh squeezed lemon juice

2 tsp. Worcestershire sauce
1 & 1/2 tsp. prepared
  mustard
dash onion powder

Combine ingredients. Use to baste hamburgers, spareribs, hot dogs, chicken, etc. *Makes about 2/3 cup.*

BLENDER HOLLANDAISE

1/2 cup butter or margarine
  (1 stick)
4 egg yolks

2 to 3 Tbsp. fresh squeezed
  lemon juice
1/4 tsp. salt
dash of salt

Heat butter or margarine until bubble. Meanwhile, place egg yolks, fresh lemon juice, salt, and pepper in electric blender. Turn blender on and off quickly. Then turn to high speed and slowly add bubbly butter in a very thin, but steady, stream. Turn off blender and serve immediately over broccoli, asparagus, or grilled tomatoes. Also good on fish or to make Eggs Benedict. *About 1 cup.*

LEMON BUTTER VEGETABLE SAUCE

3 Tbsp. butter or margarine
1 Tbsp. minced onion
1 tsp. fresh grated lemon peel

2 Tbsp. fresh squeezed lemon
  juice
1/4 cup chopped parsley

Melt butter in small saucepan; add onions, lemon peel, and juice. Let stand, keeping warm while vegetables are cooking. Pour butter over well-drained vegetables; add parsley and toss. Great on many vegetables—broccoli, asparagus, cauliflower, Brussels sprouts, zucchini, carrots, cabbage, and potatoes.

LEMON CURRY DRESSING

1 cup mayonnaise
1/4 tsp. curry powder or dry
   mustard
1/2 tsp. fresh grated lemon peel

3 to 4 tsp. fresh squeezed
   lemon juice
1 egg yolk beaten

Combine mayonnaise, curry, lemon peel, and juice. Add beaten egg yolk. Stir over low heat until thickened, about 2 minutes. *Makes about 1 cup.*

TART BAKED CHICKEN

4 chicken legs (thighs and
   drumsticks)
2 whole chicken breasts, split
   into halves
1 tsp. garlic salt
2 tsp. paprika

1/2 tsp. oregano, crushed
1/2 tsp. fresh grated lemon
   peel
1/3 cup fresh squeezed lemon
   juice
1/2 cup water

Season chicken pieces with garlic salt, rubbing well into flesh. Sprinkle with paprika. Place in a shallow baking pan, skin-side down. Combine remaining ingredients; pour into chicken. Bake, uncovered, at 400°F for about 40 minutes. Turn chicken and continue baking, basting with pan drippings once or twice, until done, about 20 minutes. Garnish with snipped parsley, if desired. *Serves four.*

DON'T SMELL UP THE KITCHEN FISH FILLETS

4 large fish fillets
   (about 1 & 1/4 lbs.)
2 lemons, thinly sliced
1/4 cup diced carrots

1/4 cup diced celery
1/4 cup chopped green onion
2 Tbsp. snipped fresh parsley

Place one serving of fish on a piece of aluminum foil about 4 inches longer than the fish. Season with salt and pepper. Sprinkle with carrots, celery, green onion, and parsley. Top with lemon slices. Bring edges of foil together and fold over several times. Twist one end to form a tail. Tuck the other end under to form point or nose of the fish. Place foil-wrapped fillets on a cookie sheet and bake at 350°F for 15 to 20 minutes or until fillets flake.

SAVORY LEMON LAMB SHANKS

4 to 6 lamb shanks
2 tsp. salt
1/2 tsp. pepper
1 tsp. paprika
1/2 tsp. thyme, crushed
3 Tbsp. flour
3 to 4 Tbsp. fat or salad oil
2 cloves garlic, finely minced

2 Tbsp. fresh grated lemon peel
1/2 cup fresh squeezed lemon juice
1/2 cup water
4 whole peppercorns
1 bay leaf, crushed
1 lemon, cut into wedges

Have butcher "crack" lamb shanks for easier browning. Thoroughly combine salt, pepper, paprika, and thyme; rub well over all sides of meat. Lightly coat with flour. Melt fat in heavy skillet or Dutch oven; add garlic. Brown shanks, a few at a time and very slowly, on all sides. When well browned, add remaining ingredients, except the lemon wedges. Cover tightly, simmer slowly for about 2 hours, or until tender. Baste and turn shanks occasionally during cooking; add small amount of water, if necessary. Serve with lemon wedges.

FROSTY PINK LEMONADE

1 cup sugar
1 cup fresh squeezed lemon juice
1 tray ice cubes

2 & 1/2 cups cold water
1 lemon, unpeeled, sliced into thin cartwheels
few drops of red food coloring

In large pitcher, combine sugar and lemon juice; stir with long-handled spoon until sugar dissolves. Add ice cubes, cold water, and lemon slices; stir briskly until pitcher is frosty. Stir in a few drops red food coloring to make the lemonade a pretty pink. *Makes 1 and 1/4 quarts, 5 to 6 servings.*

OLD FASHIONED LEMON PIE

1 & 1/2 cups sugar
1 & 1/4 cups water
2 Tbsp. butter or margarine
1/3 cup cornstarch
1/2 cup cold water
4 egg yolks
3 Tbsp. milk

1/2 cup lemon juice
1 & 1/2 tsp grated lemon peel
1 baked 9-inch pastry shell
4 egg whites
1/2 cup sugar
1 tsp. lemon juice

Combine sugar, water, and butter in saucepan and heat until sugar dissolves. Blend cornstarch with cold water and add to hot mixture; cook slowly until clear, about 8 minutes.

Beat egg yolks with milk; slowly stir into cornstarch mixture. Cook for 2 minutes, stirring constantly. Remove from heat and add 6 tablespoons lemon juice and lemon peel. Cool. Pour into a cooled baked shell.

Beat egg whites stiff, but not dry; add sugar gradually; add 1 teaspoon lemon juice at the last. Spread meringue over cooled filling, sealing to the edges of pastry to avoid shrinking. Brown in moderate oven (350°F) for 12 to 15 minutes.

LIMES

Limes are similar in nutrition to lemons. Because of their high vitamin C content, many sailors, especially British sailors, used limes to battle scurvy, a disease caused by the lack of vitamin C. Usage was so common that these sailors were given the name of "Limeys."

Bar owners have made the market for limes what it is today. They have to have their limes. The lime juice or twist of lime gives the drink that little bit of difference. It's very aromatic, very fragrant.

It's a good idea to make juice cubes, too, while lemon and limes are less expensive and plentiful. Squeeze them and freeze the juice in ice cube trays. Once frozen, they can be removed from the trays and stored in plastic bags in the freezer, and you will have juice cubes with built-in flavor for iced tea, cold drinks, or other fruit juices. Instead of dilution from regular ice cubes, you'll get additional flavor and nutrition as they melt in your favorite drink.

For those who enjoy a real good non-alcoholic thirst quencher, mix up a pitcher of fresh limeade.

FRESH LIMEADE

1/2 cup sugar
6 limes
1 cup water

ice cubes
carbonated or plain water

Combine sugar and water in a saucepan; place over heat and stir until sugar is dissolved; cool. Cut limes in half; juice. Add juice to sugar syrup; divide mixture between 6 tall glasses. Add ice cubes. Fill to top with carbonated or plain water; stir. Garnish with clove-studded lime slices. *Serves 6.*

LIME BUTTER SAUCE

3 Tbsp. fresh lime juice   1/4 tsp. Tabasco
1/2 cup butter

Melt butter; add lime juice and Tabasco. Use as sauce for seafood or vegetables such as asparagus, green beans, etc. *Yields approximately 2/3 cup.*

LIME COCKTAIL SAUCE

6 Tbsp. fresh lime juice   dash Tabasco
3 Tbsp. catsup or chili sauce   1 Tbsp. prepared horseradish

Mix all ingredients. Chill thoroughly. Serve with crab meat, shrimp, lobsters, or oysters.

SEA BREEZE LIME-MINT DRESSING

1/4 cup fresh lime juice   1/8 tsp. pepper
3 sprigs of fresh mint   1/2 tsp. sugar
3/4 cup salad oil   1 tsp. prepared mustard
1/2 tsp. salt

Remove mint leaves from stems. Cut leaves into small pieces with kitchen scissors. Combine remaining ingredients with mint leaves. Place in a small bowl. Add an ice cube. Beat with a fork until dressing thickens to the consistency of medium cream. Remove ice. Serve with fruit or vegetable salads.

LIME-CHERRY DRESSING

1/2 cup fresh lime juice   1/8 tsp. paprika
1/2 cup salad oil   3 Tbsp. maraschino cherry
1/4 tsp. salt   syrup

Put all ingredients into blender container. Cover and process at medium speed until well mixed. Serve over fruit or vegetable salads. *Yields about 3/4 cup.*

FRESH LIME PUDDING

3 Tbsp. fresh lime juice   3 Tbsp. butter
1 tsp. grated lime rind   1 cup milk
1 cup sugar   2 eggs
3 Tbsp. flour

Combine sugar and flour and butter in a mixing bowl. Add the unbeaten egg yolks, lime juice, grated lime rind, and milk. Beat egg whites until stiff. Fold into yolk mixture. Pour into buttered 1-quart mold or 6 custard cups. Place in a pan of hot water and bake for 1 hour in slow oven (325°F) or until the pudding leaves the sides of the baking pan (35 minutes for custard cups). The finished pudding has a cake-like top with a smooth, delicious lime sauce beneath. Serve warm or cold, with or without whipped cream.

FRESH LIME PIE

1 large lime   2 cups flaked or shredded
1 pt. cottage cheese   coconut
1 envelope gelatin   2 Tbsp. butter or margarine
1 cup sugar   green food coloring
1/2 cup hot water   maraschino cherries

Cut lime into pieces and remove about 3/4 of the skin. Remove seeds, if any, and blender chop until lime is finely cut. Mix in gelatin and allow to stand for a few minutes. Add hot water and blender mix until gelatin is dissolved. Slowly add 1 pint of cottage cheese and 1 cup of sugar. Mix in blender until mixture is smooth and creamy. Add food coloring, if desired, and refrigerate. Melt butter and mix with coconut. Pat firmly in bottom of a 9-inch pie plate. Pour lime mixture over coconut base and chill until firm. Garnish with bright red cherries. *Serves 6.*

FRESH LIME CHEESECAKE

2 envelopes gelatin
1 & 3/4 cup sugar
1 cup stiffly whipped topping
green food coloring (optional)
2 Tbsp. butter
1/2 cup graham cracker
   crumbs

3 cups creamed cottage
   cheese
1/8 tsp. salt
2 eggs
1 cup milk
6 Tbsp. fresh lime juice
1 Tbsp. sugar

Mix gelatin, sugar, and salt in top of double boiler. Beat eggs well and mix with milk. Add to gelatin mixture. Cook over boiling water, stirring constantly until gelatin is dissolved (about 5 min.). Using electric mixer or blender at high speed, blend until creamy. Add gelatin mixture and mix until ingredients are well blended. Stir in whipped topping. Chill mixture.

Prepare crumb topping by mixing 2 tablespoons butter, graham cracker crumbs, and sugar. Pour chilled cheesecake mixture into 8-inch round spring form pan. Sprinkle with topping and chill until firm. *About 10 to 12 servings.*

PINEAPPLE

Pineapple is a wonderful fruit known for the enzyme bromelain, which has the ability to dissolve protein efficiently, making them a perfect dessert after that steak dinner.

It's pineapple time, and I always tell people to buy golden, ripe pineapples. The outside skin color tells you the color of the flesh. If it is golden yellow outside, the flesh will be amber and ripe. A pineapple does not ripen after it's picked. Ninety-nine times out of a hundred, it has all the sugar it's going to have when it's picked from the plant.

Select a firm pineapple, one that is golden ripe in color and nice and bright. You should be able to smell the sweetness, and it will be delicious and you will love it.

FRESH PINEAPPLE MIST

1 fresh pineapple
3/4 cup ginger ale
1/4 cup chilled orange juice
1 Tbsp. lime juice

Cut pineapple into quarters. Remove fruit from shell, core and cut into large chunks. Whirl about 4 chunks at a time in blender, at high speed until pureed. Add all puree back to blender jar along with ginger ale, orange juice, and lime juice. Whirl on low speed until blended. *Makes 4 servings.*

MAI TAI MIST

1 fresh pineapple
1/3 cup light rum
1/3 cup dark rum
3 Tbsp. Curacao
1 Tbsp. lime juice

Cut pineapple into quarters. Remove fruit from shell, core, and cut into large chunks. Whirl about 4 chunks at a time in blender, at high speed until pureed. Add all puree back to blender jar along with light and dark rums, Curacao, and lime juice. Whirl on low speed until blended. Chill until frosty cold. *Makes 4 servings.*

SCANDINAVIAN HAM SALAD

1 fresh pineapple
2 cups cooked ham, cut into
  chunks
6 cherry tomatoes, halved
1 cup sliced celery
1/4 cup sliced green onions
1/2 cup dairy sour cream

1/2 tsp. dill weed
1/2 tsp. hot mustard
1/4 tsp. salt
1/4 tsp. lemon juice
1/8 tsp. garlic salt
1/8 tsp. pepper

Cut pineapple in half lengthwise through crown. Remove fruit, leaving shells intact. Core and dice fruit. In a large bowl, combine pineapple, ham chunks, cherry tomatoes, celery, and green onions. In a small bowl, combine all remaining ingredients for dressing, blending well. Spoon dressing over pineapple shells to serve. *Makes 4 to 6 servings.*

ISLAND TERIYAKI STICKS

1 fresh pineapple
2 lbs. sirloin steak
20 large fresh shrimp
1/2 cup soy sauce
1/2 cup honey
1/4 cup cream sherry

1 tsp. grated orange peel
1 clove garlic, minced
5 green onions
1 large green bell pepper,
  chunked
2 Tbsp. cornstarch

Cut pineapple in half lengthwise. Remove fruit; core and cut into 20 large wedges. Cut steak into 20 large cubes. Shell shrimp, leaving tails on. Combine soy sauce, honey, sherry, orange peel, and garlic. Marinate steak and shrimp in soy mixture for 3 to 4 hours. Drain, reserving marinade.

Cut green onions into 2-inch lengths. Skewer a pineapple chunk, shrimp, green onion, steak cube, and bell pepper chunk on each of 20 skewers. Blend cornstarch into reserved marinade. Heat to boiling, stirring constantly until thickened and clear. Place skewers on rack in broiling pan. Brush with marinade. Broil 5 inches from heat for 3 minutes until shrimp turns pink; turn, brush with marinade and broil for 5 minutes longer. Serve at once. *Makes 20 skewers.*

CHUNKY CHICKEN CURRY

4 chicken breasts
1 fresh pineapple
1 cup sliced celery
1/2 cup sliced green onions
2 Tbsp. butter
1 Tbsp. curry powder
2 Tbsp. flour
hot fluffy rice

1 & 1/2 cups Half & Half
1 Tbsp. chutney sauce or
*   chopped chutney*
4 strips bacon, cooked and
*   crumbled*
1/4 cup toasted sliced
*   almonds*

Wrap chicken breasts in aluminum foil and bake in a 400°F oven for 1 hour. Cool; remove skin and bones. Cut meat into large pieces. Cut pineapple in half lengthwise through the crown. Remove fruit, leaving shells intact. Core and dice fruit; then drain well in a strainer while making sauce.

In a large skillet, sauté celery and green onions in 1 tablespoon butter until barely tender. Remove vegetables from pan. Add remaining 2 tablespoons butter, then stir in curry. Cook for about 1 minute. Stir flour into butter until smooth. Gradually add Half & Half, stirring smooth. Add chutney sauce and cook, stirring until thickened. Fold in chicken pieces, pineapple chunks, and bacon. Cook until heated through. Spoon into pineapple shells. Sprinkle with toasted almonds. Serve with hot fluffy rice. *Makes 4 servings.*

TANGERINES

Tangerines are very high in vitamins A and C.
The two varieties most popular are the Clementine and the
Satsuma, which are easy to peal and are seedless.

Here is a special recipe that makes leftover turkey a treat. This one
has become a favorite of many of my listeners and viewers.

FRESH TANGERINE AND TURKEY SALAD

2 cups diced cooked turkey
2 cups diced celery
1 tsp. finely chopped onion
1 & 1/4 tsp. salt
1 & 1/4 tsp. salt
1/4 tsp. white pepper
tangerine sections for garnish

2 cups diced tangerine sec-
sections, well drained
(about 5 tangerines)
3 Tbsp. mayonnaise
1 Tbsp. fresh lemon juice
lettuce

Mix together first 6 ingredients. Blend mayonnaise with fresh
lemon juice; add and mix lightly. Serve on lettuce. Garnish with
tangerine sections. *Makes 4 servings.*

HEARTY TANGERINE CHICKEN SALAD

3 cups diced, cooked chicken
6 tangerines, peeled, sepa-
rated into segments, seeded
2 Tbsp. finely chopped
candied ginger
1/2 cup chopped green pepper

1/3 cup mayonnaise
1/3 cup dairy sour cream
1/2 cup slivered toasted
almonds
1/2 cup chopped celery
salad greens

In large bowl, combine chicken, tangerine segments, almonds,
celery, and green pepper. Thoroughly combine mayonnaise (not
salad dressing), sour cream, and ginger; pour over salad. Toss
lightly to mix well. Chill for at least one hour before serving on
crisp salad greens. *Makes 5 to 8 servings.*

TANGERINE MEATBALLS

1 lb. ground beef	*1/4 tsp. nutmeg*
1/2 lb. bulk sausage	*1 Tbsp. salad oil*
1 tsp. fresh grated tangerine	*Fresh Tangerine Sauce*
peel	*steamed rice*

Combine ingredients thoroughly. Shape into 1 and 1/2 inch balls. Brown well on all sides in oil, turning frequently. Cover skillet and cook until done, about 5 minutes. Remove meatballs from pan and pour off drippings, reserving 2 tablespoons. Prepare Fresh Tangerine Sauce. Arrange meatballs on platter of hot rice and add sauce.

FRESH TANGERINE SAUCE

1 Tbsp. cornstarch	*1 Tbsp. fresh squeezed lemon*
2 Tbsp. sugar	*juice*
2 tsp. fresh grated tangerine peel	*2 medium tangerines, peeled,*
1 cup fresh squeezed tangerine	*sectioned, seeded*
juice	

Thoroughly combine cornstarch and sugar. Grate tangerine peel. Blend in 1/4 cup tangerine juice; stir until smooth. Add remaining tangerine juice, lemon juice, and tangerine peel. Add mixture to reserved hot drippings in skillet. Bring to a boil over medium heat. Cook, stirring constantly, for 3 to 4 minutes. Add tangerine sections and heat for 1 minute. *Makes about 2 and 1/2 cups.*

TANGERINE HARVEST RELISH

3 tangerines
1/3 cup seedless raisins
1/2 cup firmly packed brown
  sugar
1 stick (2 inch) cinnamon
2 whole cloves

1 & 1/2 cups water
1 Tbsp. cornstarch
1 Tbsp. water
1 large apple, diced
1/2 cup diced celery
1/2 cup chopped walnuts

Grate peel from tangerines to yield 2 teaspoons. Remove peel and separate tangerines into segments, removing any seeds. Combine raisins, brown sugar, cinnamon stick, clove, grated tangerine peel, and water in saucepan. Bring to a boil and simmer, uncovered, for 30 minutes. Remove cinnamon stick and cloves. Blend cornstarch and 1 tablespoon water. Stir into raisin mixture. Add diced apple and celery. Bring to a boil and cook for 10 minutes over medium heat, stirring frequently. Add tangerine segments and nuts. Simmer for about 1 and 1/2 minutes until heated through. Serve warm. Excellent served with poultry, pork, or lamb. *Makes about 3 and 1/2 cups.*

HOLIDAY SYRUP

1/2 cup butter or margarine
2 tsp. fresh grated tangerine
  peel

1 cup maple syrup
4 tangerines, peeled, sepa-
  rated into segments, seeded

In a small saucepan, slowly melt butter with tangerine peel. Add maple syrup and tangerines. Cover and gently heat for 3 to 5 minutes. Serve warm over pancakes or waffles.

BANANAS

*Bananas are high in fructose and glucose, giving us a burst
of quick energy. They are full of many vitamins and minerals
with a good concentration of potassium.*

Bananas are available, practically all over the United States all year round. We are going to include them here because with so many of our other fresh fruits scarce at this time of year, now is a good time to enjoy bananas. Although imported, they often sell for about the same price you pay for carrots in-season, and that is reasonable.

Those brown specks must appear on the outside skin before a banana is fully ripe. That's when it talks to you and says, 'all of my starch is converted to sugar and now I'm ready.' In produce, we call the brown spots sugar spots. If you refrigerate a green banana, it will stop the ripening process, so ripen them at room temperature. Once it's ripe, you can refrigerate and it will rest at maturity. Even though the outside skin will turn black, the inside fruit will be okay.

When it comes to digestion, a banana is just about one of the easiest foods to digest, provided it is ripe. It is one of the first solid foods fed to babies. But for some reason, perhaps the sweetness or the texture, people assume bananas are fattening. They are not; in fact, one medium-sized banana contains only 85 calories, which is only ten more than a medium apple.

BANANA MILKSHAKE

1 ripe banana   *1 egg*
3/4 cup milk   *1/2 tsp. vanilla*

Peel banana and cut into quarters. Place in electric blender container and add remaining ingredients. Cover and process until smooth.

BANANA FRAPPE

2 cups pineapple of orange   *2 bananas, cut in pieces*
  juice   *nutmeg*
1 Tbsp. sugar

Combine pineapple juice and sugar in electric blender container. Add bananas and process at low speed until mixture is smooth. Serve in chilled glasses; sprinkle with nutmeg. *Serves 6.*

BAKED BANANAS

Brush whole peeled bananas with melted butter and bake in 375°F oven for 15 minutes, just until tender. Serve as a vegetable. For dessert, sweeten with honey, brown sugar, or marmalade, or sprinkle with cinnamon sugar, coconut, or nuts.

SAUTÉED BANANAS

Melt 2 tablespoons butter or margarine in a large skillet. Add 4 whole bananas or 3 bananas, halved lengthwise. Cook over low heat, turning once, just until tender, 2 or 3 minutes for halves or 5 minutes for whole bananas. For dessert, add 1 teaspoon grand lemon or lime rind and 2 teaspoons juice, and 2 tablespoons sugar. For Bananas Flambé, add 2 tablespoons cognac to dessert bananas and ignite.

BANANAS WITH LEMON SAUCE

1/2 cup sugar
1 Tbsp. cornstarch
1/4 tsp. salt
1 cup water
1 Tbsp. grated lemon rind

3 Tbsp. lemon juice
3 drops yellow food coloring,
* optional*
2 Tbsp. butter or margarine
6 bananas

Mix sugar, cornstarch, and salt in medium saucepan. Stir in water. Cook over medium heat, stirring constantly, until clear and slightly thickened. Remove from heat and stir in lemon rind and juice, yellow coloring, and butter. Peel bananas and cut into diagonal slices. Place 1 banana in each of 6 dessert dishes. Add warm sauce. Serve immediately. *6 servings.*

GINGER GLAZED BANANAS

2 Tbsp. butter or margarine
1/4 cup packed brown sugar
1/2 cup orange juice

1 tsp. ginger
3 bananas, sliced diagonally

Melt butter to skillet. Add brown sugar and orange juice; bring to a boil and cook over medium heat for 5 minutes. Stir in bananas. Serve immediately with pork or poultry. *4 servings.*

BANANA SEAFOOD SALAD

2 cups cooked seafood:
* shrimp, crab meat, lobster,*
* tuna or salmon*
salad greens

1/2 cup chopped green
* pepper or celery*
2 bananas

In a large bowl, combine seafood and green pepper. Peel bananas, cut into slices and add to salad. Add Curry Mayonnaise* (recipe on next page), mix well, and serve with salad greens. *4 servings.*

*Curry Mayonnaise:

1/4 cup mayonnaise	*1/4 tsp. salt*
1/4 cup sour cream	*1 Tbsp. chopped parsley*
1/2 tsp. curry powder	*1/8 tsp Tabasco pepper sauce*
2 tsp. lemon juice	

Blend together all ingredients in small bowl.

VEAL SCALOPPINE WITH BANANAS

1 Tbsp. margarine	*3/4 tsp. salt*
1 lb. thinly sliced veal for	*1/8 tsp. pepper*
scaloppine	*1/4 tsp. dried leaf oregano*
2 Tbsp. chopped parsley	*2 bananas, sliced*

In large skillet, melt margarine. Add veal and sprinkle with parsley, salt, pepper, and oregano. Cook over moderate heat, turning occasionally, until veal is just tender, about 7 to 10 minutes. Add sliced bananas and heat. *Serves 4.*

BANANA AND CHICKEN BARBECUE

1 broiler-fryer chicken,	*3/4 cup barbecue sauce*
quartered	*2 medium bananas*
2 Tbsp. minced onion	

Place chicken skin side up in a shallow 3-quart casserole or baking dish. Mix barbecue sauce and onion. Spoon 3/4 of sauce over chicken and bake in 375°F oven for 50 minutes. Remove from oven. Peel bananas and cut into chunks; add to casserole. Spoon remaining sauce over bananas and return to oven, bake for 10 minutes. Serve immediately. *Serves 4.*

BANANA COCONUT CUSTARD

2/3 cup milk

2/3 cup flaked coconut

2 eggs

3 Tbsp. sugar

1 cup mashed ripe bananas
(3 medium)

1/4 tsp. nutmeg

Combine milk and coconut in small saucepan. Simmer over low heat, stirring occasionally, for 2 minutes. Remove from heat. In a large bowl, beat eggs; stir in coconut, milk, and remaining ingredients. Turn into greased 1-quart casserole. Place in a pan of hot water. Bake in 350°F oven for 30 minutes, until custard is set and top is slightly brown. Serve warm. *4 servings.*

CLASSIC BANANA CREAM PIE

3/4 cup sugar

3 Tbsp. flour

2 Tbsp. cornstarch

1/4 tsp. salt

3 cups milk

2 eggs, slightly beaten

1 & 1/2 tsp. vanilla

4 bananas

One 9-inch pastry shell or
crumb crust

In large saucepan, mix together sugar, flour, cornstarch, and salt. Gradually stir in milk. Cook over low heat, stirring constantly, until mixture comes to a boil. Simmer for 2 to 3 minutes, stirring constantly, until thickened. Gradually stir hot mixture into eggs. Return egg mixture to saucepan; cook over very low heat for 2 minutes, stirring constantly. Remove from heat; stir in vanilla. Cool.

Peel and slice 2 bananas; place in pie shell. Cover with filling. Chill for several hours. Just before serving, peel remaining 2 bananas, cut in slices and place on top of pie. *8 servings.*

BANANA BREAD PUDDING

2 cups milk
1 cup mashed ripe banana
  (3 medium)
1/2 tsp. salt
2 eggs, slightly beaten

1/3 cup honey
1/2 cup raisins
1 tsp. grated lemon rind
4 slices white bread,
  cut in squares

Scald milk in large saucepan, and add mashed bananas. Add remaining ingredients and mix well. Turn into 1-quart baking dish, and bake in 350°F oven for 50 minutes, until tip of knife inserted in pudding comes out clean. Let stand for 15 minutes before serving. *Serves 6.*

BANANA OATMEAL COOKIES

3/4 cup shortening
1 cup packed brown sugar
1 egg
1/2 cup mashed ripe banana
  (1 large)
1 tsp. vanilla

1 cup unsifted all-purpose
  flour
1 tsp. salt
1/2 tsp. baking soda
3 cups uncooked regular oats
1/2 cup raisins
1/2 cup chopped nuts

In large bowl, beat shortening, brown sugar, egg, mashed banana, and vanilla until creamy. Mix flour, salt, and baking soda. Blend into creamed mixture. Stir in oats, raisins, and nuts. Drop by rounded teaspoon onto greased baking sheets. Bake in 375°F oven for 15 to 20 minutes. *Approximately 6 dozen cookies.*

BANANA POUNDCAKE

1 cup butter or margarine
1 & 1/2 cups sugar
4 eggs
1 cup mashed ripe bananas
  (3 medium)
(Continued on next page)

1 tsp. vanilla
2 & 1/2 cups sifted all-
  purpose flour
1 tsp. baking powder
1/4 tsp. nutmeg

In a large bowl, cream butter with sugar. Beat in eggs one at a time, beating well after each addition. Blend in bananas and vanilla. Sift together flour, baking powder, and nutmeg; blend into banana mixture. Turn into a greased and floured 9-inch tube pan. Bake in 350°F oven for 1 hour and 10 minutes or until a cake tester inserted in cake comes out clean. Cool 10 minutes; turn out of pan and cool completely. If desired, serve sprinkled with confectioner's sugar.

ORANGES

Oranges are very special! They are very high in the two key anti-oxidants vitamins A and C and possess good amounts of pectin, potassium, and folic acid.

One day we had a visitor from London, and she was helping my wife in the kitchen. She started to make a fruit salad since we always have a variety of fruit around. I was surprised when she squeezed fresh orange juice into the fruit salad. I didn't say anything at the time, but I thought perhaps it would be a bit sour. She served it, and it was absolutely delicious and sweet. "How much sugar did you put in it?" I asked.

"No sugar," she said. "The orange juice brings out the sweetness of the fruit." It's a wonderful thing when you can serve a fruit salad that's nice and sweet without putting sugar in it. And think of the calories that you save!

It is said that vitamin C plays an important part in the prevention of colds and viruses. That being the case, it is a good reason to start adding more oranges to your daily diet. Remember, one medium orange contains the minimum, or more than the minimum, requirement for vitamin C. Fresh oranges contain and retain more vitamin C than the processed orange juice product. One medium orange contains only 75 calories and also is low in sodium and helps calcium retention.

We are including recipes for some great new taste treats using fresh oranges, and we're sure you'll enjoy them.

ENERGY NOG

1 cup fresh orange juice,
chilled
1 Tbsp. honey or sugar

1 egg
2 ice cubes

Combine all ingredients in electric blender. Cover and whirl about 1 minute on high speed until frothy. Serve immediately. *Makes about 1 and 1/2 cups.*

CREAM FRUIT DRESSING

1/2 cup mayonnaise
1/4 cup light corn syrup
1 Tbsp. orange rind
1 Tbsp. orange juice

1/4 tsp. nutmeg
1/2 cup whipping cream,
whipped

Blend mayonnaise and corn syrup until smooth. Add rind, juice, and nutmeg; mix well. Fold in whipped cream. *Makes 1and 1/4 cups.*

ORANGE GRAND FINALE

2 large oranges, peeled
1/2 cup coffee liqueur or
Triple Sec
1 qt. softened vanilla ice
cream

1/2 cup whipping cream,
whipped
grated chocolate or fresh
grated orange peel

Cut peeled oranges in half lengthwise; core oranges, removing white membrane and any seeds. Cut into small pieces; place in electric blender with liqueur. Cover and blend on low, then high speed, until smooth. Add ice cream in 3 separate additions, blending after each addition until smooth. Pour into brandy snifters or sherbet glasses; top with dollops of whipped cream and sprinkle with grated chocolate or orange peel. Serve with short straws. *Makes 3 and 1/2 cups.*

CALIFORNIA CASSEROLE

2 oranges
1 can (16 ozs.) pork and beans
 drained
15 & 1/4 ozs. kidney beans,
 cooked and drained

1/3 cup orange marmalade,
 apricot jam or currant jelly
1 tsp. prepared mustard
5 frankfurters (1/2 lb.), cut in
 1-inch chunks

Grate 2 teaspoons peel from oranges. Remove remaining peel. Cut one peeled orange into bite-size pieces. Slice other orange into half-cartwheels. Combine both kinds of beans with orange peel, orange bite-size pieces, marmalade, mustard, and frankfurters; turn into a 1 and 1/2 quart casserole dish. Bake, covered, at 375°F for 30 minutes. Remove from oven; arrange half-cartwheels around top of casserole. Return to oven and bake uncovered for 5 minutes. *Serves 4 to 6.*

ORANGE CRANBERRY GLAZED HAM

1 Tbsp. fresh grated orange
 peel
1 center cut ham slice, about
 1 & 1/2 inches thick
1 cup raw cranberries

2 Tbsp fresh squeezed orange
 juice
2 Tbsp. butter or margarine
1 orange, peeled, divided into
 segments
1/2 cup brown sugar

Grate peel; set aside. Place ham in shallow baking pan. Cover and bake at 350°F for 1 hour. Cook cranberries in orange juice and butter for 5 minutes. Mash berries with a fork. Cut orange segments into halves. Add brown sugar, orange peel, and orange pieces to cranberry mixture. Remove ham from oven, spread orange mixture over top and return to the oven. Bake uncovered for 30 minutes. *Serves 8.*

MAPLE ORANGE SAUSAGE LINKS

2 large fresh oranges
1/4 cup maple syrup

1 lb. sausage links (about 16 sausages)

Remove peel from oranges. Cut peeled oranges in half lengthwise, and with a shallow V-shaped cut, remove center core. Place halves cut-side down; cut lengthwise and crosswise into bite-size pieces. Pan fry sausage links; drain off fat. Add maple syrup to skillet and heat several minutes until syrup is warm. Add orange pieces, stirring to coat with syrup and to warm oranges slightly. Serve over French toast, waffles or pancakes. *Serves 4 to 6.*

ORANGE TURKEY SALAD

2 oranges
3 cups diced cooked turkey
1 cup diced celery
1/2 cup toasted slivered almonds

1/2 tsp. salt
1/2 tsp. curry powder
1/2 cup mayonnaise
1 cup seedless green grapes

Peel and section oranges over a bowl to reserve 2 tablespoons juice. Combine turkey, celery, grapes, orange sections and juice, and salt. Cover and refrigerate for 1 hour. Combine curry powder and mayonnaise; blend thoroughly. Add to turkey mixture and toss to coat evenly. Sprinkle almonds over mixture. Serve in lettuce cups. *Serves 8 to 10.*

SPICY ORANGE NUTS

1 & 1/2 cups unsifted powdered
  sugar
2 Tbsp cornstarch
1 tsp. cinnamon
3/4 tsp. cloves
4 tsp. allspice

(Continued on next page)

1/8 tsp. salt
2 Tbsp fresh grated orange
  peel
2 egg whites, slightly beaten
3 Tbsp fresh squeezed orange
  juice
2 cups walnut or pecan
  halves

Sift together sugar, cornstarch, spices, and salt; stir in grated peel. Blend egg whites with orange juice; stir in nuts, coating each half completely. Drain thoroughly, then roll in sugar mixture to coat well. Spread on cookie sheet; do not allow nuts to touch. Bake at 250°F for 20 to 25 minutes, or until dry. Cool before storing in covered container.

CANDIED CITRUS PEEL

3 cups citrus peel, cut into
strips from:
4 to 5 medium oranges, or
6 medium lemons, or
2 medium to large grapefruit

8 to 9 large tangerines
12 cups cold water
2 & 1/2 cups sugar
1/2 cup honey
1 & 3/4 cups boiling water

To prepare peel, wash fruit; score peel into quarters. Remove sections of peel with fingers; cut into uniform strips about 3/8 inch wide. Boil peel with 6 cups cold water uncovered for 10 minutes; drain and rinse. Repeat process with 6 cups fresh water. (Note: if you are preparing tangerine peel, omit second boiling.)

In a large saucepan, combine 1 and 1/2 cups sugar, honey, and boiling water; bring to a boil and boil for 1 minute. Add cooked, drained peel and briskly simmer until almost all of syrup has been absorbed, about 30 to 40 minutes. Stir frequently to avoid sticking. Transfer peel to colander; drain well, about 10 minutes.

In large bowl, toss drained peel with remaining 1 cup sugar to coat well. Spread out on waxed paper to dry. Store in tightly covered container.

ORANGE BEET SALAD
Contributed by Cindi Avila

1 can of whole beets
2 small oranges sectioned
off or 1 small can of
mandarin oranges

1/2 cup pecans
1/2 cup goat or blue cheese
Balsamic Vinegar

Cut beats into quarters. Mix beets, oranges, and pecans together. Crumble cheese over mixture and sprinkle with balsamic vinegar.

AVOCADOS

*Avocadoes have it all! They have all three key
anti-oxidants vitamins A, C, and especially E.
The fat in avocadoes is the right kind of fat.
It is mono-unsaturated and similar to olive oil.*

I like avocados simple and fresh "on the half-shell." Just slice in half lengthwise, remove the pit and sprinkle with salt and pepper. A few drops of lemon juice or vinegar for flavor may also be used.

Although the avocado supply reaches its peak at this time, the tree is a natural storehouse and, therefore, the grower can "store" the fruit on the tree for months without cost and it will become even more mature, nutritious, and flavorful.

It's best to buy a solid avocado with a full symmetrical neck and let it compliment your fruit bowl for a few days while it ripens. Confinement in a paper bag or foil will speed the process. But if you need an avocado for tonight's salad, select one carefully, holding it gently in the palm of your hand. Under slight pressure, it should give a bit (like a ripe peach). In green varieties, the skin should have a velvety touch and be dull in texture. Avoid a hard avocado or one with a glistening skin...not ready. Beware of dark, soft spots or finger indentations...past prime.

Preparation: To remove from skin, use a sharp knife to make a shallow cut lengthwise through the outer skin. The skin can be peeled from a ripe avocado almost as easily as a banana. Handle the fruit gently to avoid bruising the meat. Slice around lengthwise to remove the pit and slice or dice to desired size.

THE CALIFORNIA COOLER

3 avocados, halved and
  peeled
3 & 1/2 cups unsweetened
  grapefruit juice

3/4 cup sugar
ice
mint, for garnish

Puree avocados with grapefruit juice and sugar; chill. Pour into ice filled glasses. Serve with straws. *6 to 8 servings.*

AVOCADO MARGARITAS

1 avocado, halved and peeled
1/4 cup lemon juice
2 cups crushed ice

1/2 cup tequila
1/4 cup Triple Sec or orange
  brandy

Puree avocado with remaining ingredients. Serve in chilled, salt-rimmed glasses*. *6 to 8 servings.*

* Dip glass rims into lightly beaten egg white and then into salt.

FROZEN AVOCADO DAIQUIRIS

2 avocados, halved and
  peeled
about 2 qts. crushed ice

2 cups light rum
2/3 cup lime juice
1/2 to 2/3 cup sugar

Puree avocado with remaining ingredients until fairly smooth. Serve in cocktail glasses with short straws. *6 to 8 servings.*

GUACAMOLES - DIPS AND SPREADS

Many avocado recipes come to us from Mexico, none more splendid than guacamole.

GUACAMOLE (AVOCADO DIP)
(Wah-kah-mo-lay)

2 fresh avocados
2 Tbsp. fresh lemon or lime
* juice*
2 small green onions, chopped

1/2 tsp. salt
dash of Worcestershire or
* Tabasco*

Mash avocado and add seasonings, or combine all ingredients in blender. *Makes about 1 cup dip.* This basic avocado dip is best when mixed just before serving; serve with crackers or chips.

GUACAMOLE-WITH TOMATOES

2 avocados, mashed or
* pureed*
1/4 cup sour cream
2 Tbsp. minced onion
2 tsp. salt
1 tsp. chili powder

1 clove garlic, crushed
dash Tabasco
4 tsp. lemon juice
2 medium tomatoes, peeled
* and chopped*

Combine all ingredients. Cover and chill. *Makes about 3 cups.*

GUACAMOLE-WITH BACON

4 avocados, mashed or pureed
1 Tbsp. salt
1/4 cup lemon juice
3/4 tsp. Tabasco

3 cloves garlic, crushed
1/2 lb. bacon, cooked crisp
* and crumbled*

Blend avocado with salt, lemon juice, Tabasco, and garlic. Cover and chill. Add bacon. *Makes about 3 cups.*

283

GUACAMOLE-WITH GARLIC

4 avocados, mashed or pureed
1/2 cup sour cream
1 pkg. (7/10 oz.) garlic salad
  dressing mix

1 tsp. chopped chives
1 Tbsp. vinegar
3 slices crisp bacon,
  crumbled

Combine and Chill: avocado, sour cream, dressing mix, chives, and vinegar. Sprinkle with bacon. *Makes about 3 cups.* Variation: Add 1/4 cup crumbled bleu cheese; beat or whirl in electric blender until smooth. Chill.

SALAD DRESSINGS

AVOCADO DRESSING FOR FRUIT SALADS

3 avocados, pureed
1 cup sour cream

1 & 1/2 tsp. salt
2 Tbsp. lime juice

Combine all ingredients and chill 30 minutes. *Make 3 cups.*

AVOCADO DRESSING FOR VEGETABLE SALADS

2 avocados, pureed
1 & 1/3 cups sour cream
1 & 1/2 tsp. salt
1/2 tsp. chervil

1/8 tsp. Tabasco
4 tsp. lemon juice
1 Tbsp. minced onion

Combine all ingredients and chill 30 minutes. *Makes 3 cups.*

CLASSIC AVOCADO SALAD

1/2 head Boston lettuce
1/2 head romaine
1/2 head chicory
1/2 pt. cherry tomatoes, halved
2 avocados, peeled and sliced

3 slice bacon, cooked and
  crumbled
3 ozs. crumbled Roquefort or
  bleu cheese
Herb dressing*

Into a large salad bowl, tear greens in bite-sized pieces; add tomatoes and avocados. Sprinkle with bacon and cheese. Toss lightly with Herb dressing*. *6 to 8 servings.*

*Herb Dressing:

1 cup vegetable oil   *1 tsp. sugar*
6 Tbsp. wine vinegar   *1/2 tsp. basil leaves*
1/4 cup lemon juice   *dash pepper*
1 tsp. salt   *2 cloves garlic*

Combine ingredients. Chill, covered. *Makes about 1 and 1/2 cups.*

AVOCADO HOLLANDAISE
FOR SEAFOOD SALADS

4 eggs   *2 avocados, halved and*
1/2 cup lemon juice   *peeled*
1 tsp. salt   *1 cup butter, melted (2 sticks)*
dash each: onion, salt, cayenne

Blend eggs with lemon juice in electric blender until lemon colored. Slowly add bubbling hot butter over lower speed. Blend in avocado and seasonings until smooth. Chill 30 minutes. *Makes 3 cups.*

AVOCADO AND MUSHROOM COSMOPOLITAN

2 avocados, peeled, thinly sliced   *1 Tbsp. white wine vinegar*
1/2 lb. fresh mushrooms,   *1 Tbsp. chopped parsley*
  thinly sliced   *1 clove garlic, crushed*
1/3 cup olive oil   *1 tsp. salt*
juice of 1 lemon   *few grinds pepper*

In a shallow crystal bowl, arrange layers of avocados and mushrooms. Combine remaining ingredients. Pour over avocados. Chill for at least 1 hour. *6 to 8 servings.*

SANDWICHES

THE CALIFORNIA CLUB

4 avocados, sliced	*2 large tomatoes, sliced*
1 cup mayonnaise	*8 slices cooked turkey*
1/4 cup chili sauce	*1 lb. bacon, cooked crisp*
24 slices white toast	*salt and pepper*
lettuce	*pimiento-stuffed olives*

Blend mayonnaise and chili sauce; spread on toast. Assemble 8 double-decker sandwiches with avocado and remaining ingredients. Add salt and pepper to taste. Quarter sandwiches; secure with cocktail picks and garnish with olives. *Makes 8.*

SOLVANG SANDWICH-OPEN-FACE

3 avocados, thinly sliced	*crumbled bleu cheese*
Boston lettuce	*1 can (2 ozs.) rolled anchovy*
2 lbs. shrimp, cooked, shelled	*filets, drained*
and cleaned	*8 large slices rye,*
Watercress Cream Dressing,	*pumpernickel or white*
below	*bread, buttered*

Top bread with lettuce, then rows of avocado and shrimp, then a sprinkling of cheese and a garnish of anchovies. *Makes 8.*

Watercress Cream Dressing:

1 & 1/2 cups sour cream	*1/4 tsp. dill weed*
1/4 cup chopped watercress	*1 Tbsp. lemon juice*
1/2 tsp. salt	

Combine and chill. *Makes 1 and 1/2 cups.*

ON THE HALF-SHELL

The opened avocado makes a perfect small, golden cup from which to serve any number of chilled or hot fillings. Avocados on the half-shell may be served…as an appetizer, salad, dessert…or as a meal in themselves.

WITH GARLIC SALSA

3 cloves garlic, crushed　　　　*1/8 tsp. white pepper*
1 Tbsp. basil leaves　　　　　　*1/4 tsp. salt*
1/2 cup olive or salad oil　　　　*2 Tbsp. wine vinegar*
2 Tbsp grated Parmesan cheese

Combine and chill all ingredients. Spoon into avocado halves.

WITH TOMATO SALSA

6 medium tomatoes, coarsely　　*3/4 tsp. basil leaves*
　chopped　　　　　　　　　　*1/4 tsp. rosemary leaves*
9 green onions, chopped　　　　*1/3 cup Italian dressing*
1 & 1/2 Tbsp. chopped parsley

Combine and chill all ingredients. Spoon into avocado halves.

BAKED STUFFED AVOCADO

3 avocados　　　　　　　　　*dash salt*
1/4 cup lime juice　　　　　　*dash of cayenne pepper*
1 cup flaked crab meat　　　　*1 tsp. minced onion*
1 cup cream sauce　　　　　　*1 cup grated cheese*

Cut avocados in half lengthwise. Remove seeds. Sprinkle avocado with lime juice and salt. Combine crab meat and cream sauce. Season to taste with salt, pepper, a pinch of cayenne, and onion. Fill avocados with mixture. Sprinkle with grated cheese. Arrange avocados in a baking pan with half an inch of water. Bake in a moderate oven (350°F) for 15 minutes, or until cheese melts and avocado is heated through.

CHICKEN OR TUNA CURRY

1/2 cup chopped pared apple
1/4 cup chopped onion
1 clove garlic, crushed
1 Tbsp. curry powder
1 tsp. salt
1/8 tsp. pepper
1/4 cup butter or margarine
1/4 cup flour

2 cups cubed cooked chicken
* or 2 cans (7 oz. each) tuna,*
* drained and flaked*
3 or 4 avocados, halved and
* peeled*
3 to 4 cups hot cooked rice
1 cup light cream
1 cup chicken broth

In a saucepan, cook apple and onion with garlic, curry, salt, and pepper in butter until tender. Blend in flour. Gradually stir in cream and broth. Cook, stirring constantly, until sauce is smooth and bubbly. Fold in chicken or tuna; heat slowly, stirring occasionally for 10 minutes. Meanwhile, spoon rice into shallow baking dish; arrange avocado halves on rice. Bake at 350°F for 5 minutes. Spoon curry over avocado halves. Serve with any of these suggested condiments: chopped hard-cooked egg, crumbled cooked bacon, sweet pickle relish, coconut, raisins, chutney, or chopped peanuts. *Makes 6 to 8 servings.*

CHUNKY GUACAMOLE
Contributed by Cindi Avila

2 ripe avocados (just
* starting to get soft, but*
* not mushy)*
1 large tomato or 2 plum tomatoes

1/2 small onion
2 tablespoons cilantro
2 teaspoons sea salt

Finely chop onion. Dice tomatoes. Coarsely chop cilantro. Mix together in serving bowl. Cut avocado in half. Remove pit by stabbing it carefully with the side of a knife. While avocado is still in skin, use knife to cut rows. Cut rows up and down and side by side creating a checkerboard. Scoop cut avocado out of skins and mix with other ingredients. Add salt (add extra if you like it salty). Mix thoroughly, but don't mash. Serve chunky with tortilla chips.

AVOCADO CAKE

1/2 cup mashed fresh avocado
1/2 cup shortening
1 & 3/4 cups sugar
2 eggs
1/2 cup buttermilk
1 & 1/2 cup flour
1/2 cup raisins

1/2 cup chopped nuts
1 teaspoon soda
1/2 tsp. salt
1/2 tsp. nutmeg
1/2 tsp. cinnamon
1/2 tsp. cardamom (ground)

Cream shortening and sugar. Add eggs and beat thoroughly. Sift dry ingredients together and add alternately with buttermilk. Soak raisins in hot water for a few minutes, drain well and flour lightly to avoid sinking in batter. Stir in avocado, nuts, and raisins. Bake in loaf pan at 375°F for 1 and 1/4 hours until done. Let cake stand a few minutes in pan before removing.

AVOCADO LIME PIE WITH MERINGUE

1 fresh avocado, pureed with
1/2 cup fresh lime juice
  (about 5 limes)
1 & 1/2 cups sugar
1/2 cup cornstarch
1/4 tsp. salt

1 & 1/2 cups water
4 eggs, lightly beaten
1 Tbsp. grated lime peel
9-inch baked pie shell
meringue, given below

In a saucepan blend: sugar, cornstarch, and salt; gradually stir in water. Stir to boiling over medium heat and boil 1/2 minute. Gradually beat half of hot mixture into egg yolks; then return to saucepan. Stir and boil 1 minute longer. Remove from heat and stir in lime peel. Blend in avocado puree. Turn into pie shell. Top with

Meringue. Bake in 350°F (moderate) oven for 10 to 15 minutes until golden. *Makes one 9-inch pie.*

Allow to mellow at room temperature for about 30 minutes before unmolding.

Meringue: Beat 4 egg whites (at room temperature), 1/4 teaspoon cream of tartar, and 1/8 teaspoon salt until foamy. Continue beating gradually adding 1/2 cup sugar, until stiff, but not dry.

Note: Lemon peel and juice may be substituted for lime. Also, the avocado filling may be turned into 8 baked 4 and 1/2 x 1 and 1/4 inch tart shells for individual desserts. For very high meringues, double the meringue recipe.

AVOCADO HONEY CUP
Contributed by
Simla Somturk Wickless

*1 ripe avocado, cut in
half and seed removed*

*1 Tbsp. raw pumpkin seeds
2 tsp. honey (get locally made
honey)*

Prep avocado. Drizzle honey over both sides. Sprinkle with pumpkin seeds. Marvel at how pretty it looks. Grab a spoon and scoop away! *Makes enough for 1 breakfast serving. Have 1/2 for a snack or appetizer, or dessert!*

Variations:

- Use ground walnuts, almonds, hazelnuts, or whole sunflower seeds instead of pumpkin seeds.

- Sprinkle with 1 tablespoon ground flax seed.

- If you're really hungry, add a side of brown rice bread, toasted, spread with 1 tablespoon of organic goat cheese or creamy sheep's milk cheese.

SOUPS AND STEWS

SOUPS AND STEWS

Most of the items that go into soups and stews are very reasonable in price, and believe me, a bowl of homemade soup is an extremely nutritious meal. Nowadays, it's so easy for people to reach for a can, and there is no question about the fact that canned or prepared soup has a place in our life, but it just can't compare with homemade soup.

Soups and stews also provide one of the best ways in the world to use leftover turkey or chicken or beef. You'll find your soup or stew will have a better flavor if you include the bones along with the meat while cooking and remove them before serving. This gives additional flavor from the bone marrow.

Another thing that will make a tremendous difference in the flavor of your soups and stews is to use herbs. This is something you have to experiment with to find the right ones to suit your family's taste. Many gourmet cooks tie the herbs into a cheesecloth bag so that it may be easily removed. This is called bouquet garni. A bay leaf, fresh parsley, and thyme are generally included, plus any of your specific herbs in the recipe. You'll be amazed at the flavor this will add to your soup or stew.

The important thing about soup or stew is that it is a one-plate meal. Nutritionists tell you not to throw the water away when you cook vegetables because much of the nutrition is contained in the water. With homemade soups and stews, you don't throw it away, so your family gets the full food value.

It's important that I share one of my mother's secrets of success with soups and stews. She showed me how to do this with minestrone because minestrone is supposed to be a thick, vegetable soup, but I think it applies to any soup where consistency is important. You control the amount of liquid in a soup by using the lid of the pot. At the beginning, you have quite a lot of water, and
294

by keeping the lid off, you allow the steam to escape and the liquid to boil down. If you have to add more liquid, go ahead, and leave the lid on again for a while. As the soup is about done cooking, you must watch it carefully. If it's a little too thin, remove the lid and let it cook down to just the right rich, thick consistency.

COLD CREAM OF ARTICHOKE SOUP

4 artichokes
1 cup heavy cream
2 cups chicken stock or
   bouillon

1 tsp. salt
1/4 tsp. pepper
1/4 tsp. basil

Remove artichoke leaves and scrape fleshy pulp from bottom of leaves with a metal spoon; discard leaves. Remove hearts and discard chokes. Force pulp, hearts, bottoms, and stems through food mill. Combine artichoke pulp and remaining ingredients; mix well. Chill. Stir well before serving. *Makes about 4 cups.*

AVOCADO SOUP

1 large avocado
1 Tbsp. butter or margarine
1 Tbsp. minced onion
3 Tbsp. flour
1 qt. milk

2 chicken bouillon cubes
1 cup diced cooked chicken
dash pepper
salt to taste
1 Tbsp. lime juice

Cook onion slowly in butter or margarine until lightly browned. Blend in flour; stir in milk. Add bouillon cubes, diced chicken, seasonings. Cook and stir until mixture thickens. Sieve avocado; blend with lime juice. Just before serving, pour hot mixture slowly over avocado, stirring until well blended. Serve at once. *Serves 6 to 8.*

CREAM OF BRUSSELS SPROUT
AND GARLIC SOUP

*1 & 1/2 lbs. fresh Brussels
sprouts, cooked
3 cups chicken broth
1 pt. heavy cream*

*1/4 cup lime juice
1 clove garlic, crushed
salted whipped cream*

Puree Brussels sprouts with all ingredients; chill thoroughly. Serve with cream. *Makes 6 to 8 servings.*

A HEARTY WINTER SOUP

*2 Tbsp. butter
1 small onion, chopped
2 Tbsp. flour
2 cans (10 1/2 oz. each)
condensed chicken broth
1 & 1/2 lbs. fresh Brussels
sprouts, halved*

*1/4 tsp. marjoram leaves
dash each: nutmeg, pepper
1 egg
1 cup light cream
2 Tbsp. dry white wine
8 oz. diced carrots
1/2 tsp. salt*

Sauté onion in butter until golden. Stir in flour, then broth. Stir to boil. Add Brussels sprouts and seasonings; cover and cook for 5 minutes until sprouts are just tender. Reduce heat. Beat together egg, cream, and wine. Stir into soup. Add carrots. Cook for 5 minutes longer. *Makes 6 to 8 servings.*

CREAM OF CARROT SOUP

*1 lb. carrots
1 stick celery
1/4 small onion
1 oz. butter
pepper and salt*

*1 oz. flour
1/4 pt. milk
2 Tbsp. cream
chopped parsley
1 & 1/2 pts. stock
bouquet garni*

Prepare and cut up the vegetables and sauté them in the butter for 10 minutes without browning. Add the stock, bouquet garni, and seasoning. Cover and simmer for about an hour, or till the vegetables are quite tender. Remove the herbs and strain the soup. Blend the flour with milk, add to the soup, and bring to a boil, stirring. Cook for 2 to 3 minutes, re-seasoning to taste. Before serving, stir in the cream and add the parsley.

POTAGE CRECY

3 cups sliced carrots
1 cup diced potatoes
6 cups chicken or beef stock
1 tsp. salt

1/8 tsp. ground black pepper
2 Tbsp. butter or margarine
chopped fresh parsley
cooked carrot rings

Cook carrots and potatoes in stock until they are tender, about 25 minutes. Push through a sieve. Add seasonings and butter or margarine. Serve hot, garnished with chopped fresh parsley and a few cooked carrot rings. *Serves 4.*

CHICKEN GUMBO

3 Tbsp. oil
1 fricassee chicken
   (about 3 & 1/2 to 4 lbs.) cut
   into serving-size pieces
1 cup diced onions
1 lb. tomatoes, crushed
10 ozs. chicken stock
1 cup water
10 ozs. whole okra

1 bay leaf
1 tsp. salt
1/2 tsp. thyme leave
1/4 tsp. ground red pepper
1 qt. sliced celery, cut into
   1 & 1/2 inch pieces
1 lb. cooked, smoked ham,
   cut into 1-inch pieces

In a large pot, heat oil. Add chicken, a few pieces at a time, and brown well on all sides. Remove chicken; set aside.

Add onions; sauté for 5 minutes. Add tomatoes, broth, water, bay leaf, salt, thyme, and red pepper. Bring to boiling. Return chicken to saucepan. Cover; reduce heat and simmer for 45 minutes. Add celery and ham; cook 15 minutes longer or until chicken and celery are almost tender. Bone chicken, if desired. Return to boiling point.

Add okra and cook for 4 minutes. Serve with rice, if desired. *Serves 8.*

GARDEN PATCH MEATBALL SOUP

2 medium potatoes, peeled
and cubed
2 medium carrots, peeled and
sliced
4 medium celery stalks and
tops, coarsely chopped

1 lb. tomatoes, peeled and
diced
2 tsp. salt
1 lb. lean ground round
1 egg
1/4 cup chopped parsley

In large kettle or Dutch oven, combine potatoes, carrots, onion, celery, tomatoes, salt, and 3 cups water. Cover and simmer for 30 minutes.

Meanwhile, combine ground beef, egg, and parsley. Shape into 1-inch balls. Add to soup. Simmer, covered, for 15 minutes longer or until meatballs are tender. *Makes 4 servings.*

L.B.J.'S RECIPE FOR
PEDERNALES RIVER CHILI

2 lbs. ground or cubed beef
1 medium onion, chopped
1 clove garlic, minced
2 tsp. ground oregano
1/2 tsp. cumin seed

3 tsp. chili powder
3/4 cup whole tomatoes
2 drops hot pepper sauce
salt
1 cup hot water

Have beef ground through the chili plate or cut into 1/2-inch cubes with sharp knife. Place meat, onion, and garlic in large, heavy skillet or Dutch oven. Cook until meat is lightly browned. Add oregano, cumin, chili powder, tomatoes, pepper sauce, salt to taste, and hot water. Bring to a boil, reduce heat and simmer for about 1 hour. Skim off fat while cooking. *Serves 3 or 4.*

COUNTRY CHICKEN STEW

1 broiler-fryer (about 3 lbs.),
* cut up*
3 Tbsp. red wine
3 medium stalks celery,
* cut up*
1 medium onion, quartered

1 tsp. salt
1 tsp. thyme leaves
3 medium potatoes, peeled
* and quartered*
4 medium carrots, peeled
* and cut in large chunks*

Under broiler, brown chicken pieces, skin-side up. Drain off fat. In large, heavy kettle or Dutch oven, place chicken, 1 & 1/2 cups water and remaining ingredients, except potatoes and carrots. Cover and cook for 30 minutes, stirring occasionally. Skim off surface fat. Add potatoes and carrots; cook for 30 minutes more or until chicken and vegetables are tender. Thicken, if desired. *Serves 6.*

MANHATTAN CLAM CHOWDER

3 cans (7 ozs. each) minced
* clams*
3 medium potatoes, peeled
* and diced*
3 medium carrots, peeled and
* diced*
4 medium stalks celery,
* chopped*

2 cups tomatoes, peeled and
* diced*
1 Tbsp. crumbled bacon
2 tsp. salt
1/2 tsp. thyme leaves
1/4 tsp. pepper

In large kettle or Dutch oven, combine all ingredients and 4 cups water. Cover and simmer for 1 hour. *Makes 8 servings.*

NEW ENGLAND CLAM CHOWDER

3/4 cup chopped onion
1 Tbsp. margarine
2 cups cubed potatoes
1 tsp. salt
1 Tbsp. crumbled bacon

dash pepper
2 cans (7 ozs. each) minced
   clams
1 cup evaporated skim milk

In large saucepan, cook onion in margarine until tender. Add potatoes, salt, bacon, pepper, and 1 cup water. Cover and simmer for 30 minutes or until potatoes are tender. Stir in clams and milk. Heat. (Do not boil.) *Makes 6 servings.*

LAMB AND VEGETABLE STEW

2 & 1/2 lbs. bone-in-lamb stew
   meat, cut into chunks
1/4 cup flour
1 & 1/2 tsp. salt
1/8 tsp. ground black pepper
2 Tbsp. oil or shortening
3/4 cup chopped onions

2 cups boiling water
1 lb. potatoes, peeled and
   quartered
2 small carrots, peeled and
   sliced
3 cups celery, sliced 1 inch
   thick

Dredge lamb with flour mixed with salt and black pepper. In a large saucepan or Dutch oven, heat oil. Add lamb; brown well. Add onion and sauté until lightly browned. Gradually add water. Cover and cook 1 and 1/2 to 2 hours or until almost tender, stirring occasionally. Add potatoes and carrots; cook for 15 minutes. Then add celery; cover and cook 15 minutes longer or until vegetables and meat are tender. *Serves 6.*

ITALIAN VEAL STEW

8 pieces of veal shank, well-
 trimmed
1 Tbsp. olive oil
1 medium onion, diced
1 clove garlic, minced
1/2 cup white wine
2 Tbsp. ketchup
1 Tbsp. lemon juice
2 chicken bouillon cubes
1 tsp. oregano

1/2 tsp. rosemary
4 medium potatoes, peeled
 and quartered
8 small white onions, peeled
4 medium carrots, peeled and
 chopped
2 medium stalks celery,
 chopped
1 Tbsp. chopped parsley

In large, heavy, non-stick Dutch oven, brown veal in olive oil. Add chopped onion and garlic; cook for 5 minutes. Stir in wine, ketchup, lemon juice, bouillon cubes, oregano, rosemary, and 1 cup water. Cover and simmer for 1 hour or until meat is almost tender. Add remaining ingredients; simmer, covered, 30 minutes longer or until meat and vegetables are tender. *Serves 8.*

The cranberry bean has nothing to do with the red berries at Christmastime. The cranberries we use during the holidays are a fruit. The cranberry is a favorite with all the old-time Italian cooks. When you buy the cranberry bean fresh, you don't have to soak it overnight as you do with the dried beans. This recipe is another one of those old Sicilian gems that have been handed down from generation to generation in my family.

CRANBERRY BEAN SOUP

3 lbs. cranberry beans (fresh)
3 qts. of water
1 medium-size onion, sliced
2 or 3 cloves garlic, sliced

1 tomato, cut into small
 pieces
2 Tbsp. olive oil
salt
pepper

(Continued on next page)

Shell the beans and place in water with sliced onion, garlic, and tomato. Then add the olive oil, salt and pepper and let it cook slowly until the beans are softened, about 2 hours.

Get the fresh cranberry beans when you can, but if you can't, get the dried ones. If you use the dried beans, you'll have to soak them overnight before you use them for the soup.

GARDEN SOUP

1 medium onion, chopped
1 Tbsp. margarine
3 medium potatoes, peeled and diced
2 medium carrots, peeled and sliced

1 medium stalk celery, sliced
2 Tbsp. chopped parsley
4 chicken bouillon cubes
salt
dash pepper

In large, heavy, non-stick kettle or Dutch oven, cook onion in margarine. Add remaining ingredients and 5 cups water. Cover and simmer for 40 minutes or until vegetables are tender. Serve as is, or puree in an electric blender and reheat. *Makes 8 servings.*

When I finally decided to put together a collection of fresh fruit and vegetable recipes, one of the first and finest uses I thought of for fresh vegetables was in soups and stews. Of course, I proceeded to solicit from the members of the various Carcione families recipes for the delicious minestrone soups I have been enjoying at their homes over the years. Much to my surprise, I found that from three different Carcione kitchens, I've been getting three different recipes for Minestrone. One is from my house, one is from Fran, my brother Sam's wife, and the third, of course, is from my mother, who makes the greatest Sicilian soups in the world. But I'm not going to play favorites. I'm not even going to identify which is which. I'm going to give you all three, keep peace in the family, and keep on enjoying Minestrone.

MINESTRONE

2 medium onions, sliced
3 medium tomatoes, sliced
3 carrots, sliced
3 stalks celery, sliced
3 or 4 leaves cabbage,
  coarsely chopped
4 medium zucchini, sliced
2 medium potatoes, coarsely
  sliced

1 lb. fresh peas
1 lb. fresh green beans, cut in
  1 inch lengths
4 Tbsp. oil
1 & 1/2 qts. water
2 to 3 leaves basil
1 cup Tortellini or other
pasta

Sauté onion in oil until golden brown. Add tomatoes and cook for 10 minutes over low heat, stirring occasionally. Add water, carrots, celery, potatoes, and green beans and continue cooking until tender. Add zucchini, cabbage, peas, and pasta during last 15 minutes. For added flavor, stir in 1 or 2 tablespoons pesto sauce.

MINESTRONE

4 qts. water
1/4 cup olive oil
1 onion, sliced
4 soft tomatoes, peeled and
  mashed
3 stalks celery, cut up
1 cup red cabbage
1 cup white cabbage
2 leeks

2 cups carrots, sliced
1 Tbsp. chopped parsley
3 large potatoes, diced
2 bay leaves
2 bouillon cubes
salt and pepper to taste
1/2 cup small shell pasta
1/4 cup Parmesan cheese

In large pot, sauté onion and garlic in hot oil until lightly browned. Add water to pot, and when water comes to a boil, add vegetables and seasonings. Simmer for 1 and 1/2 hours. Add pasta shells for about 15 minutes or until tender. Add cheese and stir thoroughly until cheese melts.

STRICTLY VEGETABLE MINESTRONE
(My favorite, says Pete)
Contributed by Gail Carcione

The two most important ingredients in this family minestrone soup are: Cranberry beans (found dried in most grocery stores) and curly or Savoy cabbage. These two items are very important in the development of the perfect flavor and texture.

1 green onion with tops
2 large leaves of curly cabbage*
2 large ripe tomatoes
2 cups of cranberry beans*
1 clove garlic
1 large potato
1 cup or enough grated Romano
   cheese to cover each serving

1 leek with tops
10 to 12 green beans
1 carrot
3 tablespoons olive oil
2 tablespoons parsley
1 tablespoon of dried or
   fresh basil

Soak dried cranberry beans overnight in 2 quarts of water. In the morning, add 1 teaspoon of salt and boil for about 2 hours until tender. Drain half the beans out of their liquor and put them in a colander or purée sieve; then return the resultant purée to remaining beans and the liquor. Set this aside. In another pot, large enough to hold at least 3 quarts of water plus the vegetables, put finely minced dry onions and garlic, stir well, and cook slowly for 10 minutes without browning.

Peel tomatoes and add them. Add parsley and basil and cook for 10 minutes more. Put in the set-aside purée and liquor, and black pepper. Stir well. Mince all green vegetables, mince squash and carrots, peel and dice potatoes, and add all these to the pot. Add enough cold water to amply cover the vegetables. Cover, bring slowly to a boil, and then add salt to suit taste. Simmer until vegetables are very tender, which will take about 2 hours. When three quarters done, add more salt, if needed. This soup will be at its best cooked one day and eaten the next. It keeps well in a refrigerator, so one can safely make twice as much as is needed for one meal, put away what remains, and serve it several days later. *Makes 8 servings.*

MINESTRONE

4 qts. boiling water
3 Tbsp. oil
1 onion, chopped
1 clove garlic, minced
3 potatoes, diced
2 cups fresh string beans,
*   cut up*
4 stalks celery, cut up

1 cup fresh peas
2 tomatoes peeled and
*   mashed*
1 Tbsp. chopped parsley
2 bay leaves
salt and pepper to taste
1 cup Ditaline pasta
1/4 cup Parmesan grated
*   cheese*

Pour oil in pot and when oil is warm, sauté onion and garlic until lightly browned. Add water and bring to a boil. Then add vegetables and spices, and let simmer for about 25 minutes. Add pasta and cook for 15 minutes. Sprinkle cheese on each serving of soup.

GOURMET MUSHROOM VEGETABLE SOUP

3 cups chicken broth
1 large carrot, very thinly
*   slivered*
1/4 lb. sliced fresh mushrooms

1/4 lb. fresh chicken, chopped
1 tomato, diced
1 Tbsp. dry sherry, optional

In a medium saucepan, combine broth and carrot. Bring to boiling point. Reduce heat, cover and simmer for 5 to 8 minutes. Add mushrooms, spinach, and tomato. Cook covered for 5 minutes longer. Add sherry, if desired. *Serves 6.*

305

FRENCH ONION SOUP

1 Tbsp. butter
2 & 1/4 cups thinly sliced onions
6 cups beef broth
1 tsp. salt

1/8 tsp. pepper
few grains cayenne
3 dry rolls, toasted
3/4 cup grated Parmesan
  cheese

Melt butter in saucepan. Add onions and cook for 8 minutes, or until yellow. Add broth, salt, pepper, and cayenne. Cook slowly for 20 minutes, or until onions are tender. Do not cover. To serve, place half a toasted roll in each of 6 soup plates. Top each roll with 2 tablespoons cheese. Fill plate with soup and serve at once. *Serves 6.* Beef broth may be made by dissolving 6 bouillon cubes in 6 cups boiling water.

Sorrel is one of those items that we don't seem to get in volume, at least not here on the West Coast. Supply is limited and sales are limited, but if you do come across, it, do try this recipe for Cream of Sorrel Soup. It is really delicious.

CREAM OF SORREL SOUP

3 1/2 cups chicken stock
  (3 & 1/2 cups hot water)
  (3 & 1/2 cubes chicken stock)
1/2 cup butter
2 to 3 leeks (white only,
  chopped fine)
1/4 cup celery (optional)

4 medium potatoes, sliced
  fine
1 tsp. salt
1/8 tsp. pepper
3 to 4 bunches Sorrel,
  washed
1 lemon, sliced
2 cups cream

Prepare chicken stock and set aside. Melt butter in a large saucepan. Add leeks and celery and cook low for about 5 minutes. Add remaining ingredients. Cook for about 15 to 20 minutes until potatoes are done. Simmer. Put mixture through a fine sieve and blend in the cream. Cool soup a little before adding cream.

SUNCHOKE SOUP

The salted water in which sunchokes (Jerusalem Artichokes) are boiled has a superb and intriguing flavor. It is yellow to yellowish green in color, depending upon the variety of the sunchokes.

You may season it to taste with a little more salt and pepper and serve it as a clear soup. Float thin slices of fresh sliced sunchokes on top.

Prefer a heartier soup? Melt 2 tablespoons of butter in a heavy saucepan. Add 2 tablespoons flour and stir until smooth. Add 2 cups of sunchoke liquid, stirring rapidly. Continue stirring until thickened. Salt to taste. The texture will be similar to split pea soup, but with a flavor similar to artichokes.

YAM CHICKEN SOUP

1 & 1/2 qts. chicken stock	*4 medium yams, peeled*
1 cup diced cooked chicken	*and diced*
2 medium carrots, diced	*1/8 tsp. poultry seasoning*
3/4 cup diced celery	*thyme to taste*
1 medium onion, thinly sliced	*1 & 1/2 tsp. salt*

Combine chicken stock, chicken, carrots, celery, and onion. Heat to boiling point. Cover and simmer for 10 minutes. Add yams and cook, covered, about 20 minutes, or until vegetables are tender. Add seasonings.

LOUISIANA YAM GUMBO

1/4 cup ham drippings or
butter
1 cup chopped onion
1 qt. chicken bouillon
1 lb. tomatoes, peeled and
diced
1 lb. fresh, sliced okra

2 cups diced cooked ham
1 lb. fresh peas, shelled
4 medium yams, cooked
peeled and diced, fresh or
canned
1/2 tsp. thyme

Heat drippings or butter and add onion. Cook until lightly browned. Add bouillon, tomatoes, okra, and ham. Heat to boiling point and add peas, yams, and thyme. Cook over low heat, stirring occasionally, for 30 minutes. *Makes about 2 and 1/2 quarts.*

COLD APPLE SOUP

4 apples, pared and diced
1/2 cup sugar
1 lemon rind, finely chopped
3 cups hot water

1/2 cup red or white onion
2 Tbsp. flour
2 Tbsp. cold water
1/2 cup heavy cream

Combine apples, sugar, lemon ring, and hot water. Cook until apples are tender. Add wine, blend flour and cold water until smooth. Thin with few tablespoons of hot soup, then mix into soup. Simmer for 5 minutes. Chill. Add cream before serving.

COLD SWEET AND SOUR CHERRY SOUP

2 lbs. sour cherries, pitted
1 cup or more sugar, to taste
1 stick cinnamon
3 cups water

2 Tbsp. flour
1 cup heavy cream
1 cup red wine

Simmer cherries, sugar, and cinnamon in the water until the cherries are tender. Remove cinnamon stick. Blend flour with 3 tablespoons of cold water until smooth. Thin with 3 more tablespoons of water and stir into hot soup. Heat to boiling. Chill before serving. Stir in cream and wine.

NUTRITIOUS LENTIL-BEAN SOUP
Contributed by Connie Umbenhower

This recipe uses black lentils, which are the most nutrient rich of the lentil family. It is an easy, delicious and nutritious dish, perfect for a cold, rainy day.

1 lb. black lentils
1 can black beans
2 cups chopped celery
2 medium tomatoes chopped
1/2 large red onion
4 slices fresh ginger
  (or chopped finely)
1 tsp. ground cumin
1 tsp. ground cloves
Salt 1 tsp. (or to taste)

1 can garbanzo beans
1 can vegetable broth
2 cups chopped carrots
1 bunch cilantro, finely diced
3 cloves garlic
2 Tbsp. canola oil
1 Tbsp. ground coriander
1 tsp. ground turmeric
1 Tbsp black pepper

Add lentils and broth to 8 cups of cold water and bring to a boil. Lower heat to medium and continue to cook lentils for another 10 to 12 minutes.

While lentils are cooking, chop tomatoes, celery, and carrots. Add to lentils. Drain and rinse garbanzo and black beans and add to pot, together with all the spices, salt, and pepper.

In saucepan, sauté onions, garlic, and ginger in oil. Add to cooking mixture, add chopped cilantro and cook for another 10 minutes. Serve with Pita bread or whole grain rolls.

ROASTED CAULIFLOWER, CARROT, GINGER SOUP
Contributed by Kristin Hoppe

1 head cauliflower,
sliced 1" thick
2 whole onions, chopped
1 tablespoon ginger, minced
5 tablespoons olive, coconut,
or grapeseed oil
1 tablespoon sea salt, to taste
1/2 whole lemon, juiced

6 whole carrots, sliced 1/2"
thick
2 whole apples, chopped
6 cloves garlic, minced
12 cups water or vegetable
stock
1 teaspoon pepper, to taste
1 bunch cilantro, chopped

Preheat oven to 415° F. Line a baking sheet with parchment paper. Toss cauliflower and carrots with 2 tablespoons oil and dash of salt and pepper. Place on baking sheet and roast until tender and edges browned, approx. 45 minutes.

In a large sauté pan, heat oil over medium heat. Saute onions, apples, garlic, and ginger until soft and caramelized.

In batches, blend both veggie mixtures and water or vegetable stock until smooth. Return to stove and simmer over low heat. Season to taste with salt, pepper, lemon, and cilantro. *Makes 12 servings.*

CARAMELIZED ONION, ZUCCHINI, CILANTRO SOUP
Contributed by Kristin Hoppe

2 large sweet onions, sliced
1 bunch cilantro, chopped
6 cups stock

2 pounds, zucchini, chopped
1/4 cup olive oil
salt and pepper, to taste

In a large sauté pan over medium heat, add olive oil, onions, and dash of salt. Saute onions until very soft and edges become golden brown and caramelized, about 20 minutes. In a large stockpot, place stock and chopped zucchini. Bring to boil, reduce to simmer and wait until zucchini is soft. Add caramelized onions and cilantro to zucchini stock mixture. Turn off heat. Blend using immersion blender or blend in batches using a blender. Return to stove, add additional stock if required for desired consistency. Season with salt and pepper to taste. *Serving Size: 8*

SQUASH, ASIAN PEAR, APPLE, AND GINGER SOUP
Contributed by Kristin Hoppe

2 medium squash, butternut-
  kabocha, delicata; halved
  and seeded
1/4 teaspoon cinnamon, ground
1/8 teaspoon nutmeg, freshly
  ground
1 tablespoon fresh ginger, minced
1 large apple, peeled, cored,
  and chopped
8 cups vegetable mineral broth

1/4 cup coconut oil
1/4 teaspoon allspice, ground
1/4 teaspoon sea salt
1/4 teaspoon red pepper
  flakes
1 medium onion, chopped
1 large asian pear, peeled,
  cored, and chopped
1 cup coconut milk
Cilantro, minced

(Continued on next page)

Preheat oven to 425° F. In a small bowl, whisk 2 tablespoons of coconut oil and spices. Brush the inside flesh of the squashes with the oil/spice mixture and place cut side down on a baking sheet lined with parchment paper. Roast in oven for 45 minutes, until tender. Remove from oven and cool.

In a large pot over medium heat, add 2 tablespoons of coconut oil. Add onion and sauté until golden brown. Add ginger, asian pear, and apple and sauté until fruit softens and turns golden brown.

Deglaze pot with 1 cup mineral broth. Add additional 4 cups of broth. Allow to simmer for 15 minutes.

Scoop the flesh of the squashes into the apple mixture. Mash the squash into the mixture. Stir coconut milk into squash-apple mixture and let simmer for 15 minutes, allowing flavors to blend.

Using a blender, puree the soup in small batches. If soup is too thick, add additional mineral broth while pureeing. Return pureed soup to stove over low heat, add additional mineral broth to achieve desired consistency. Season to taste with sea salt. Garnish with cilantro or ground nutmeg. *Serving Size: 12*

TIP: Vegetable Mineral Broth

Over the span of a few weeks, I gather most of what I need for a mineral broth. I keep a bag in the freezer where I put vegetable compost, such as onion and garlic peels, carrot and celery ends, potato peels, leek tops, and parsley stems. You will be amazed how quickly you gather a pot worth of veggies.

When I make the mineral broth, I add the contents of the freezer bag and then add additional onions, carrots, celery, sweet potatoes, and garlic. I also add a piece of kombu for extra minerals. I then fill the pot with water, bring to a boil, and then let simmer for a minimum of 4 hours.

When you are satisfied with your broth, allow to cool and then strain to remove the veggies and kombu. You can use your mineral broth now or freeze for later.

CREAMY POTATO SOUP
Contributed by Beatrice Johnson

3 potatoes
1 teaspoon oregano
Salt and pepper to taste

1 pearl onion
3 cups vegetable broth
1/4 cup Kalamata olives
(optional)

Scrub potatoes, and pierce each one several times with knife midway through potato. Bake potatoes in 350° degree oven for 90 minutes, wrapping each one individually in aluminum foil. Once potatoes are done, unwrap, split open and allow to cool for 20 minutes.

Place potatoes (skins and all) and vegetable broth in high-powered blender or food processor. Blend until mixed, but chunky.

Add onion and oregano and blend. Taste, and depending on your broth, add salt and pepper to suit tastes. Garnish with minced kalamata olives.

EXOTIC
FRESH FRUITS
AND
VEGETABLES

EXOTIC FRESH FRUITS AND VEGETABLES

One definition of Exotic is: introduced from another country or not native to the place where found. Another is: strikingly or excitingly different and unusual.

We are starting to find fresh fruits and vegetables in our produce departments which qualify on both counts. The reason for this is the new, improved methods of packing and shipping, and of course, jet air cargo, which can bring fresh produce from all over the world right to our local markets.

You have to have an adventuresome spirit. That's what life is all about. Try new things; enjoy new experiences. It keeps you young and alive! So when you see something unusual in your fresh fruit and vegetable department, buy a small amount and try it. Who knows, you may introduce your family to a new and delightful eating experience.

APPLE PEARS: Also known as Japanese, Chinese, or Oriental Pears. They have long been a favorite of the Oriental people, but because not very many have been commercially grown and the market is limited, the price has been quite high. There seem to be more available and at more reasonable prices recently. If you see something that looks about halfway between an apple and a pear, about one to three inches tall, round shaped and green in color with a russet texture, try it. It certainly might be worth your while. You are most likely to see them from August through March.

BELGIUM ENDIVE: Also known as the French endive, witloof and chicory. This has long been a prestige item, considered a delicacy and very popular with gourmets and gourmet restaurants. Now, with the controlled temperature and refrigerated containers, prices have dropped considerably, and it arrives fresh and beautiful. In New York, it is handled on a volume basis because it is the closest point of entry for most of the United States and sells at lower prices there since the freight cost is less. It has a mildly bitter tonic flavor, but is tender and crisp. It is generally served braised or makes a delightful salad. The retailers who have handled it in the past would like to keep it as a specialty item, but it has become so popular and there are many people who really want it that stores are featuring it at a reasonable price.

CARAMBOLA: This is also called Five Finger Fruit, Bali-Bing, or Star Fruit. It is the strangest fruit I have ever seen in my life, and I have only seen it recently. It has a waxy looking appearance and is two to five inches long and as much as one and a half inches in diameter. It is all solid meat, and when you slice it crosswise, like a cucumber, believe it or not, it makes a perfect five-pointed star out of each slice. I understand the fruit is widely grown in China, and the Chinese buyers are delighted to see it. It is also grown in the islands of the South Pacific. It is considered a great delicacy, and I am sure you ladies will delight in using it for garnishes and decoration. I am told it has a very delicate, good flavor when ripe. If you find it, try it, and you'll have a tremendous surprise.

CELERY ROOT: This has to be one of the roughest, toughest looking root vegetables found anywhere in the world and is also known as celery knob or celeriac. Like many ugly ducklings of the fresh produce world, the outside appearance is deceiving. It is fragrant and delicious and can be used in salads or served cooked. It should be peeled before cooking and either boiled or steamed and served with butter or Hollandaise sauce, or it can be dipped in egg batter and fried. Celery root also adds extra flavor to soups and stews.

CELERY ROOT CELEBRATED
Contributed by
Simla Somturk Wickless

Celery root is an underappreciated root vegetable. It tastes like a mix between turnip and celery and has a consistency similar to that of starchy potatoes when cooked. It is an excellent source of potassium, and also phosphorus, magnesium, iron, and vitamins B6 and C. It's usually available in the fall and winter months and is a wonderful dish to have in colder weather, especially accompanied by a whole grain dish and green vegetables or garbanzo beans.

*1 large celery root, with its
tough outer layer peeled off
& cut into bite-size chunks
1/4 cup olive oil
2 cups vegetable or chicken
broth or water, if broth not
available
Sea salt & pepper to taste*

*1 medium onion, peeled and
sliced
1 medium carrot, sliced – can
leave the peel on for added
nutrients and fiber
1/2 a lemon, squeezed
3 Tbsp chopped fresh parsley*

Sautee onions and carrots on medium heat in olive oil for 3 to 5 minutes. Add chopped celery root, lemon juice, sea salt, and pepper and stir well to coat with olive oil. Add broth, bring to a boil, then reduce to a simmer (low-medium heat). Let simmer until celery root is tender.

Serve warm or chilled. *Serves 2 to 4, depending whether it's served as a main dish or side dish. Double the recipe for several side dishes or meals.*

CHERIMOYA: Also called custard apple and shaped like a huge strawberry. It is oval in shape and green in color. The skin texture varies from smooth to spiny depending on the variety. This is another one of those fruits which is not too attractive from the outside, but the inside is an entirely different story. Inside, it is white and has black seeds that resemble watermelon seeds. It is an excellent fruit and has a delicious, very delicate, flavor. The flavor is a combination of fresh pineapples, strawberries, and banana, plus a quality all its own. Unfortunately, it is quite expensive, and one of the reasons for that is it has to be hand pollinated two or three times a week through the blooming period. But if you have an opportunity, try it. It's good in fruit salads or sprinkled with a little lemon juice, as a dessert.

COCONUTS: The meat of the coconut is quite familiar, but the fresh coconut itself it still a specialty item, although it is becoming more popular. Unless you know how to open a coconut, it may remain a stranger forever. But there are easy ways. There is a soft eye in the largest of the three sections of a coconut. Push a screwdriver or a nail into that eye and drain the liquid or coconut milk. Place the coconut in an oven preheated to 300°F for about an hour. If it hasn't cracked completely in that time, tap it with a hammer. Or should you wish to use the coconut halves as serving dishes, instead of baking it, simply hold it in the palm of your hand with the ridges running lengthwise. With a hammer, rap it sharply in the center on one of the ridges until it splits in half. Use a grapefruit knife to remove the meat and any brown inner shell attached to it.

You can make coconut curls by using a vegetable parer to cut strips. Spread a single layer on a shallow baking pan and toast at 300°F for just a few minutes until brown and sprinkle with salt. Store tightly covered.

Grated fresh coconut keeps several days in the refrigerator or indefinitely in the freezer. Or, you can dry grated coconut in the oven at 150°F for three or four hours. Shreds will dry, not brown, and may be used instead of packaged processed coconut.

JERUSALEM ARTICHOKES: Also known as sunchokes, they are being rediscovered as a versatile and delicately, nutlike flavored vegetable. It is a knotty tuber of the root of a variety of the sunflower plant.

Served raw and sliced, they make an excellent crisp, crunchy finger food just sprinkled with salt or served with your favorite dip. Here are some other serving suggestions:

Boiled: Scrub tubers well in cold, running water, using a very stiff brush. Cook in boiling, salted water to cover for 10 to 12 minutes, or until just tender-crisp. If the tubers are quite large, they may take up to 5 minutes longer. DON'T OVERCOOK. Remove sunchokes from the liquid, setting liquid aside to use in soups, aspics, or stews. Peel or rub the skin off and cut in cubes or slices, season with melted butter, salt and pepper. 1 pound serves 3 to 4.

Steamed: Scrub tubers as above. Cook in a small amount of water in a heavy saucepan with a tight lid. As soon as the water comes to a boil, turn the heat down to avoid scorching. Steam for approximately 20 to 25 minutes until tender-crisp. Don't overcook. Peel and serve like boiled sunchokes.

Creamed: Serve hot cooked cubes of tubers in a cream sauce. For variations, a dash of nutmeg or sweet basil added to the sauce brings out the delicate flavor of the sunchokes.

A quarter cup of grated cheddar cheese added to the sauce provides a hearty accent.

Try putting creamed sunchokes in a casserole dish, top with slices of cheddar cheese and buttered crumbs. Put under the broiler for 2 to 3 minutes until cheese is bubbly.

Sautéed: Scrub thoroughly with a stiff brush and cut in fairly thin slices. It isn't necessary to peel them, but you may if you desire. In a heavy skillet, melt two tablespoons of butter for each pound of sunchokes. Add sunchokes and sauté in melted butter, stirring frequently. Sprinkle lightly with salt. Cook until crisp-tender.

Mashed: Boil or steam sunchokes until tender. Rub off skins and mash or put through a food mill. Season with butter, salt, and pepper. The texture will be more moist and not as fluffy as mashed potatoes.

For a change, blend a cup of mashed sunchokes with a cup of mashed, cooked carrots, season to taste.

With Salad: Mix 2 cups of cubed cooked sunchokes with 1/2 cup of your favorite French or Italian dressing. Chill. Add 1/2 cup diagonally sliced celery and 1/4 cup chopped pimiento. Toss lightly to blend. Serve on individual salad plates on a bed of lettuce.

Green salads come to life with the addition of slices or cubes of crisp sunchokes.

With Vegetables: Raw sliced or diced sunchokes may be added to almost any other vegetable. Try them with cooked carrots, string beans, peas, or spinach. Just add a cup of sunchokes to the cooked vegetable, heat through and serve. The sunchokes will give every-day vegetables an Oriental flair.

With Meat: Sunchokes are an excellent extender for meatloaf. Nutritious, economical, and flavorful, a cup of cubed sunchokes will give your meatloaf new interest.

Scrub sunchokes and put them around a roast for the last 30 minutes of cooking time. They are an excellent substitute for potatoes. Serve with roast gravy or juices.

Add a cup or two cubed sunchokes to beef stew during the last 15 minutes of cooking.

JICAMA: Also described as the Mexican potato or Chinese potato, this root vegetable is brown in color and looks something like a turnip. It is very crisp and crunchy and is very good raw, sliced with lemons, served with a dip, or is sometimes used as you would use water chestnuts. The principle supply comes from Mexico and is generally available between November and June.

KIWI FRUIT: This is actually the Chinese gooseberry grown in New Zealand, which the New Zealanders renamed after the native Kiwi bird. This fruit is about the size of the small potato, dark brown in color and has little fine hairs on it. Inside, the fruit is lime green with a creamy colored center and tiny seeds spreading from it, like the rays of the sun. It is a surprisingly good flavor, kind of mild and not too sharp. I like it best sliced up in a fruit salad, or jello, or even in a fruit punch. This fruit is high in vitamin C.

MANGOS: As far as I'm concerned, this tropical fruit is one of the finest fruits from anywhere, anytime, or any place. They can hardly be called an exotic fruit on the West Coast anymore because in the past few years, sales have increased by leaps and bounds. They are now becoming popular throughout the United States and are moving in tremendous volume and at reasonable prices. The mango has a delicious flavor. It is so juicy it is wise to eat it standing over the kitchen sink. You can eat them out of hand on the half shell, mix with any fruit salad, or alternate mango slices with layers of dairy sour cream for a delectable parfait. Kids of all ages love to stick a fork in one end and eat the peeled mango like a popsicle. Believe me, when the good Lord made the mango, He threw the mold away!

PAPAYAS: The papaya is also known as the tree melon, and believe me, they are sunshine from Hawaii. Here is another wonderful tropical fruit. If you haven't introduced your family to

322

the papaya, you're really missing something. Like the mango, the papaya is becoming very plentiful and is now being carried in most large produce departments across the country, year round, and at reasonable prices. In addition to having a sweet delicate flavor, papayas are very easy to digest—a perfect food for the very young and very old. They contain twice as much vitamin C as an orange, as much vitamin A as a carrot, and lots of B1 and vitamin D.

Never buy a green papaya. Select one with as much light yellow color as possible, but always be sure it is firm. They may be stored in the refrigerator for several days.

A classic breakfast in the Islands will include half a chilled papaya with wedges of lime, which brings out their delicate tropical flavor. After cutting it lengthways, scoop out the seeds and this will leave a natural cavity. Eat it plain, with lime or add cottage cheese. Delicious with a seafood salad, or for an exotic dessert, your favorite ice cream.

We are delighted to be able to offer a good variety of recipes for this wonderful taste treat.

PANCAKES WAIKIKI

2 tsp. baking soda
1 cup buttermilk
2 eggs, beaten
1 very ripe banana, mashed
1 Tbsp. sugar

1/2 tsp. salt
1 Tbsp. melted butter
1 cup sifted flour
sliced papaya
whipped honey butter

Dissolve baking soda in buttermilk and mix with eggs, banana, sugar, salt, butter, and flour. Bake pancakes on griddle and top with thin slices of papaya and whipped honey butter. *Makes 12 small pancakes.*

PAPAYA CROWN SALAD

1 can (6 1/2 oz.) tuna
1/2 cup green onions, finely
  chopped
1/2 cup cucumber, finely
  chopped
1 large chili pepper, seeded
  and finely chopped

2 Tbsp. capers, drained and
  chopped
salt and pepper to taste
4 papayas
1 lemon

Combine tuna, green onions, cucumber, chili pepper, and capers in a mixing bowl. Season with salt and pepper and chill for several hours. Make papaya crowns by cutting each papaya in half and removing seeds. With cut side down, cut a wedge 2 inches deep from the stem end of each half. Sprinkle each half with lemon juice and refrigerate until ready to serve. To serve, place 2 papaya halves in a small cup (custard cup, etc.) and fill with tuna salad mixture. *Makes 4 servings.*

PAPAYA STUFFED WITH HAM SALAD

1/2 lb. cooked ground ham
1/4 tsp. ground cloves
2 Tbsp. brandy

2 papayas
salad greens

Try this with chicken and shrimp, too. Combine ham, cloves, and brandy. Blend thoroughly. Cut stem ends off papayas and scoop out seeds with an ice tea spoon. Firmly pack ham into papayas. Cover and refrigerate for several hours. Slice into rings and serve on greens. *Makes 4 servings.*

PAPAYA FRUIT BASKETS
WITH RUM LIME SAUCE

4 papayas
2 bananas, peeled and sliced

1 box strawberries, washed
and sliced

To make papaya baskets, cut fruit 1/3 from top, leaving 3/4 inch of the fruit in the center to form handle. Remove seeds and fill baskets with strawberries and bananas.

Rum Lime Sauce:

2/3 cup sugar
1/3 cup water
1 tsp. grated lime rind

6 Tbsp. lime juice
1/3 cup light rum

To make sauce, combine sugar and water in a small saucepan and bring to a boil. Reduce heat and simmer for 5 minutes. Add lime rind and let cool to room temperature. Add lime juice and rum. Pour over papaya baskets and fruit. Cover with plastic wrap and chill for several hours. *Makes 4 servings.*

HAWAIIAN PAPAYA MUFFINS

2 cups sifted flour
2 tsp. baking powder
1 tsp. salt
2 Tbsp. sugar

1 egg, beaten
1 cup milk
3 Tbsp. melted butter
1 cup papaya pulp*

Preheat oven to 375°F. Sift dry ingredients together. Mix egg with milk, butter, and papaya. Fold lightly into dry ingredients, taking care not to overstir. Bake in small greased muffin tins, filled 2/3 full, for 20 to 25 minutes. *Makes 12 small muffins.*

*To make papaya pulp: Into blender jar, put chopped, seeded and peeled papaya. Puree until smooth.

GREEN PAPAYA POMELO SALAD
Contributed by Diem Doonan

Salad:

3 cups green papaya,
  peeled, julienne cut
1 cup red cabbage, shredded
1/3 cup mint leaves, rough chop
1/3 cup Thai Basil, rough chop
Salt and pepper to taste

1 medium pomelo or
  ruby grapefruit, peeled,
  segmented, remove skin,
  tear into bite-size pieces
2 to 3 Tbsp. fried shallot
  flakes (optional)

Dressing:

1/4 cup lime juice
1/4 cup sugar
1 to 2 garlic cloves, minced

1/4 cup fish sauce
1 Thai chili, thinly sliced
1/2 cup warm water

In a small bowl, combine dressing ingredients and stir until sugar is dissolved. In a salad bowl, add salad ingredients and gently mix. Add dressing, making sure it is well incorporated. Add salt and pepper to taste. Top with fried shallot flakes.

Fried Shallot Flakes (optional):
6 shallots, thinly sliced   1 cup vegetable oil

Heat oil in pan over medium heat, add shallots and slowly fry until shallots are rich brown and crispy. Remove and let drain on paper towel. Shallots should be light and crispy. Store in air-tight container in refrigerator. *Servings: 4 appetizer plates or 2 entrees.*

PRICKLY PEARS: This is a delicious fruit of a species of cactus. It is about the size and shape of a lemon and comes in greens, yellows, reds, and mixed. Usually the flesh is the same color as the outside skin. However, that outside skin is covered with many, many tiny little spines. Years ago, if you would pick one up in a store, these spines would stick to your hands. They are practically invisible. If you touched your face, they would go into your face and were a real annoyance. Now, however, all of the spines are completely removed by mechanical brushes, and you can handle this fruit just like you would an apple. They have a very good flavor and are probably best known for the jams, jellies, and preserves which are made by the Indians of the Southwest.

SNO PEAS: Also known as Sugar Peas, are a flat Chinese pea or pea pod, three or four inches long, one inch wide, and available generally from May through September. They are similar to China Peas, which are smaller in size and more tender than sugar peas and often eaten raw. It looks like a very immature pea; in fact, the shape of the peas in the pod is barely visible, but, of course, the pod is what you want—it must be nice and fresh, crisp, and green.

KUMQUATS: The Kumquat is the tiniest of all citrus fruits and is shaped like a football. It can be eaten out of hand, used for preserves, or as a decoration. The Chinese people have a wonderful custom when they go visit a friend, particularly at the time of the Chinese New Year. They bring their friend fruit, and it is very important that the fruit be nice and bright and has healthy green leaves still attached. Kumquats and tangerines are both popular for this purpose. When they give it, they are saying, "Good Luck to you for the balance of the year." Isn't that great! It is often difficult to find the fruit with the leaves still on, but that is very important because the leaves represent good luck, good health, and good prosperity.

WATERCRESS: Here is another item that people think is way, way out there—gourmet and exotic, but it shouldn't be. It is

327

something you can use just like lettuce. It is loaded with zest and gives you a little bit of zip you don't get in any other item. The English absolutely love watercress, and they use it to make wonderful watercress sandwiches.

Every 3 and 1/2 ounces of watercress contains 900 units of vitamin A, 79 units of vitamin C plus iron, and protein. Believe me, the nutritional content of watercress is very, very good. They say it will bring back the bloom to the young and put color in old ladies' cheeks. Now that's doing something!

To get you started, try these recipes:

PEAR WATERCRESS BOWL

4 fresh Bartlett pears　　　　　　*2 tsp. lemon juice*
3 bunches watercress　　　　　　*1 tsp. onion slat*
1/2 cup bottled Italian-style　　　*1/4 tsp. white pepper*
*　dressing*　　　　　　　　　　　*1/4 tsp. salt*
1/4 cup fresh onion,
*　finely chopped*

Halve, core, and slice pears. Wash and trim cress; break into bite-size pieces. Mix dressing, onion, lemon juice, onion salt, pepper, and salt in bottom of salad bowl. Add pears and toss well to coat; add cress and toss gently.

WATERCRESS ARUGULA SALAD
WITH THYME VINAIGRETTE
Contributed by Diem Doonan

Salad:

2 cups watercress,
washed, dried and picked
1 Granny smith apple,
matchstick cut

2 cups arugula, washed
and dried

Dressing:

2 Tbsp. Dijon
1 garlic clove, minced
1 tsp. fresh thyme, minced
Salt and pepper to taste

2 tsp. honey
Zest & juice of 1 lemon
1/3 cup extra virgin olive oil

In a wooden salad bowl, combine dressing ingredients except oil. Slowly drizzle oil, using a whisk to stir constantly. Add watercress, arugula, and apples, tossing and making sure each leaf is dressed. Add salt and pepper to taste. *Servings: 4 appetizer plates or 2 entrée.*

ENDANGERED FRESH FRUITS AND VEGETABLES

ENDANGERED FRESH FRUITS AND VEGETABLES

The world continues to change, and when you think about it, the same thing is true of fresh fruits and vegetables. When you have new developments in old vegetables, when they are changed from their original color, suddenly sales take off. Pretty soon, the old variety just seems to disappear. Take, for example, white asparagus, white corn, and white celery. Years ago, white was all you could buy, and everyone was satisfied. But then they developed the green asparagus and the green celery, and that was it for the white varieties. The growers used to build up mounds of earth over the plant so the asparagus grew underground, and that was why it was white. When it was big enough, they would take a knife and cut it off under the mounds. But now it just grows up through the ground, so it is green and probably more nutritious from exposure to the sun. They used to wrap celery so it would grow white, but now it is allowed to turn green, and that is how we know celery today.

Once all sweet corn was white, but when they started growing yellow sweet corn, people fell in love with both the color and the taste. So, you seldom see white corn anymore, not even as much white grapefruit. About 30 years ago, white grapefruit was all that was available. When they developed the pink and the red grapefruit, the sales took off spectacularly. We still get some white grapefruit, and it is very good. I would recommend it, but generally speaking, there is not much white grapefruit around in comparison to pink and red.

We are creatures of habit, and once people start eating one variety of a thing, they hate to change. As far as the supermarkets are concerned, they are going to go with the tide. They are not going to buck it. If it's what the customers want, it is what they are going to get.

Blood oranges are very hard to find anymore. The name describes them perfectly; they are blood red inside. This is a favorite of the European countries especially around the Mediterranean. They are one of the finest oranges for making marmalade because they have a slightly bitter quality.

There is a variety of peaches called blood peaches which have gradually been phased out. Although they were never a big seller, there were usually some around in season; but in the past few years, they have been disappearing. The outside skin has many tine red stripes over a greenish or amber base. When you cut it in half, the flesh is white with many red stripes running completely through it. Directly under the skin, the flesh is a deep red, and it measures about an eighth of an inch thick. The red fans out into thin stripes into the white flesh. It's an interesting peach and worth buying. They have an excellent flavor, kind of a strawberry-peach flavor. It's a very, very peachy peach, you might say, but there aren't many around anymore.

The crabapple is a very, very scarce apple now, although it was very common many years ago. It's a small apple, about half the size of a ping pong ball. If you like a sour or tart apple, then you will certainly enjoy the crabapple. When they are ripe, they take on a red blush and the skin may be slightly amber in color.

Years ago crabapples and currants were in high demand for jelly. They are a good combination and make a great jelly. Currants used to be big business, but now very few currants or crabapples are grown. If you ever get the opportunity to make crabapple-currant jelly, try it because it is fantastic.

FIGS

*Figs are a storehouse of energy, with simple sugars,
calcium, magnesium, iron, copper and manganese.*

They say figs are phasing out. This is an unfortunate set of circumstances, but the younger generation, in all probability has not tried too many figs. That's a shame because they are a wonderful fruit. Figs are a storehouse of energy, with simple sugars, calcium, magnesium, iron, copper, and manganese.

When you buy Mission figs, you have to go for the color of the skin. The blacker the skin, the riper and sweeter the fig will be. Most of the time, we say to avoid any fresh fruit or vegetable that is shriveled and doesn't look too good, but Mission figs are one of the exceptions to the rule. Of course, there are other varieties also, and you should give them a try. The Calimyrna is a large, luscious, yellowish-green-skinned fig, and the Kadota has a thick yellow skin and very few seeds.

MARISA'S FIG PIE
Contributed by Marisa Riparbelli

3 Tbsp. Minute Tapioca
1/2 cup brown sugar
1/4 tsp. nutmeg
2 Tbsp. butter cut into pieces,
  plus extra to butter pie plate
1 package All Ready Pie
  Crust or your favorite
  homemade pie crust recipe

2 Tbsp. flour
1/2 cup granulated sugar
1/2 tsp. cinnamon
4 to 6 cups quartered fresh
  figs (or as many as it takes
  to fill pie plate until slightly
  mounded)

Blend dry ingredients. Add fruit. Stir gently until fruit is completely coated. Butter Pyrex pie plate. Place one crust in bottom of plate. Fill with fig mixture. Dot with butter. Top with second pie crust. Crimp edges as usual. Poke holes in top. Bake at 450 for 45 to 50 minutes. Enjoy!

RHUBARB: I can remember when we used to ship carloads of rhubarb to the East Coast in 20-pound boxes. But that business has gone right down the river, you might say. You make rhubarb sauce like you make applesauce, and it is delicious and it's good for you. It is known as the spring tonic. Rhubarb is also called pieplant, because you can make tremendous pies out of it. But we don't see too much rhubarb anymore, and that's a shame.

In the interest of bringing back the popularity of rhubarb, we have some fantastic recipes for you. Maybe we are going to see an increase in the use of rhubarb. I, for one, would certainly like to see that happen.

RHUBARB SAUCE

1 lb. (4 cups) rhubarb   *1/4 cup hot water*
1 cup sugar

Stewed: Cut stalks in inch pieces without peeling. Cook in covered saucepan with hot water until tender. Add sugar. Stir to dissolve.

Baked: Cut rhubarb in inch pieces, without peeling. Put in baking dish. Dissolve sugar in hot water then pour over rhubarb. Bake in moderate 350°F oven until tender, about 30 minutes.

RHUBARB FESTIVE SPRING SALAD

2 cups rhubarb (1 1/2 inch pieces)   *1/2 cup water*
1/2 cup sugar   *1/3 cup chopped nut meats*
1 Tbsp. lemon juice   *1 pkg. apple Jello*
2/3 cup sliced green celery   *1 3-oz. pkg. cream cheese*

Cook unpeeled rhubarb with sugar and water. Bring to boil and reduce heat to low for 10 minutes. Dissolve the gelatin in the

335

boiling hot rhubarb sauce. Add the cream cheese which has been mashed to break it up, and stir until dissolved in the hot mixture. Chill until it begins to thicken. Whip until light and fluffy, then add lemon juice, celery and nut meats. Turn into a salad mold or into individual molds. Chill.

RHUBARB FRUIT WHIP

2 cups rhubarb	*1 cup sugar, divided*
1/2 cup sugar	*1 tsp. grated lemon rind*
2 Tbsp. water	*1 Tbsp. lemon juice*
1 Tbsp. gelatin	*1 tsp. vanilla*
1/4 cup cold water	*4 egg whites*
1/4 cup boiling water	*1/8 tsp. salt*

Cook unpeeled rhubarb, sugar, and 2 tablespoons water together for 5 minutes. Soak gelatin in cold water and then dissolve it in boiling water. Stir in 1/2 cup sugar and lemon rind until sugar is dissolved. Add lemon juice, cooked rhubarb, and vanilla. Place saucepan with these ingredients in ice water. When chilled, whip with an egg beater until frothy. Whip egg whites until stiff, adding 1/2 cup sugar gradually. Fold whites into gelatin mixture. Chill. *Serves 6 to 8.*

RHUBARB PINWHEEL COBBLER

1 & 1/2 lb. diced rhubarb	*2 Tbsp. butter, melted*
1 & 1/2 cups sugar	*juice of 1 lemon*
2 & 1/2 Tbsp. cornstarch	*1/4 cup water*

Mix sugar and cornstarch in saucepan. Add lemon juice and water. Bring to boil, dissolving sugar. Add butter and unpeeled rhubarb. Pour into 2 and 1/2-quart baking dish. Set into heated oven while preparing Pinwheels in the following recipe.

PINWHEELS

1 & 1/2 cups biscuit mix   *2 Tbsp. cooking oil*
4 Tbsp. sugar, divided   *grated rind of 1 lemon*
1/3 cup milk

Combine biscuit mix and 1 tablespoon sugar. Stir oil into milk; add to dry ingredients. Mix lightly. Roll into 1/2-inch thick rectangle. Spread with butter. Mix remaining sugar with lemon rind. Sprinkle half over dough. Roll jelly-roll fashion. Cut into 8 pieces. Place Pinwheels on rhubarb in baking dish. Sprinkle with remaining sugar-peel. Bake at 450°F for 25 minutes. *Serves 8.*

TAPIOCA RHUBARB PUDDING

3 cups rhubarb   *1/4 tsp. salt*
1/2 cup quick-cooking tapioca   *1 & 3/4 cups sugar*
2 cups boiling water   *2 tsp. grated orange rind*

Cut unpeeled rhubarb in 1-inch pieces. Bring water to boil in saucepan and add tapioca and salt. Cook over low heat, stirring until thickened, about 5 minutes. Add rhubarb and cook for 10 minutes more, stirring occasionally. Add sugar and orange rind; stir until sugar is dissolved. Cool. Serve with whipped cream.

RHUBARB PIE

4 cups diced rhubarb   *few grains salt*
1/3 cup flour   *1 Tbsp. butter*
1 & 1/2 cups sugar

Prepare pastry and roll out undercrust; fill into 9-inch pie pan. Combine flour, sugar, and salt with unpeeled rhubarb and place in crust. Dot with butter. Cover with top crust which has been priced. Bake at 425°F for about 40 minutes.

RHUBARB CUSTARD PIE

3 cups diced rhubarb
1 & 1/2 cups sugar
3 Tbsp. flour
few grains salt

1/2 tsp. nutmeg
2 eggs
2 Tbsp. milk
1 Tbsp. butter

Wash and dice unpeeled rhubarb and mix with sugar, flour, salt, and spice. Beat eggs slightly, add milk. Combine with rhubarb mixture. Place in pie shell and dot with butter. Bake at 400°F for 50 to 60 minutes. *Makes 1 single-crust 9-inch pie.*

DATE SWEETENED NO-BAKE BROWNIES
Contributed by Beatrice Johnson

1 cup raw walnuts
1/4 cup raw cacao powder
1/2 teaspoon vanilla extract
dash salt

8 medjool dates (pits
  removed)
2 teaspoons water
2 teaspoons shredded
  coconut (optional)

Blend the almonds, dates and salt together in a food processor until it mixture begins to stick together. Add the dates, cacao powder, and vanilla until evenly distributed. Slowly add in water, 1/2 teaspoon at a time until it's the right consistency. Spoon mixture into small container lined with plastic wrap or heart-shaped cookie mold. Sprinkle with coconut and press coconut into brownie. Store in refrigerator for up to five days.

PRODUCE QUESTIONS FOR
THOSE IN THE KNOW

1. Why is some asparagus white?

   White asparagus is picked under the ground. Sunlight turns it green.

2. What is an edible flower of a thistle plant called?

   Artichoke

3. What seeds of a common melon were found in Tutankhamun's Tomb?
   Watermelon

4. What spice found in Tutankhamun's Tomb was good and useable today?

   Nutmeg

5. What is found represented in the cabbage family that makes them strong infection fighters and cancer fighters and so beneficial for us?

   Sulfur compounds

6. What food contains the sunshine vitamin "D" that helps build strong bones and helps with cancer protection? This food also is a good source of niacin and copper, and some even have a decent amount of protein.

   Mushrooms

7. What vegetable do we eat, but throw its poisonous leaves away?

   Rhubarb

8. What is a Pluat?

50% plum and 50% apricot

9. Dandelion greens are known to be very high in vitamins and minerals, but they are best known for the effect they have after eating?

Very strong diuretic or spring tonic

10. The delicious orange flesh honeydew is a combination of what two melons?
The cantaloupe and honeydew

11. The honeydew will possess what outward sign to tell that it is ripe and ready?

Tackiness of the skin. Sugar comes right through the skin.

12. We have navel oranges in October in our stores and they are out of season. Where are they coming from?

Australia

13. To measure temperature of most things, we use B.T.U's or British thermal units, but how do we measure the heat given off by chili peppers?

We use the Scoville scale, developed by Wilber Scoville in 1912.

14. How does the Scoville scale work?

It measures the reaction with saliva and nerve endings of mucous membranes to determine the amount of capsaicin present.

15. Why is spinach so good for us? Popeye says so?

    Spinach is a good source of niacin, zinc and dietary fiber. It has protein, vitamin A, C, E, B6, folate calcium, iron magnesium, phosphorus, copper, and manganese. That's why!

16. What is the world's hottest chile?

    Naga Jolokia is the world hottest chile, measuring 1,040,000 scoville units, found in northeast India, Bangladesh, and Sri Lanka. Habaneros have 100,000 to 350,000 scu's; Jalipinos have only 2,500 to 2,800 scu's.

17. What is the least hot of the pepper family?
    Bell pepper

18. Law enforcement capsacin spray contains 5,000,000 to 5,000,300 unit of capsacin. Pure capsaicin is 15,000,000-16,000,000 units.

19. What fruit is named after a bird?

    Kiwi

20. What two produce items possess very strong anti-bacterial properties, as well as anti-viral properties?
    Garlic and Ginger

21. What is the main quality that an apple possesses that brings truth to "An apple a day keeps the doctor away"?

    It possesses a good amount of pectin that attaches itself to cholesterol to clean our veins and arteries.

CARCIONE PRODUCE HISTORY
February 3, 2010

I have been part of the wholesale produce business for 40 years. I began in December, 1969 at the Golden Gate Produce Terminal in South San Francisco, California. My grandfather was the first of three generations of Carcione's who worked in produce. My grandfather, Pete Carcione, was only a teenager in the early 1900's when he came to San Francisco from Sicily. He met a young man by the name of Eugene Da Massa, and the two soon became friends. Together, they opened a grocery store at Columbus and Powell Streets. There was no refrigeration in those days, so my grandfather would have to go to the produce market, located on the embarcadero, every day to pick up fresh produce for their market. All the produce came in hot, that is, it still had field heat. Produce had to be sold daily because it would not last. The produce market then was called a commission market. Everything was sold on consignment. There was no price on anything. The price was determined by supply and demand on that day.

A few years went by, and their retail business was a success. Pete's journey to the market each morning led to other friendships. One of those friends was George Giannini, the brother of A.P. Giannini, who later founded the Bank of Italy, which later was renamed Bank of America. The two brothers were running the wholesale produce firm of Scatena, Galli Produce Company. It was founded by Lorenzo Scatena, their stepfather. George knew that Pete, with his booming voice, would make a great salesman. He asked my grandfather, Pete, to join the firm, which he did.

I guess I must backtrack a little so that you might discover how Lorenzo became their stepfather. The Giannini family had a farm in Alviso, south of San Francisco, where one of the Scatena Galli's company barges would pick up their vegetables and bring them to market. Scatena Galli Company had three barges which made daily trips down the three waterways—the Sacramento River, the San

342

Joaquin River, and one that traveled along the peninsula to San Jose. One of the stops was Luigi Giannini's ranch in Alviso. The story is told that one day Luigi had a disagreement with one of the workers over wages and he was shot and killed. Their mother continued using the barge to get the produce to market. She was befriended by Lorenzo Scatena, and after some time, they were married.

My grandfather loved being part of the wholesale produce business, and as his children grew up, they too worked in the business. My Uncle Sam specialized in citrus and strawberries and developed a wonderful following. My aunt became a skilled bookkeeper. My grandfather depended on her talent for many years. This, of course, was before the computer, fax machines, or copy machines. My dad, Joe, loved to sell. His specialties were lettuce and cantaloupes, and just about anything else. Joe was definitely a man of vision. He knew that if the public only knew when to buy and what to buy, it would be better for the farmer and the consumer, as well as the wholesaler. Being in the wholesale produce market each day, he could see for himself what was in and available, and what people should buy that particular day.

This was the beginning of a nationwide love affair with Joe and his recommendations. Joe was convinced that if produce was fresh and the quality was good, it would have the flavor and would taste good. Flavor is everything. Soon, people throughout the nation waited for Joe's recommendations. Joe could be trusted! If he told you to buy something, he believed it with all his heart. His sincerity and passion about his produce suggestions led him to talk to every grower he knew, telling them that picking too early to be first on the market was wrong and it would hurt their business in the long run. It would be very shortsighted if their product did not have the proper sugar or flavor. Singlehandedly, Joe changed the thinking of many growers in regard to fresh produce, while he changed and improved the eating habits of America.

ACKNOWLEDGEMENTS

I would like to thank my many friends for their assistance and encouragement in this project. Those who have contributed recipes are:

Aaron French
Alex Lopez
Barbara Carcione Erle
Barbara Malinowski
Beatrice Johnson
Bruce Riezenman
Caryl Christiansen
Cindi Avila
Connie Umbenhower
Deborah Dal Fovo
Diem Doonan
Florence Lang
Florence Wennes
Frances Carcione
Gail Carcione
Hazel Edwards
Irma Moulton
Ivy Marenco
Jeanne McElhatton

Jo Davolt
Joseph Carcione
Josephine Wilson
Judy Baker
Katherine Carcione
Kristin Hoppe
Larry Cooper
Lenora Wennes
M. Elaine Murphy
Madeline Carcione
Marisa Riparbelli
Myrtle Clark
Patti McKenna
Peggy Schramm
Roberta Carcione
Simla Somturk Wickless
Vera Tomic
Zuzy Martin Lynch

American Mushroom Institute
   Kennet Square, Pennsylvania
Apricot Advisory Board
   Walnut Creek, California
Artichoke Advisory Board
   Santa Cruz, California
Avocado Advisory Board
   Newport Beach, California
The Banana Bunch
   New York, New York
Bostford Ketchum, Inc.
   San Francisco, California
Brussels Sprouts Program
   Committee Santa Cruz, California
Bush Berry Advisory Board
   Fresno, California
Calavo
   Los Angeles, California
Lewis/Neale, Inc.
   New York, New York

Dole – Castle & Cooke Foods
   San Francisco, California
Dole Nutrition Institute
Florida Avocado Administrative
   Committee, Homestead, Florida
Florida Celery Exchange
   Orlando, Florida
Florida Lime Administrative
   Committee, Homestead, Florida
Fresh Bartlett Promotion
   Advisory Board, Sacramento,
   California
Fresh Peach Advisory Board
   Sacramento, California
Fresh Plum Promotion Advisory
   Board, Fresno, California
InterHarvest
   Salinas, California
Produce Specialties
   Los Angeles, California

Louisiana Sweet Potato and
  Yam Commission
  Opelousas, Louisiana
Martin Produce, Inc.
  Salinas, California
Pierre Vireday, MGM Grand Hotel
  Las Vegas, Nevada
National Banana Association
  New Orleans, Louisiana
National Onion Association
  East Lansing, Michigan
National Peach Council
  Martinsburg, West Virginia
Nectarine Administrative
  Committee
  Sacramento, California
North American Blueberry Council
  Marmora, New Jersey
Ocean Spray Cranberry Kitchen
  Hanson, Massachusetts
Papaya Industry Association
  Honolulu, Hawaii
Plum Commodity Committee
  Sacramento, California
The Potato Board
  Denver, Colorado

Raisin Advisory Board
  Fresno, California
  Theodore R. Sills, Inc.
Standard Fruit and Steamship
  New Orleans, Louisiana
State of Maine Apples
  Augusta, Maine
State of Maine Potatoes
  Augusta, Maine
Strawberry Advisory Board
  Watsonville, California
Sunkist Growers, Inc.
  Van Nuys, California
Victor J. Bergeron, Trader Vic's
  San Francisco, California
Washington Rhubarb Grower's
  Association
  Sumner, Washington
Washington State Apple
  Commission
  Wenatchee, Washington
Western Iceberg Lettuce, Inc.
  San Francisco, California

NEW CONTRIBUTORS TO
THE NEW GREENGROCER COOKBOOK

Chef/Ecologist **Aaron French** is Executive Chef of The Sunny Side Cafe in Berkeley and Albany, CA. He has an MA in Ecology from San Francisco State University and is studying sustainable business at U.C. Berkeley. Visit his website at www.eco-chef.com.

Alex Lopez, The Food Diva, is a graduate of the prestigious Le Cordon Bleu culinary program. Alex works as a freelance chef teaching cooking classes, developing recipes and food styling. Alex has appeared on several local news channels, The Food Network, and Fine Living Network. Visit her website at www.thefooddiva.net.

Beatrice Johnston is the founder of HealthySparks.com, a site dedicated to helping people transition to adding natural foods for healthier meals, one step at a time. To download free tools, visit the website at healthysparks.com.

Chef **Bruce Riezenman** is the author of *Pair It! Food & Wine Pairing App* and the Executive Chef/Owner of Park Avenue Catering. To learn more, visit his website at www.pairitapp.com.

Chef **Cindi Avila** is a graduate of the country's top natural cooking school, "The Natural Gourmet Institute" in NYC. She has had her cooking spotlighted on networks, such as The Food Network and TLC. Cindi created and hosted her own cooking show, "Green Goddess". She shares her meat-free recipes and blogs about food on nomeatnoproblem.com.

346

Connie Umbenhower is the author of *The Deity Diet* and founder of Himalayan Boot Camp. Her wellness programs motivate people to live a lifestyle of optimal health and vitality. Learn more by visiting her website at www.thedeitydiet.com.

Deborah Dal Fovo is an accomplished Italian chef and cooking instructor who mastered her culinary education hands-on while living in Italy for 20 years. Deborah teaches authentic Italian cooking on television and DVD cooking shows and at nationally-acclaimed cooking schools. Visit her website at www.deborahdalfovo.com.

Diem Doonan is a California Culinary graduate and has been cooking professionally for over seven years. While incorporating the traditional Le Cordon Bleu training, her flavors lend tribute to her Vietnamese background. She now resides and works as a personal chef in the Napa Valley area. Her website can be found at www.diemdoonan.com.

Kristin Hoppe is a Certified Nutrition Consultant, Educator, and Natural Chef. Her nutrition consulting practice, Food Therapy, is dedicated to improving people's health through an inspiring and comprehensive nutritional approach that celebrates food. Visit her website at www.foodtherapysf.com.

M. Elaine Murphy: Although Elaine has been a business owner for many years, her passion outside of work is cooking. She is the author of a cookbook, *Food With No Name*, and has been cooking since she was nine years old. Her cookbook is available at http://www.foodwithnoname.com.

Marisa Riparbelli is a stay-at-home mother of two whose passion is cooking and entertaining friends and family. Having lived in Saratoga for 28 years with husband David, an avid gardener, she is always striving to find and create new recipes in which to feature the fruits of his labor.

Simla Somturk Wickless, MBA, CHC, CNE, is a holistic health coach, nutrition educator, speaker, writer, and the founder of Delicious Health. She helps busy professionals, entrepreneurs, and those with autoimmune conditions tame stress, increase energy, and take back control of their health. Learn more at www.EnjoyDeliciousHealth.com.

Zuzy Martin Lynch is co-founder of Cooking for the Clueless®, a DVD set, website, and blog to help people bring life into the kitchen. Host Zuzy works alongside popular chefs, asking questions audiences want to know, such as the proper way to chop, wine pairing, pantry must-haves, and how to achieve a restaurant-quality presentation. Visit her website at www.cookingfortheclueless.com.

Index

LaVergne, TN USA
18 January 2011
212874LV00001B/76/P